D1561929

PERSONAL CONSUMPTION IN THE USSR AND THE USA

Also by Igor Birman

THE TRANSPORTATION PROBLEM OF LINEAR PROGRAMMING
OPTIMAL PROGRAMMING
METHODOLOGY OF OPTIMAL PLANNING
SECRET INCOMES OF THE SOVIET STATE BUDGET
THE ECONOMY OF SHORTAGES

Personal Consumption in the USSR and the USA

Igor Birman

St. Martin's Press   New York

All rights reserved. For information, write:
Scholarly and Reference Division,
St. Martin's Press, Inc., 175 Fifth Avenue, New York, N.Y. 10010

First published in the United States of America in 1989

Printed in Hong Kong

ISBN 0–312–02392–8

Library of Congress Cataloging-in-Publication Data
Birman, Igor' IAkovlevich.
Personal consumption in the USSR and USA.
Bibliography: p.
Includes index
1. Consumers—Soviet Union.   2. Consumers—United
States. I. Title.
HC340.C6B55   1989   339.4'7'0947   88–15808
ISBN 0–312–02392–8

To Albina

Contents

List of Tables

Preface

Soviet propaganda paints the CIA as the worst enemy of the regime.[1] I do not know enough about the Agency's agents, but many of its analysts have presented too rosy a picture of the USSR, particularly of the economy.

A few years ago, Andrew W. Marshall (Director of Net Assessment, Office of the US Secretary of Defense) commissioned me to review the CIA's work *Consumption in USSR: An International Comparison*. I did, and here is the text of my report. But why is my Pentagon Paper appearing only now? My report was officially sent to the Agency, and I hoped that serious people would take my criticism earnestly. Apparently they did and decided on no public response. The task of the report was published then in Russian;[2] no response followed. Neither could I detect any reaction to the summary of the report in English.[3] This encouraged me to present to a seminar, at Harvard's Russian Research Center in March of 1985, a paper in which my major disagreements with the CIA's economists (and the community) on personal consumption were put into the much broader context of Soviet economic performance. My opponents just stated their objections. No criticism was expressed in the literature when I published the paper in a few journals.[4] In Russian we say: 'Silence is a sign of agreement', so I could proudly think that my opponents quietly agreed with me; however, they have kept stating in their publications very much the same. Well, the public should have a fair chance to evaluate the quality of the analytical work done to benefit us.

In publishing the report now (only Appendix II is added to the initial text), I ought to explain at least the following. First of all, the situation with personal consumption in the USSR has not changed. Statements by Gorbachev admitted *stagnation* of the economy as a whole, and of consumption in particular, since the end of the 1970s. No real progress is expected within the next several years. In other words, my book is fully contemporary and applicable. It was possible to update it, but the more I familiarise myself with the recent data the more I see that my arguments, estimates, and conclusions still hold.

Further, my report, I hope, has methodological significance, demonstrating what you could extract from the Soviet literature even before glasnost. I also hope that my theoretical discourses at least deserve discussions. Furthermore, apparently I was influenced by American government propaganda! After another trip to Moscow I recognised that the Soviet lag is much greater than I had thought previously.

Lastly, Gorbachev said recently: 'in two–three years, with appropriate effort' it will be possible to compare the military expenditures.[5] Apparently, indeed, the Soviets will publish some figures and we in the West should be able to check them. With all modesty, I think that many methodological issues considered in the book directly relate to the comparison of military expenditures.

The reader should not expect leisure reading, but he will be rewarded by tons of concrete facts and figures. Those who want to know how the Soviets really live, what the comparative size of the Soviet economy is, what the American intelligence knows about all this, etc., are welcome. I especially welcome those who will indicate disagreements; I do not think that consensus of opinions is healthy in science.

It is my pleasure to thank my friend and translator James Gillula, Jack Alterman and David Epstein of the Office of Net Assessment, the most attentive readers of the manuscript.

Silver Spring, Maryland   IGOR BIRMAN

Introductory Remarks

'The age-old motto of every Russian is:
the worse, the better.' – Pushkin

Strictly speaking, the reader has in front of him nothing more than an 'extended review'. That, in any case, is how I initially conceived this work on a recent CIA report on Soviet-American consumption.[1] But the extreme importance of the topic, the interest of the public, to say nothing of specialists, and the scarcity of literature led me to expand my overview to the point that it may be longer than the reviewed work itself. Since the genre of this CIA study limits its accessibility to the public, I try first of all to retell its contents in my overview of the problem, and to identify and comment on (explain) its main numerical results. They were calculated by various methods, and I begin the overview with detailed (and, I hope, understandable) methodological explanations. The authors wrote, in my opinion, too little about the significance of their work, and I start with just this point. And, naturally, how can there be a review without criticism? None the less, the study contains much interesting material and my overview is not a substitute for the work itself. On the other hand, I also present a mass of statistics, mainly from primary sources, and hope that this review can be read separately from the study.

The text of the study indicates that the authors are a professor at the University of Virginia, Gertrude E. Schroeder, commissioned by the Office of Economic Research of the CIA to direct the study, and Imogene Edwards. But the study is so large that, no doubt, it required the very sustained, hard work of several specialists for several years.

Overall, I rate the study very highly. The very attempt to deal with this exceedingly difficult topic deserves great praise. And this is a pioneering publication.[2] The work has been done very carefully; the authors used a huge amount of information of all sorts – nearly all the available literature[3] – and they made not too many mistakes (my disagreements don't count; where is the guarantee that I am right?). The authors saw the object of their research only during short business (tourist) trips, but I have no great cause to attribute to them errors arising from a lack of knowledge of Soviet life.[4] The text is capacious, written expressively, and has almost no scientific jargon. But I should warn against a possible illusion – the CIA study is not easy reading; many concrete items, due to the complexity of the topic and the brevity of explanations, are difficult to sort out even for an economist: the authors presume their readers are professionals.

It is also impossible to overemphasise the significance of the simple fact that the publication provides the starting point for moving further in the direction of 'quantifying the truth'. Before, we had to work with scattered observations and estimates such as 'a little more', 'maybe twice as much', and 'it makes little sense even to compare'. Now we have calculations, figures, some objective basis not only for judging but for quantitatively evaluating and measuring. Hopefully, specialists will examine the work carefully, indicate imperfections in the approach and computations, discuss all this and make suggestions, and new estimates will follow. We should also hope for the appearance of other books on this most interesting and important topic.

One more point must be made. Studying the Soviet economy is becoming more and more labour-intensive. A lone person such as myself has less and less chance of success, especially with such fundamental problems as the national product, military expenditures, capital investment, and the standard of living. The quality of an economic study is usually judged by its results: were they expected, do they contradict known facts? But such judgements are not necessarily correct. Moreover, if the results of research are easily confirmed by common sense, then their scientific value could be questionable. 'Scientific' means a result that is unexpected, if not paradoxical, which contradicts widely accepted impressions and which cannot be obtained without special methods, new approaches, and time-consuming work. To speak more concretely about our case, the authors' conclusion that the Soviet population's level of consumption is much lower than the American is, in itself, obvious, trivial, and this is not why the work is of interest. Of interest are the concrete figures – the fact that the level is exactly one third (or one fifth) of the American, and the specific gaps for various individual components of consumption – and the substantiation of conclusions with economic measurements. But just on the basis of 'general impressions' or common sense, it is difficult to check the authors' calculations and their conclusions. Intuition prompts me to say that the relative level of Soviet consumption is lower than the study concludes, and the authors themselves think so. But references to intuition are not arguments in a scientific debate. And to confirm such suspicion, to support belief with figures, would require carrying out practically the same work that the authors did, carefully checking all sources and calculations, and making new ones, which of course is beyond the capacity of a solitary researcher.

I do not wish, and am unable, to belittle the significance of the intricate labour of CIA economists. However, their monopoly position is of no help. Not in the US, not anywhere in the West, is there another group that could carry out similar work. There are specialists outside the CIA, primarily in universities, but they are atomised, and jump from topic to topic. An urgent need is for another, definitely non-governmental, organisation in this country that has been built on competition, to study the Soviet economy and develop its own opinions. But such an organisation does not exist, and we are limited to imperfect reviews and overviews.

With that, the first draft of the preface is concluded. But in response to the reactions of several of its readers,[5] I will make a few more remarks. First, I warn that Chapters 2 and 3 deal with dull, special methodological matters, but without them it can be difficult for a layman to follow the discussions of concrete facts and figures. I was advised to shorten the description of methods and to lengthen it, to begin with the results and shift the discussion of methods to a specific appendix, to move my methodological discourse from Chapter 12 to the beginning – I got a lot of advice. Having thought it over, and remembering that the best is the enemy of good, I leave the text as it is.

In general, for the intelligent reader (the non-economist) who works through those chapters the rest should be understandable. The exceptions are Chapters 12 and 14. They deal with quite important issues, but are intended for those who have at least a minimum of economic preparation and an interest in the problem examined there.

For the reader not familiar with the special literature and statistical handbooks, it may be irksome to follow all the various statistical references and calculations, but they are intended primarily for specialists, and the 'ordinary' reader, if he trusts me, may skip them (they are mostly in footnotes). At the same time, I considered one of the main tasks was to give *a statistical picture of Soviet consumption in comparison with American* as complete as possible.

Anatole France wrote in *Penguin Island* that Perot's (Dreyfus's) case was absolutely splendid as long as there were no proofs of his guilt, and therefore, nothing to refute. But when a large number of 'proofs' was accumulated, the charges collapsed under their own weight. Perhaps the interest and attention of the reader will collapse under the weight of my proofs, but I do support all my judgements and evaluations, my disagreements with the CIA study and with Soviet statistics, as solidly as I can.

The next point relates, so to speak, to the theoretical basis of the CIA work and to my position regarding this basis. The concept of standard of living (level of consumption) is complex, many-faceted, and debatable. Especially intangible is the category 'quality of life', and particularly meaningful in international comparisons is the influence of cultural traditions on the level of consumption. Of cardinal significance is the fact that various people perceive the same level of well-being differently, and therefore in political analysis what is important is not how people objectively in fact live but how they evaluate their standard of living.[6] The composition of consumption – for example, whether health and education should be included, and, if so, to what extent – is open to debate. Also debatable is, for example, including personal automobile transportation in estimates of the level of consumption. All these and certain other questions are directly connected with our topic, but I have avoided them, One reason is that they would swell the scope of the overview and increase the area of disagreement with the authors, which is already large. Second, there is no special need for such discussions here. The authors have stated their position clearly and identified their methods, and these disagreements, so to say, are my own business. The comparison of the standard of living in the USSR and the US certainly merits a special study. However, as I understand the various CIA economic publications, the agency's economic research is aimed primarily at calculating the total volume of Soviet national product and comparing it with the American. Directly connected with this is the task of clarifying Soviet military expenditures. Although the work under review does not directly say so, it is not a secret that Soviet consumption was studied mainly as a component part of national product, which predetermined the approach to many debatable problems. Precisely this, in particular, fully justifies the authors' approach to health, education, and the like, and there is no point in arguing with them. The fact that I do not consider their concrete computation of Soviet national product to be irreproachable is another matter (see Chapter 14).

One reader thinks my criticism is not very justified because I did not offer my own concepts in place of the authors' and because in many cases, while not agreeing with their concrete results, I did not give my own figures. I must say that, *overall*, the methodological approach used by the authors, in spite of all its shortcomings, is the best; no other method is apparent. The central idea of comparison on the basis of sample goods, the calculation of price ratios, and their application to subgroups seems to be the only possible approach for international comparisions. The idea was not invented by the CIA but has been widely used by economists, including the United Nations, and in part, by Soviet statisticians for decades. Therefore, I have not too many conceptual differences with the authors. However, I not only bring out disagreements on relatively isolated methodological questions, but in several cases, I try to offer constructive criticism and some alternative approaches for consideration (Chapter 12).

Regarding alternative figures, I repeat that there is no competition for the authors. No organisation is capable of making a 'double' of their work, and alone I certainly cannot do this. However, the publication of the work under review has created a unique possibility to deal with the topic concretely and, using the results the CIA obtained, to offer corrections and alternative rough estimates.

This point must be clearly understood. Below I present a mass of concrete material – on the quantities of mayonnaise and coffee per capita, on the number of nights in hotels and kilometres of road, on the cost of burial and the number of phonograph records. However, reducing all this material to one or a few summary estimates, to an overall indicator of the standard of living in one country *vis-à-vis* another, requires exceptionally time-consuming and complex calculations. The CIA economists took such an effort upon themselves and, in doing so, made criticism possible. For instance, in disagreeing with the authors' estimate of the relative 'volume of consumption of tobacco products', I propose to correct it by a factor of two, but without their estimate I would have no basis for the correction.

Precisely for this reason my overview was written in the form of review of the CIA study. Although I use many primary sources, although I disagree with the authors in many of their particular calculations and in the final conclusions, the basic line of my arguments none the less follows the authors' material and, to a certain extent, relies on it even when contradictory evidence is given.

Some readers of the manuscript questioned the appropriateness of my references to impressions, personal evaluations, and statements such as 'it seems to me', 'to my understanding', and 'I am convinced'. It seems to me such comments are justified. Where I could, I based my opinion on data from the literature, on logical reasoning, and on examples. But in some cases data are lacking and logical constructions, to my understanding, offer little – so, what can be done? I am convinced that my own life experience and my professional intuition can guide me. But in fact not much in the overview is based on such 'non-proving' material.

The statistical base I present includes many different indicators and practically always I cite the source. References to figures that are taken directly from the reviewed work are given in the text itself – *by placing the page number in brackets.* All other sources are cited in footnotes. I use the following abbreviations for the main statistical handbooks:

a) Tsentral'noye statisticheskoye unpravleniye SSSR, *Narodnoye khozyaystvo SSR v 19–godu: statisticheskiy yezhegodnik* is cited as *Narkhoz* with the year indicated: thus, the yearbook for 1977 (published in 1978) is cited as *Narkhoz-77.*

b) Sekretariat SEVa, *Statisticheskiy yezhegodnik stran-chlenov Soveta Ekonomicheskoy Vzaimopomoshchi*–the volume for, e.g. 1981, is cited as *SEV-81.*

c) Ministerstvo vneshney torgovli SSSR, *Vneshnyaya torgovlya SSSR v 19–godu: statisticheskiy sbornik* – the volume for, e.g. 1976, is cited as *VT-76.*

d) References to two American statistical sources are also shortened: US Bureau of the Census, *Statistical Abstract of the United States, 1978, 99th Annual Edition* is cited as *StAb-78*, etc., US Department of Agriculture, *Agricultural Statistics, 1980* as *AgSt-80*, etc.

The reliability (trustworthiness) of Soviet statistics will come up in the text more than once. But then not everything is perfect with American statistics. I did not succeed in locating some needed figures in the standard sources and I have my doubts about some others. Some indicators are reported differently in various statistical handbooks without sufficient explanation.[7]

It was necessary to convert all American figures to the metric system. American statistics distinguish 'total population', which was 215.1 million on 1 July, 1976, and 'civilian population', 213 million. The latter is used for a number of calculations including per capita consumption. Because of this, some small inconsistency of figures is possible. In my own calculation of per capita consumption, I used 215.1 million.

Presenting a huge amount of statistical data, I try to refrain from exclamation marks, italics, and epithets – the figures themselves are sufficiently expressive and eloquent.

And finally, in spite of all my efforts, errors and inaccuracies undoubtedly remain, and I apologise for them in advance. I would be truly grateful to readers who inform me of their disagreements and my mistakes.

1 What For?

Even without the CIA discoveries, everyone knows that the Soviet people live a lot worse than Americans. And the question that the CIA study tries to answer – precisely how much worse? – may appear to be not significant. If the USSR were just a little behind, placing the Soviet standard of living somewhat in the range of France, then the question might look different. But the lag is so great that being more precise about its extent does not seem necessary.

Still, a knowledge of the *measure* of this difference is very important. Having the measure, we can compare the Soviet level with the Spanish, Greek, Polish, i.e., with countries for which the results of such a comparison are not too obvious. Measurements for various years make it possible to determine the direction of development – is the USSR catching up to America or falling further behind? An accurate measurement is also needed for a comparison for the total amount of national (social) product of the two countries. While observant people can, and often do, give a rough estimate of the standard of living of this sort (the standard of living in West Germany is lower than in Sweden), the measure of difference must be determined only by a specialist. And only he, of course, can substantiate his conclusion.

Knowledge, an exact figure instead of an approximate conjecture, is needed not only to satisfy curiosity, which itself is not sin. At least two such needs are apparent. The first is propaganda. The word has an unpleasant after-taste (if not taste). None the less, soberly, one of the reasons for the many failures of American foreign policy is the neglect of propaganda, the illusion that people are not affected by it, the foolish hope that people will figure out for themselves what is true and what is a lie. On many occasions I have written that Soviet propaganda is the regime's most powerful and successful weapon. But almost nothing opposes it. I am in no way calling on the West to engage in propaganda in the worst sense of the word. I am only saying that it is a must to oppose persistently, purposefully, and skilfully the contentions of the Soviet propaganda machine with actual facts, correct figures, and truthful interpretation. In particular, about the standard of living this has hardly been done.

Even among the elite Moscow intelligentisia I often heard: of course there are a lot of private cars in America, but then our education and medicine are free and our housing is not expensive; they have no queues, but then we have no unemployment. A Harvard economist told me in Moscow: 'My apartment is no better that yours'. Western tourists are amazed by the fact that Muscovites are dressed almost better than Washingtonians; they admire the public transport and the cheapness of taxis. It is conceivable that my guest's apartment was no better; I do not dispute the taste of fashionable Moscow ladies, and the high cost of the Washington Metro dispirits me. However, such facts, not correctly compared with others, not *measured against* others, distort the overall picture.

The difficulties of measuring the standard of living, even with full information available (we will soon see them) mean that despite the best intentions and efforts, reliable *generalising* results are hard to get – a fact which Soviet propaganda uses beautifully. Open, for example, the latest statistical yearbook. You will learn that between 1940 and 1980, 'real income per capita' increased by a factor of 5.8; that the average number of issues of newspapers printed increased 5.2-fold during this period and 'housing space put into use' 4.4-fold; that Soviet national income amounted to two-thirds of American in 1980; that in 1980 the USSR constructed 2 050 000 apartments and the US only 1 627 000; that the USSR is ahead of all other countries except the US and Yugoslavia in the number of students per capita; that the Soviet ratio of doctors per capita is 1.7 times greater than that of the US, and the number of hospital beds two times greater; and that life expectancy is only slightly less than in the US and the birth rate is higher.[1] These figures should give assurance (and they do!) that things in general are not all that bad. Not everyone notes that this voluminous handbook has no summary indicator characterising the relative standard of living in the USSR and other countries; although total production is compared. This absence is no accident: the real difference is disgracefully large for a country of 'developed socialism', and it is risky to lie – you could get caught.[2]

I conducted a sociological survey of sorts among emigrants on how far below the US the standard of living in the USSR is. Disregarding non-serious answers (one is in the next chapter), here are their estimates. Several immediately answered that the Soviet level is one-fifth to one-seventh of the American. Others answered with questions, trying to establish some methodological basis for the comparison, and then refused to answer or claimed a modest difference – one-half to one-third. Those who are acquainted with the CIA estimate – per capita, the USSR produces a little more than half of the American national product – say approximately the same thing.[3]

The survey reveals some points that are rather important for our topic. It is next to impossible to solve the problem simply on the basis of personal impressions, and the more a person ponders, the more factors he tries to consider, the more difficulties he faces. A person's own standard of living – there and here – affects his answer, naturally. But of course, the main problem is simultaneously comparing the various components. Imagine (this, incidentally, is an actual case) the respondent says that the Soviets eat one-half as well, dress one-fifth as well, and have housing one-third as good. What should the aggregate estimate be? Scientifically speaking, what weights should be given to each of the factors? If one somehow manages to resolve this, then taking into account eduction and health as well presents insurmountable barriers, especially since in the unanimous opinion of all the emigrants Soviet secondary school education is better than American.

Be that as it may, although the standard of living is no distant matter but something everyone encounters every day, far from everything is obvious here and you will not get far with common sense. And if that is so, in order to get figures that are worthy of discussion and which, I will not stop repeating, should be used in Western propaganda, special efforts and special means of measurement are required.

Why have I said all this? Because individual examples and general declarations are not enough to oppose Soviet propaganda. The persuasiveness and effectiveness of counter-propaganda can and should be imparted only by figures based upon special calculations. Let the Soviet propagandists refute the figures obtained in this study. If the lag in the Soviet standard of living were only 25 or 30 per cent, one might think that things are not all that bad in the USSR, that by overcoming the constant 'temporary difficulties' the country will gradually, and even quickly, catch up with America. But the simple fact that the difference in the standard of living is much greater immediately demonstrates the real state of affairs in this state.

The second need for such calculations is political analysis. Whether we like it or not, in most cases people evaluate political systems not by the degree of freedom but by their standard of living. Since an absolute measure of the standard of living (consumption) is meaningless, people compare the standard with what it used to be, with their neighbours', bosses', and co-workers', and, if they know, with other countries'. In general, the attitude of people and how they relate to a political-economic situation in society must be determined by, so to speak, the opening of 'scissors': the position of one blade characterises people's desires, their impression of how they wish and expect to live, and the position of the other is the actual level of consumption. What is the position of the scissors, which is what the real standard of living is irrelevant; of importance is the appearing of the scissors. If the scissors close, everything is all right, but if they spread, there is increased dissatisfaction – a cause of serious political consequences.[4]

In people's evaluation of their actual level of consumption and especially in their impression of the level they would like to have, much is subjective and not less depends on how well-informed they are (we just spoke of propaganda). None the less, at bottom are the objective facts – the actual standard of living. Western observers write about the queues in the USSR and about rising prices, but they avoid characterising the overall standard of living no less carefully than the Soviet Central Statistical Administration. I do not blame them; in fact, the reviewed work gives, for the first time, an empirical basis for such estimates. And just this basis enables one to judge the extent of the Soviet people's satisfaction with their material well-being and their attitude towards the regime.

I do not share the enthusiasm of contemporary analysts with models, scenarios, and mathematical formulas, but analysis must be based on facts. We cannot conduct a survey of the Soviet people to determine their estimate of how far the scissors have spread and people's real attitude towards the regime. But the reviewed work allows us to judge the position of at least one of the blades. And comparing Soviet consumption with that in other countries permits us to at least indirectly judge the 'objective basis' for the spread.[5]

At the same time, we should not exaggerate the significance of exact figures or the precise results of such comparisons. Accuracy is needed for the calculation of national product, rates of growth, etc. However, for, so to speak, general use, a more or less approximate estimate is quite sufficient. I say this because the CIA, as we will soon see, had to make various assumptions and conditional statements, and the results they obtained are not precise; the authors admit a number of uncertainties in the study. To some extent, this is no cause for alarm. What is important is only that these estimates should not be grossly in error and that a multiplicity of mistakes did not have a 'cumulative effect'.

The main thing is that a single objective, true and precise indicator of the standard of living, does not exist in nature. Much depends upon the methodology used and on its different possible variants. Therefore, we must first turn our attention to the methodology on which this study was based.

2 Methodological Basis

The concept of *standard of living* itself must be defined first – a lot depends on one's point of view, on a country's cultural traditions – no objective truth exists here.[1] Clearly this standard is largely determined by the quantity and quality of food, clothing, various services, and by the size and comfort of housing. But it is somewhat less clear with respect to entertainment and sport – recreation in general. Rejuvenating relaxation is an important element of the standard of living, but without a concrete statement of what it is, one might conclude that the unemployed live better than everyone else.[2] Therefore, the assumption is made that entertainment, sport, and recreation can be measured by expenditures on them, i.e., other things being equal, the more we spend for these pursuits, the better we live. Including health and education in the standard of living is no less questionable,[3] but it is intuitively clear that, again, other things being equal, by spending more on universities, schools, and hospitals, people live better. Be that as it may, all these are components of consumption, and it is the total expenditures for consumption that characterises the standard of living.

The standard of living must include the length of the working day, provisions for retirement, social mobility, and, in general, everything subsumed by the capacious but difficult to define term 'quality of life'.[4] Proud statements in the Soviet literature that 'a feeling of security about tomorrow' should also be included here are not groundless. All this is indeed important and to a large degree determines the living standard, but it is not easy if at all possible to measure for inclusion with consumption as such. For example, in what units should we measure certainty of constant employment to relate the result with the quantity of food? Pensions, to be sure, can be compared with various elements of consumption, but not everything is so simple here either.[5] And what about the length of the working day (week)? It differs little in the US and the USSR now,[6] but one cannot say how much the standard of living rose in the USSR when average working time was reduced in the 1950s.

Attempts to measure the standard of living with income encounter difficulties that are hardly surmountable. Even if we ignore people who, like Balzac's Gobseck, accumulate everything, the difference in the way people use their income is great. In the West a significant part of personal income is invested, and in the USSR the population has accumulated colossal monetary savings.[7] On the other hand, there are rentiers; many retirees live on previous income. Therefore, although the higher per capita income, the higher the standard of living, this correspondence is far from always proportional. For international comparisons this approach is even less suitable.

Thus, the CIA study is concerned not with the standard of living or incomes but with consumption, and it is no accident that both that work and my overview are titled accordingly.

Soviet statisticians prefer to operate with measures of the population's income ('real income') to indicate the standard of living.[8] This could be due to technical problems (income is easier to count) and possibly to the fact that a growing part of money incomes is now going for saving in savings banks and 'under mattresses'.

Western researchers include in consumption everything that is bought for this purpose as well as received free of charge (or with partial payment) from the state and what is consumed of the consumer's own production (in particular, non-commercial food production). The accounting of imports and exports corresponds to this approach; for example, US grain used in the USSR is considered Soviet and not American consumption. Thus, consumption may (and does) differ from production of consumer goods and services.

This is not the place to get into subtle economic matters, but I will mention that since the measurement is based upon expenditures, results are measured by expenditures. However, there is no better alternative to this; practically every economic measurement is done this way.

I have already said that measurement of the absolute standard of living (consumption) in itself has no substantive meaning – a comparison is always needed. The principal difficulty is the multiplicity of diverse and heterogeneous elements of consumption. Suppose people eat only oranges and wear only shorts. Consuming nothing else, Ivan eats two oranges and has two pairs of shorts. Does he live well? It is impossible to answer; we must compare. With what? His requirements? But they change (grow), and we are not able to measure them.[9] So we have to compare either with his consumption in the past or with someone else's consumption. Suppose John eats 125 oranges and has three pairs of shorts: it is clear that Ivan lives poorly and John much better. But just how much better? If John were to eat not 125 but 150 oranges, the answer would be '50 per cent better', but with differing structures of consumption it is necessary to compare shorts with oranges, or, as the saying goes, to 'add apples and oranges'.[10]

We can add apples and oranges only with the aid of a monetary measure – prices. One of my friends reasons with the utmost simplicity that in Moscow he earned R2000 a year and here in New York $30 000. On the black market in Moscow, one dollar goes for five rubles. Thus, his standard of living increased $(30 \times 5) \div 2 = 75$ times. Clever? Not very. My friend ignored a lot. He did not consider at all the differing structures of consumption of which I have just spoken. We should not measure the standard of living by income. His consumption both there and here is not determined only by wages, there are taxes, free goods and services (for example, his children's education), property income here and additional earnings from 'private' dealings there. He invests part of his income here (pays off his mortgage). The ruble–dollar ratio on the black market in Moscow does not reflect the actual relation of prices on many goods. His calculation takes no account of the quality of goods and services. And, of course, my friend's standard of living is his purely personal business; the subject of comparison is the consumption of social (or other) groups or the population as a whole.

In general, comparisons of standard of living (consumption) are clever business: you will not get far on elementary common sense. Therefore, one proceeds with the help of a special method of international economic comparisons,[11] which is applicable to countries with market economies and open statistics. Our authors followed this method with all of its merits and limitations. Their real (and appreciable!) achievement lies primarily in solving the riddles and silences of Soviet statistics, in drawing out of the Soviet literature practically everything that can be extracted and, I would say, in the very fact they boldly undertook this cumbersome and difficult research.

Thus, with reference to this method: economists (Western!) take as a postulate that the ratios of prices reflect the consumer qualities (values) of goods. If 10 oranges cost one dollar and the price of 10 apples is 50 cents, then just this (two to one) is the summary ratio of the value, usefulness (importance, nutritiousness, palatabilty, prestige, etc.) of these fruits for the purchaser. Based upon this fundamental premise, consumption is compared using figures on spending. For food, various other goods and many services, this is obviously clear. Although it is somewhat less clear, entertainment and recreation are also compared the same way – according to expenditures on them. Health and education are also measured by expenditures (Chapter 11).

Strictly speaking, the postulate is not indisputable,[12] but there is no other way. Following it, if my same friend spends (not earns!) $20 000, his level of consumption is considered to be twice as high as someone who spends $10 000 (with corrections for medicine and education if they are not fully paid for). However, a special difficulty arises in international comparisons. Its source is that the relationship among prices of various goods (the structure of prices) is not identical across the globe. Thus, in the US, chicken is much cheaper than beef, while in the USSR it is the opposite; here fatty meat is usually cheaper and there its price increases in correspondence with 'fatness'; a ride on the New York subway costs 75 cents, and in Moscow 5 kopecks; a fur coat (*dublenka*) is much more expensive in rubles than in dollars, etc. Because of differences in the structure of prices, because of cultural and national traditions and for many other reasons, the structure of consumption also differs a lot. If the shares of individual elements in total consumption were the same, differing structures of prices would not create any problem. But this is not the case. Moreover, we want to ascertain not only the overall volumes of consumption in various countries but their structures as well. Precisely because of the differing ratios of prices, the simple translation of an amount of consumption expenditures in rubles into dollars using a coefficient based upon the ruble–dollar rate on the Moscow black market (setting the exchange rate on only a few goods) leads to the ridiculous result obtained by my friend. Also precisely for this reason, even if we could determine more or less accurately the total (or per capita) amount of consumption in the USSR in rubles, and that for the US in dollars, these amounts cannot be directly compared.

How can this difficulty be overcome? We compile a list of every single good and service acquired by the average Soviet consumer. The amount that all this costs him and the amount that it costs the state for services that he receives without paying are established directly. Then we compile an analogous list of all the goods and services consumed by the average American and price each item on the list in Soviet prices, in rubles. This way we know that total consumption of the average Soviet and how much the average American spends on consumption, also in rubles. By comparing these two sums, we establish how much one figure differs from the other, i.e., by how much (how many times) consumption in one country is greater (less) than in the other. Or, it would appear (why 'appear' we will see in a moment) that we could get the same result by pricing Soviet consumption in dollars and comparing the amount obtained with total American consumption also in dollars.

The method is not bad, but in practice inapplicable. There are literally hundreds of thousands of diverse goods and services (considering all varieties), and such a calculation would be extremely unwieldy.

Statistics, considering all these variations, are not available even for America. Many goods are not of comparable quality, many goods are consumed in only one of the two countries. Therefore, we cannot directly apply American prices to the entire list of Soviet goods (or the opposite). One other snag is that depending upon which currency – rubles or dollars – is used for the comparison, the result will differ.

So that the latter point, which is of utmost importance for all of our further arguments, will be understood, let us examine the following hypothetical example. Suppose we have the data in Table 2.1.

Table 2.1 Example of calculation

	USSR				US		
	Price, rubles	Consumption		Price, dollars	Consumption	
		Quantity, kg	Amount, rubles			Quantity, kg	Amount, dollars
Beef	2.0	200	400	2.5	250	625
Chicken	2.7	100	270	1.0	300	300
TOTAL	2.23	300	670	1.68	550	925

In kilograms, the total American consumption of meat is 183 per cent (550 ÷ 300) of that in the USSR. Now let's calculate in money terms. First we price American consumption in rubles – (250 × 2.0) + (300 × 2.7) = 1310. Thus, in rubles, Soviet consumption amounts to 51 per cent of American (670 compared with 1310). Calculating now in dollars, we find that Soviet consumption is (200 × 2.5) + (100 × 1.0) = 600, that is 65 per cent (600 ÷ 925) of American.

Hence it turns out that the measurements in rubles and dollars are not mirror images; the result depends upon which currency is used for the comparison. This phenomenon, long known to economists, is called the 'index number problem'.[13] What causes it? The structure of consumption in each country shifts naturally toward those goods that are least expensive there. The correlation of the initial figures in our example is not accidental. The share of consumption of less expensive chicken in America is much larger than in the USSR where consumption leans toward beef which is cheaper there. Similarly, a lot of bread and potatoes are eaten in the USSR because they are relatively cheaper.[14] According to the authors' calculations, five times more is spent on shoe repair in the USSR than in the US, not because, as they state, Soviet shoes are worse (although they indeed are) but because the correlation of prices of new shoes and shoe repair is greatly different in the USSR.

That is why, in comparisons in rubles, we should not forget that Soviet consumption is shifted toward the goods that are cheaper there, while American consumption is not; therefore, in this comparison the latter is, sort of, overstated (why 'sort of', we will see below). And with comparison in dollars, the estimate of Soviet consumption is overstated *vis-à-vis* American.[15] In general, the volume of consumption of a country always looks lower when comparison is done in its currency (prices).[16] This is what happened in our example in Table 2.1 – in rubles the USSR lags behind the US more than in dollars. Overall, in Soviet-American comparisons of the level of consumption, the gap is greater when measured in rubles than in dollars.[17]

This is all fine, but then which indicator – calculated in rubles or in dollars – is right? Should we consider in our example in Table 2.1 that Soviet consumption of meat is 51 per cent of American, or is the 65 per cent figure more correct? The answer may seem unexpected, but theoretically speaking there is no reason to prefer one indicator over another; both are correct.[18] Therefore, in economic studies, both indicators are usually calculated, and an average of them is taken – the geometric mean.[19] The general public is usually given not two or three results, but precisely the geometric mean. I will not go into the technical details of why this is a geometric and not an arithmetic mean, especially since the difference between the two in our example is not so great (and the *real* difference is not too significant). Instead I will say that it is rather difficult to find a physical (natural) equivalent of the concept of geometric (or arithmetic) mean. Economists have agreed upon its use because nothing better is apparent, and one should accept this average as a sort of statistical abstraction, which is very suitable for international comparisons. If the indicators in rubles or dollars themselves are used, then it is necessary to make reservations about the index number problem, which is not trivial, as we saw already in Table 2.1.

Precisely because the geometric mean is an abstraction, I said above that comparison in rubles 'sort of' overstates American consumption (and comparison in dollars overstates Soviet consumption) with respect to the geometric mean. At the same time, I repeat again that this 'abstract' indicator is completely applicable; it is necessary only to understand its sense. In fact such an abstraction is not one iota worse than the very measurement of consumption in money terms. Throughout the text I will work primarily with geometric mean indicators.

Now it is high time to address the techniques of comparison. All consumption, the entire totality of goods and services that compose it, is broken down into groups and they in turn into subgroups. For each subgroup, *sample goods* are selected. Such a good (or service) should be typical and characteristic of its subgroup and account for a significant or, better, a dominant share of it. Another important property of a sample good is that its qualitative characteristics for both of the compared countries should be, if not identical, then as close to each other as possible.

For each sample good, a *price ratio* is calculated, which characterises the relation of prices in the different currencies. The ruble–dollar price ratios for the goods in Table 2.1 are 0.8 for beef and 2.7 chicken (and the dollar–ruble price ratios are correspondingly 1.25 and 0.37). This is how price ratios are determined when the compared goods are of identical quality in both countries. If quality is not identical, a corresponding correction of the price ratios is made. How this is done concretely is described in Chapter 3. Here I will emphasise that a change in a ratio due to a difference in quality is equivalent to a change in the relative volume of consumption of the corresponding good. I will explain. We found the ruble–dollar price ratio for beef to be 0.8. This means (I ask the reader to think this through; otherwise much below will not be understandable) that for the same quantity of beef is bought in the USSR for R1 it is necessary to spend $(1:0.8) = \$1.25$ in the US. Further, we somehow establish that the quality of American beef is 15 per cent better. Therefore, we make a corresponding change of the ratio: $1.25 \times (1.0 - 0.15) = 1.06$, and in further calculations it will indicate that the quality of beef that can be bought for R1 in the USSR (taking into account differences in quality) costs $1.06 in America. But the amount that Americans spend on beef has not changed, hence, in practice the correction for quality results in an increase in the relative volume of American consumption of beef in the comparison.[20]

Then, for each individual group a *price parity* is calculated, which enables us to compare consumption in different currencies not for individual goods but for aggregates of them. While, for example, a price ratio is determined for each particular type of beef, a price parity for 'meat' as a whole is computed. We already saw that the results of comparison depend upon the currency in which they are made. The price parities will also differ. Let us calculate for our example in Table 2.1 the price parity for the subgroup 'meat', and for simplicity we will not make the correction for quality. The volume of Soviet consumption was R670, and in American prices it amounted to $600. Hence the ruble–dollar price parity for the subgroup is 670 ÷ 600 = 1.117. This is calculated on the basis of the Soviet quantities of consumption in kilograms, that is, as economist say, on the basis of Soviet weights. The ruble-dollar parity calculated on the basis of American consumption (by American weights) is different – 1130 ÷ 925 = 1.416.

Since not everything said is too simple, I will repeat it in other words. The ruble–dollar price parity for a given group (subgroup) of goods and services shows how many rubles must be spent in the USSR in order to buy the quantity of goods that can be bought for $1 in the US. The dollar–ruble parity is calculated in just the opposite way. Given the conditions of our example and using the Soviet structure of consumption as shown there, R1117 will buy as much meat in the USSR as $1000 in the US. If we take the American structure of consumption, it turns out R1416 must be spent in order to buy as much meat of given quality as can be bought in the US for $1000. The substantial difference between the two figures in rubles – R1147 and R1416, both of which are equated with $1000 – clearly demonstrates the effect of considering the structure of consumption on such measurements.

It is easy to see that the difference between a price ratio and a price parity lies not only in the fact that the first is established for a single good and the latter for several goods. The ratio depends upon price and quality, but the parity upon the values of the ratios and upon the structure of consumption.

Now, the next step. Assume it is known that a total of, say, R50 m. is spent on meat in the USSR, and in the US $40 m. Without price parities these figures are not comparable, but with them the calculation is elementary. The price parities are 1.117 and 1.416. If we use Soviet weights, American consumption is equal to 40 × 1.117 = R44.7 m. That is, Soviet consumption is 112 per cent of American. If we use the American structure of consumption, Soviet consumption is 50 ÷ 1.416 = $35.3 m. In other words, calculations according to the American structure per Soviet consumption in this example at 88 per cent of American. The goemetric mean is 99 per cent.

Thus, the main role of price parities is to avoid comparison of the 'complete list' and to limit the comparison to only sample goods and services. For example, in the study reviewed, the consumption of fish (not counting canned fish) was compared on the basis of data for 3 types, and milk and milk products on the basis of 9 types. I am not discussing the correctness of limiting the calculations to only three types of fish and two types of cheese (processed and Swiss), but obviously without such limits and, correspondingly, without the use of price parities, the comparison would be altogether unfeasible.[21]

Price parities are determined not only for groups and subgroups of goods but overall for total consumption. My friend's figures, in the example quoted earlier, would have been more correct if he had included in the calculation those components of consumption that the state pays for and, most important, if he had used the overall purchasing ratio price parity (parities) for Soviet–American consumption instead of the exchange rate of Moscow black-marketeers.

The reader should also note the extreme importance of the shares of various sample goods in their subgroups and the shares of subgroups in groups, i.e., the structure of consumption. If we, for example, assumed in Table 2.1 that chicken amounts to not one-third, but one-half, or two-thirds, of Soviet meat consumption in kilograms, then, other things being equal, the result would have changed.

In international comparisons, determining the shares is one of the hardest problems. In many cases the statistics are lacking, and as a result it is not very easy to 'combine' the sets of various goods into subgroups. Therefore, assumptions and arbitrary estimates are always necessary.

In practice, the method described can be different in procedure. Indeed, knowing somehow price ratios and parities we may avoid operations with quantities of particular goods and use instead data on the population's expenditures by group and subgroup. In Table 2.1, using prices and quantities we calculated 'amounts of consumption' and price parities. But if we knew the parities, we could operate with the amounts of consumption by subgroup, for which we could use the population's expenditures with some adjustments.

In the statistics of various countries, amounts of consumptions are easier to obtain than quantities of particular goods. American statistics give 'sales' by various groups of goods much more often than quantities of physical units sold (even less consumed). Soviet statistics also give data on retail sales rather than quantities. For example, the statistical yearbooks publish retail sales of herring in rubles but not quantities of herring caught and sold.

Therefore, in international comparisons so-called direct and indirect approaches (methods) are used.[22] The first was described above in detail; the second should also be clear to the reader – it is based on price parities and amounts of consumption in rubles and dollars by subgroup. There is no reason why both of these methods cannot be used in the same study (calculation) simultaneously for different components (subgroups). Depending on the available statistics, calculations for some subgroups can be made on the basis of amounts of consumption.

We do not know which method – direct, indirect or both – the authors used, but this is not so important. A part of my critique is based on comparisons of quantities of certain goods and services. Although, possibly, the authors did not use such data in these concrete cases, this does not mean that my arguments are invalid. The essence of both methods is the same and the results should be identical. In other words, it is completely legitimate to analyse the results supposing the use of either of these two methods. To give an example, in Chapter 8 I use quantity data to demonstrate that the real Soviet consumption of leather footwear is, because of statistical tricks, much less than it seemed to the authors. Possibly, they did not in fact base their computations on the number (quantity) of shoes (leather or other), but on the population's expenditures. However, by itself this does not invalidate the conclusion from my analysis: in such a case my results should be interpreted as a criticism of the price parities.

A substantial stipulation is needed. The cornerstone of the international comparisons method is the premise that price ratios for various goods and services are determined by consumer preferences. This premise makes it possible 'to add apples and oranges' or, in other words, to use price ratios of sample goods for subgroups. This is precisely the reason why both direct and indirect methods must give the same results. However, this premise, while essentially correct for market economics, does not work in Soviet-type economies where prices are determined not by consumer wishes but by administrative actions of bureaucrats. Let us return again to Table 2.1. The reader, of course, understands that 'beef' is an aggregate of various types with different prices for each component. Since, I repeat, prices in a Western economy depend on consumer wishes (predilections, inclinations, utilities, etc.) it is not terribly important which particular type (types) of beef was (were) sampled to characterise the aggregate. But for the Soviet economy it is important, which is most evident from the fact that various goods have quite different availability for the consumer – some goods are easier to 'get' then others.

I would like to say even now (we will address the issue in Chapter 12) that this fact reduces the significance of international comparison with the USSR (and other Soviet-type economies) on the basis of the methodology described (but other methods do not exist). And, obviously, for a comparison with the Soviet economy, the direct and indirect methods will give *different* results: the direct method is more accurate. Therefore, if the authors indeed used the indirect method and my estimates differ from the CIA results, it means, above all, that the price parities used by the authors must be checked very scrupulously. The most critical issue for the entire study is precisely the correctness (validity, reliability) of the price ratios, and especially price parities, determined and used by the authors.

3 Methodology Employed in the CIA Study

The authors' main difficulty in the concrete utilisation of the methodology described in the CIA study was, of course, the struggle with Soviet statistics – sparse, fragmented, unexplained, unreliable, and sometimes deliberately distorted. In addition to everything else, its various classifications do not correspond to those employed in the West. Although it complicated their work, the authors strived to follow Western classifications in order to ensure the international comparability of their results.

Consumption was divided into goods and services. *Goods* were further divided into such groups: food (including beverages and tobacco); durables, e.g., automobiles, refrigerators, furniture, watches, etc.; and all other goods, termed 'soft goods'. Each of these groups was in turn broken down into subgroups.

Services were divided into 'household' and 'communal'. The former included housing, utilities, public transport, communications, various personal services (shoe repair, appliance repair, barber-beauty shops, funeral homes, etc.), recreation, and automotive services. The latter included health and education.

The sample goods (services) were selected for each subgroup. The selection included 110 food products, 105 soft goods, 58 types of durables, and 59 services.[1] For the meat and poultry subgroup 16 samples were selected, 3 for bread and bakery products, 4 for alcoholic beverages, 20 for apparel, 12 for footwear, 6 for drugs and other medical supplies, 10 for furniture and rugs, 5 for communications services, etc. The availability of information determined the selections. In the USSR price lists are published 'for official use only' and there are few prices in the literature. Therefore, part of the prices were taken from tables of lotteries, but most were obtained in the following way. In the summer of 1976, the CIA undertook a 'spy' operation – various goods were bought in ordinary stores (not in foreign currency stores – *Beryozka*) in Moscow, Leningrad, Murmansk and Minsk, and the prices were written down.[2] The goods (other than perishables) were shipped to America, and experts of major firms evaluated them. In comparing Soviet and American prices of a good of the same kind, 'quality coefficients' were determined and then applied to the American

16

prices in computing price ratios. For example, in order to consider the difference in packaging, the prices of all American foodstuffs were reduced by 5 per cent.

In many cases, special calculations were made in order to determine differences in quality.[3] These comparisons considered primarily functional characteristics of the goods; their external appearance and correspondence to style and taste were regarded as secondary factors [52].

Undoubtedly there could be errors in such evaluations; cultural differences must also have had an impact.[4] None the less, judging from the examples presented by the authors, the quality of goods was compared carefully in many respects. The correctness of the conclusions obtained in the process is another matter.

The fact that the spy operation was undertaken in 1976 determined to a large extent that the estimates relate to that year.[5]

A rather large part of Soviet food products is sold not in state and cooperative stores but in collective farm markets. Not knowing the corresponding prices, the authors did the best they could. Using the statistical yearbook for 1976, price indexes for so-called commission sales of agricultural products by consumer cooperatives can be calculated, and a special statistical handbook on trade gives the relation of these prices for 1963[6] to those in collective farm markets. The rest is, so to speak, a matter of simple techniques. Without at all blaming the authors, I note that not everything works out all right here. During the 13 years after 1963, the food situation in the country got worse (the blades of the scissors about which we spoke in Chapter 1 moved apart), and prices in collective farm markets began to differ sharply from those in state and co-operative (including commission) trade. The prices the authors derived for colective farm markets – R2.95 per kg of meat and poultry and R0.43 per kg of milk and dairy products – appear obviously underestimated.[7] I will note some other errors in prices below.

In the US, prices differ sharply in different stores, during sales, in various seasons, depending upon the amount purchased, etc., while in the USSR they are more or less identical.[8] The authors proceeded from the assumption that in Washington, prices are average for the country, and used some studies on prices.

A complete list of sample goods and services, together with the Soviet and American prices used, is given in the study. To illustrate, part of this list is presented in Table 3.1.

In analysing the Soviet prices, the reader must bear in mind that the

18

Table 3.1 The CIA data on prices[a]

| | Price | | Price ratio |
	Soviet, in state stores, rubles	American, dollars	(rubles per dollar)
Beef, shoulder roast, kg	1.62	1.96	0.827
Lamb (mutton), leg, kg	1.88	2.79	0.674
Pork, leg roast, kg	1.88	2.67	0.704
Frankfurters, kg	2.48	1.87	1.326
Chicken, whole fresh, kg	3.40	1.27	2.677
Boiled ham, whole, kg	3.66	1.84	1.989
Herring, kg	2.60	4.02	0.647
Orange juice, kg	1.85	0.79	2.342
Butter, kg	2.41	2.85	0.846
Whole milk, litre	0.48	0.52	0.923
Ice cream, kg	1.92	1.93	0.995
Chocolate candy, kg	11.70	4.24	2.759
White bread, kg	0.30	0.68	0.441
Rye bread, kg	0.24	1.18	0.203
Beets, kg	0.13	0.57	0.228
Onions, kg	0.52	0.51	1.020
Vodka, litre	8.00	6.82	1.173
Bath towel, each	1.90	1.58	1.203
Man's wool suit, each	97.00	102.00	0.951
Man's sweater, each	20.50	22.60	0.907
Man's street shoes, pair	12.30	21.75	0.566
Woman's dress shoes, pair	33.50	17.45	1.920
Shampoo, 8 oz bottle	0.50	0.47	1.064
Lipstick, 0.1 oz tube	1.10	0.38	2.895
Electric razor, each	23.00	19.31	1.191
Typewriter, each	135.00	44.99	3.001
College textbook, each	1.45	13.45	0.108
Hot water bottle, each	1.28	9.48	0.135
Multiple vitamins, bottle of 50	1.59	1.45	1.097
Sleep sofa, each	142.00	199.85	0.711
Boy's bicycle, each	39.30	52.49	0.749
Tape recorder, each	220.00	78.16	2.815
Motorcycle, each	300.00	900.00	0.333
Refrigerator, each	347.74	232.50	1.496
Auto, *Zhiguli*, each	5500.00	3564.00	1.543
Auto, *Volga*, each	9200.00	3743.00	2.458

[a][40–43, 55–60].

average yearly wage of workers and employees (excluding collective farmers) in 1976 was R1816,[9] and in examining the American prices recall that they are adjusted downward by the 'quality coefficients'.

Clearly, the selection of sample goods and the determination of their prices is the critical point of the entire work. Overall, what the authors have done appears rather impressive, and one is amazed at how they managed to deal with Soviet trade, services, and life in general. None the less, some questionable figures jump out at you, although they are difficult to judge since the authors did not describe the goods in the majority of cases. For example, there is no indication which camera the price of R64.04 relates to or which American camera it was contrasted with. The discount applied to American prices for the quality of Soviet goods is not reported in all instances.

As an illustration of questionable figures, the prices of chicken (R3.40) and plums (R0.80) are overstated, but the price of herring at R2.60 is too high. The price of potatoes in state stores is not 12 but 10 kopecks, but the average price which the authors use for potatoes in state trade and collective farm markets, 13.8 kopecks, is apparently low. Greatly understated are the prices of chocolate candy, butter, mens' shoes and motorcycles.[10]

Among tobacco products, the selection included only 'Yava' cigarettes for 60 kopecks and 'Feniks' for 35, Cuban cigars for 95 kopecks each and pipe tobacco (no mention of what kind) for 62 kopecks per 100 grams. Practically no one smokes cigars and very few smoke pipes in the USSR; and the choice of cigarettes leans heavily toward the most expensive types – not one of those included in the selection is a brand of truly mass consumption.

The selection of fish included catfish (I never ate it in the USSR), codfish and tuna, which also (especially the latter) are not the most representative in the USSR. Herring was included in another subgroup, but, as I already said, its price was overstated.

Watches in the comparison included digital watches, which even now, six years later, are not widespread in the USSR, and in America in 1976 they had just entered the mass market.

It looks (one cannot say exactly since the weights are not given) that the authors took the Soviet price of beef to be higher than pork. However, in the USSR it is not as in the West.[11]

They took the prices of white and rye bread to be 30 and 24 kopecks, but 'in 1970 the average retail price of all bread (rye and wheat) was 215.6 rubles per ton',[12] i.e., 21.56 kopecks per kg.

They show 'men's wool slacks' for R40.20 and 'men's work trousers' for R27.20 [55]. This is too expensive for work trousers and, as an authoritative journal says, the overall price of a pair of men's wool slacks was R23.[13]

The list of such examples could easily be lengthened.[14] Instead I want to emphasise that the principle used to select sample goods and their particular varieties is not clear. For some goods the maximum price was used,[15] while for others it does not appear to be the highest – for example, the price of movie tickets – 20 kopecks.[16]

The need to be more precise about both the selection of sample goods and their prices poses a natural question – how did this affect the final results of the study? Generally speaking, overstating Soviet prices should lead to a corresponding understatement of the volume of consumption, but more expensive goods are in principle closer in quality to American, and thus it is not necessary to discount the American prices greatly when computing price ratios.[17]

Moving to the next element of the concrete methodology used in the study, I regret to say that there is practically no information in the shares (weights) of the sample goods within their subgroups,[18] which makes it impossible to check the basic calculations directly. Precisely for this reason my further criticisms are addressed primarily to the *results* of the authors' calculations, although, as I said above, the correctness of economic calculations can far from always be judged by their results. The authors did not show us the details and steps of many of their calculations, and they did not describe the concrete method of getting from sample goods and price ratios to the summary results for subgroups of goods (services) and purchasing power parities.

An exception is, perhaps, the calculations for foodstuffs. All consumption of food in the USSR can be divided (simplifying a little) into purchases in state and cooperative trade (which includes public dining and also consumption in hospitals, kindergartens, the army, etc.), sales in collective farm markets, and 'own consumption', i.e., that which is produced on private plots for one's own use. In working on meat consumption, the authors did some complicated side calculations, complicated because the statistics are incomplete. As a result, they found [46] that meat and poultry were distributed as follows (in rubles): state and cooperative trade 53 per cent, collective farm markets 11 per cent, and own consumption 36 per cent. Bear in mind that for meat and meat products co-operative trade accounts for one-seventh of all state and cooperative trade,[19] and very crudely we may assume that cooperative trade takes place primarily in the countryside.[20] In 1976 the rural population was 39 per cent of the total, i.e., the percentage is a little higher than the rural own share of meat consumption. But we must add to this at least part of cooperative trade; besides, some collective farm workers serve rural, not urban, areas. Thus, the average rural person consumes, at a minimum, at least as much meat as an urban dweller. For anyone who knows the Soviet countryside[21] this looks suspicious.[22] Without going deeper into calculations here, I will say that Soviet statistics in all likelihood overstate the total volume of meat production in the country, and the overstatement relates to the rural population.[23]

A layman would exclaim: 'But of course; Soviet statistics can't be trusted at all! And if the CIA work is based upon them, then that's what the study is worth!' This question is not at all a simple one, and in any event you will not get far on nihilism alone. There is no doubt that much in Soviet statistics cannot be trusted, but we have nothing else. The art and skill of an economist working on the Soviet economy consists partially in being able to sift the statistical wheat from the chaff. Overall, the authors have this ability; in analysing concrete data they managed to cope with the riddles and the oddities, and where they erred I try to note it. Among the least reliable are these very agricultural statistics, which distorted several of the authors' calculations. In spite of this, carefully following official statistics (and the no less official Soviet economic literature) has an unquestionable advantage – it will be difficult for Soviet propagandists to refute the conclusions of our efforts.

Thus, the example of food tells us that not all of the shares of consumption of sample goods within their groups determined by the authors are faultless. For other components of consumption, the authors give insufficient information for a detailed examination.

Several other comments on methods follow in the analysis of concrete results. I repeat that the authors had to overcome many problems, but it would hardly be of interest to my readers to know, for example, how the share of purchases in drugstores by organisations rather than individuals was determined. The authors had to take into account that Soviet statistics include libraries in cultural services and day-care centres in health, that expenditures on education include subsidies to school breakfasts, etc.

In many instances, the authors had to make arbitrary assumptions; for example, separate estimates of canned fruits and vegetables were determined by simply dividing the total of the two in half [47].[24]

I will discuss the most significant items of this type later (particularly in Chapter 12 we will address some of my principal methodological disagreements). Here we turn to what is not in the study, what its methods do not envision.

All types of illegal economic activity – everything that in sovietological literature has become the fashion after G. Grossman to call the 'second economy' – are practically ignored. The obvious reason is the absence of even slightly reliable evidence. Another reason is that people are not saints in the West either; the drug trade, income not reported on tax returns, shoplifting, and pilferage at work amount to tens of billions of dollars,[25] and if the Soviet 'second' economy were considered, all these things in America would also have to be taken into account.

One other reason is that the 'second' economy is primarily a redistribution of income between different groups of the population, which does not affect the average per capita level of consumption.[26]

A significant exception is the production of *samogon* (home-made hard liquor). But there is no suitable information for calculations here, although a (small) part of its value was taken into account in the volume of the sugar from which *samogon* is made in the city and the value of other products that are processed into it in the countryside. Another exception is the services of private individuals for car repair, housing repairs, etc., but the authors tried to take them into account. No doubt, private music teachers, profiteers in scarce goods, semi-private plumbers and others who pay on the side do participate in creating the standard of living, but only very arbitrary estimates can be made here, and the total volume of these services is rather modest on the scale of our calculations.

The authors did not examine differences in the levels of consumption of various population strata – ethnic groups, professions, social groups, etc. – but this is a separate topic. Regarding ethnic differences, there is almost no information, but the following figures show per capita state and cooperative trade (including public dining) in 1976 for republics as a percentage of the USSR as a whole (100 per cent):[27]

Estonia	144	Armenia	80
Latvia	143	Georgia	79
Lithuania	113	Kirgizia	71
RSFSR	110	Turkmenistan	69
Belorussia	96	Uzbekistan	63
Ukraine	91	Azerbaijan	60
Kazakhstan	85	Tadzhikistan	59
Moldavia	82		

To comment on these figures is difficult. They must, of course, be affected by different sizes of families, small regional price differences of food products, varying rural shares of the population and differing shares of 'own' consumption, proportions of visitors to the republics, different consumption of alcohol, etc. Still, such factors alone cannot explain the difference between 144 per cent in Estonia and 59 per cent in Tadzhikstan. Although, of course, state and cooperative trade turnover forms only a part of the standard of living, a sharp economic inequality of republics is demonstrated here.

Regarding social differences, the authors, referring to a work by a well-known sovietologist, say [36] that at the end of the 1960s, the degree of economic inequality in the USSR was about the same as in Western Europe, a little less than in Great Britain, and significantly less than in Italy and the US. I have complete respect for this well-known specialist, but such an evaluation does not seem very convincing. Of course, a lot depends here on definitions and methods of calculation. Still we should remember that there are abundant Western statistics but only very scarce and fragmentary Soviet data on the subject. Even if the data were available they would not show that economic inequality in the USSR grew sharply in the 1970s due to the accelerating growth in 'unofficial' incomes and benefits, and corruption. Certainly, economic inequality in the US is great, but the economic stratification of the Soviet population is not small either.[28]

A few words on pensioners in the USSR. By the beginning of 1977 there were 45.9 million pensioners (about 18 per cent of the total population), and in 1976–7 pension benefits averaged R26.4 billion a year. In other words, an average pension was R575 a year. This must be compared with the average pay of all Soviet employees in 1976 of R1514[29] and with various data in this overview on expenditures of the Soviet population for various goods and services.

The authors also ignored the diversity of goods in the US and the complete incomparability of Soviet and American retail trade. They admit that not accounting for the diversity of goods overstates the estimate of Soviet consumption relative to American but do not attempt any sort of quantative estimate of its effect. We will discuss this in Chapter 12.

It is also worth noting that family size has an effect on the level of consumption – a large family requires relatively less income per capita.[30] The average size of the Soviet family is larger – 3.5 persons, compared with 2.75 in the US –[31] which somewhat lessens the inequality in amounts of consumption per capita.

It would be an oversimplification to think that all consumer goods produced in a country (taking into account exports and imports) are used only in consumption. A certain amount of milk is used to feed calves, and a certain number of eggs go to incubators; many chairs go to institutions; business trips do not pertain to consumption, etc. In Chapter 9, I demonstrate that in 1976 22 times more rugs were sold in the US than in the USSR, but certainly, some of the rugs in both countries were used for non-personal consumption.

Both American and Soviet statistics differ therefore from the accounts of a national product and personal consumption. These differences hampered many of the authors' calculations. I refer to such cases in my analysis.

Finishing this desription of the methodology used by the authors, I should say that in principle there are two possible approaches to reviewing such studies. One is to follow step by step the methodology of the work under review, checking all the data and calculations. But I did not have such a possibility and chose another way. First of all, I address the results the authors obtained and consider them, taking into account various additional information and some analytical tools. In doing so I consider the results chiefly within the authors' methodology. But afterwards, in Chapter 12, I discuss those methodological issues on which I differ with the authors.

Finally, a few words about my 'methodology'. As the reader will see, I try to check the authors' results from different angles, and using various approaches. To summarise all of them is difficult. It is worth noting here a few basic points.

One of my main 'tools' is making simple calculations for subgroups with 'homogeneous' goods, in order to establish 'quality ratios' (see Chapter 5).

In considering food comparisons, I use some data on city-country consumption.

In appropriate cases, I question the results, indicating that the prices are not right.

In many cases, I put into the picture additional information about the quantities and qualities of goods and services.

As I already said, in Chapter 12 I address a number of methodological issues on which I disagree with the authors.

In a great many cases, although feeling the authors' results cannot be right, I cannot present some calculations and quantify my opinion. In such instances, I try to provide a lot of concrete material (figures, facts, observations), and hope that the material adequately supports my criticism. In other words, though some critics may say that such material is of an 'anecdotal nature', I hope that if one considers this material without preconceptions, it will be persuasive enough.

4 General Results

Briefly about the major conclusions: The study starts with a reminder that about 20 years ago the CPSU promised to provide 'the highest living standard in the world by 1980'. In October 1961, the Twenty-Second Party Congress adopted a new programme which stated: 'the CPSU poses a task of worldwide historical significance – to provide the highest standard of living in the USSR compared with any country of capitalism'.[1] Although the text does not speak precisely of 1980, other parts of the programme and also Khrushchev's speech presenting the programme to the Congress leave no doubt here.[2] The CIA study says (v–vi):

> Events have turned out quite differently. Real per capita consumption in the USSR currently is less than a third of that in the United States. The gap was narrowed in the 1960s, but began to widen in the 1970s. The Soviets also lag far behind the major West European countries and Japan, and except for the United Kingdom, the differences have increased considerably since 1960 ... Over the past 20 years, the Soviets have made the most progress in 'catching up' in food, soft goods, and durables, but have retrogressed relative to the United States in housing, recreation, education, and health ... We estimate ... the Soviet level [of per capita consumption] to be roughly half that of West Germany and France, about two-thirds of that in Japan, and about three-fourths of the level in Italy ... Soviet consumers are also less well off than consumers in most of Eastern Europe ... The pattern of expenditures on consumption in the USSR is markedly different from that in the United States and Western Europe, and the differences are greater than might be expected from levels of development ... The Soviet pattern in many respects conforms to that in the less developed countries, and remarkably little progress toward a more modern pattern has been made in recent decades. In this and other respects, the USSR is indeed the world's most underdeveloped developed country.

Let us turn to the concrete figures upon which all of the above statements are based. We begin with Table 4.1, which shows the basic results of the authors' comparison of consumption in the USSR and the US, both overall and by individual components. The figures are

Table 4.1 Per capita consumption, 1976[a]

| | In rubles | | | In dollars | | | Geometric mean |
	USSR	US	USSR as percentage of US	USSR	US	USSR as percentage of US	USSR as percentage of US
Food	546	1092	50	651	1131	58	54
Soft goods	240	740	32	312	652	48	39
Durables	102	1031	10	133	749	18	13
All goods	888	2863	31	1096	2532	43	37
Household services	116	822	14	438	1956	22	18
All goods and household services	1004	3685	27	1534	4488	34	30
Education	70	111	63	457	491	93	77
Health	42	243	17	405	620	65	33
Total	112	354	32	862	1111	78	50
Grand total	1116	4039	28	2396	5599	43	34

[a] Due to rounding and regrouping, these figures may differ slightly from those in the source.

rather curious. We see first of all a significant difference in the ruble and dollar estimates, and it varies sharply for individual groups. The smallest gap between the estimates in rubles and dollars is for food, and the largest is for health.

The USSR lags behind, and quite significantly, for each of the groups, coming closest to the US in education and lagging the farthest behind – by a factor of eight according to the geometric mean – in durables. The Soviet lag in housing and services is also extremely large – less than one-fifth of the US level, which is twice as bad as the lag for all goods combined.

Note also that although the lags for health and education are not small either, including them in the calculation improves the general picture for the USSR somewhat. Without them the lag for all consumption would be several percentage points greater (especially in dollars).

Overall, as is apparent in the last line of table 4.1, Soviet per capita consumption is about a quarter of American (28 per cent) when both are measured in rubles, 43 per cent when measured in dollars, and about a third (34 per cent) according to the geometric mean.

Later we will evaluate in detail the results of the comparison for each component; for now we will limit ourselves to the summary indicators. As I just said, due to differences in classification, rounding, etc., the summary indicators of consumption in other tables of the CIA study are a little different. These, in particular, are the sort of figures that we see elsewhere [20]:

Total annual per capita consumption	
Soviet, rubles	1153
American, dollars	5583
Ruble–dollar price parity	
with American weights	0.748
with Soviet weights	0.483
USSR consumption as a percentage of the US	
calculated in dollars	42.8
calculated in rubles	27.6
geometric mean	34.4

Let us examine the meaning of the price parities for this concrete example with not hypothetical but real figures. In order to express Soviet consumption in dollars, its sum R1153 must be *divided* by the price parity with Soviet weights – 0.483. We get $2387. This is the annual per capita amount of Soviet consumption in dollars taking into account differences in the quality of goods and services. The indicator means that if the standard of living of the average American was exactly the same as that of the average Soviet, the American's consumption would be $2387, which is 42.8 per cent of his actual level – $5583.

Doing the same operation from the other end, we take American consumption in dollars and calculate how much it was necessary to spend in rubles in order to provide the same standard of living in the USSR. We *multiply* $5583 by 0.748, which gives R4176,[3] but Soviet consumption was R1153 of 27.6 per cent.

Thus, the price parity, as was demonstrated also in Chapter 2, makes it possible to directly translate the volume of consumption from one currency into the other.[4] To say it simply, the price parity shows the exchange rate (purchasing power) of one currency *vis-à-vis* the other. In our case, depending upon whether calculations are weighted on the basis of the Soviet or American structures of consumption, one dollar is equivalent to either 0.748 or 0.483 rubles. Now we understand why my friend in the example in Chapter 2 was so wrong. In his calculations he overstated the dollar–ruble exchange rate by a factor of 7–10. But was he really so far off?

Please ponder whether in fact, in 1976, as the parities assert, 75 (or even 48) kopecks could buy in the USSR on the average as much of a consumer good as could $1 in the US. And even if this is so, why was this ratio so different from the black-marketeers'? We know that the official Soviet exchange rate is approximately the same (about 72 kopecks per dollar)[5] and that everyone leaving the USSR tries to obtain as many dollars as possible, while foreigners groan in harmony about this exchange rate. What is going on?

Undoubtedly this overall exchange rate is affected by the inclusion of housing, health, education, and some durables, which do not participate in actual exchange on the black market, that pull the average rate down. None the less, this exchange rate (price parity) itself raises doubts about the correctness of the entire calculation, i.e. about the fact that the standard of living in the USSR is as much as one-third of the American (according to the geometric mean). Later, in examining the concrete results of calculations for subgroups one at a time, I display all my doubts and disagreements. Now, taking the results as they are, we will look at them in a little more detail.

Some interesting data on the relative levels of consumption, and its structure in different countries, are given in Table 4.2. The reader sees that consumption in the USSR lags far behind not only that in the US

Table 4.2   Level and structure of consumption, dollar comparisons, per cent[a]

	US 1976	USSR 1976	Italy 1973	United Kingdom 1973	Japan 1973	France 1973
1. Level of consumption, as percentage of the US	100	43	54	69	57	74
2. Structure of consumption, Total	100	100	100	100	100	100
Food	20	47	40	30	37	32
Clothing and footwear	6	17	9	8	10	8
Gross rent and fuel	18	5	13	17	15	13
Household furnishings and operations	7	5	6	7	9	8
Transport and communications	15	6	10	12	5	10
Recreation	7	5	7	9	6	9
Education	9	6	6	7	8	6
Medical care	12	4	6	6	8	11
Other expenditures	6	5	7	4	4	3
3. Share of consumption in GNP	71	54	69	71	55	64

[a][21, 23]

but also that in other developed countries. Don't forget that we are comparing the 1976 levels in the USSR and US with 1973 levels in other countries, where in the following three years it moved ahead. And, the comparison is in dollars: in rubles the indicators would be much worse for the USSR.[6]

Glancing at the last row of Table 4.2, one might think that the serious Soviet lag is due primarily to the use of too small a part of the national product for the population's consumption. To some extent this is indeed true, but Japan, having in 1973 only a 1 per cent larger share of consumption, far outdistanced the Soviet level. Hence, the distribution of the national product is only a part of the story, and I must add that the calculations of the Soviet national product made by the CIA do not seem too convincing (see Chapter 14).

Regarding the structure of consumption, the USSR, with the lowest overall absolute level, also has the smallest share of expenditures on housing, household furnishings and services, health, recreation and education. But the shares of expenditures on food,[7] and also clothing and footwear, are very large. This sort of structure is characteristic of a lagging country, and the USSR is indeed a backward country in consumption.

The figures in Table 4.3 for 10 countries are also of interest. Analysing the indicators for different countries, the authors note [19] that 'the USSR has a long way to travel to catch up even with socialist Hungary[8] or with capitalist Italy, the least affluent of the market economies compared. All the others are far more distant; overtaking and surpassing them in living standards may be an impossible dream.' This conclusion is quite consistent with even official Soviet data. According to them, per capita 'real' income of the population increased by 46 per cent during the 1970s. This is clearly overstated,[9] but suppose it is true. Then, by increasing consumption at the same rate the USSR will reach the 1976 level of consumption in the US only after 30 years (taking the lag according to the geometric mean, i.e. one-third; calculating in rubles, much more time would be required). But even this is extremely unlikely since the rate of growth in the USSR is declining, and without the most fundamental and radical structural changes of the entire system, will soon fall to zero. And the US will not stand still but will hopefully move forward in these 30 years. Thus, even if we use official Soviet data on the growth of consumption, it is unlikely that the USSR will succeed in catching up to America for many decades.[10]

The last comparison. Since 1960, data have been published in the US on the 'poverty level'. For example, in 1976 almost 12 per cent of the

Table 4.3 Indicators of various countries, 1976[a]

	Meat, kg per year	Potatoes and grain products, kg per year	TV receivers, units per 1000 persons	Telephones, units per 1000 persons	Passenger cars, persons per car
USSR	46	166	223	66[b]	46
US	118	66	571	695	2
W. Germany	92	84	305	317	2
France	102	92	235	262	3
Italy	67	134	213	259	4
United Kingdom	70	90	315	379	4
Japan	26	126	233	405	6
Poland	70	159	198	108	27
Czechoslovakia	81	128	253	?	9
Hungary	68	134	233	?	14

[a][22]
[b]See Chapter 10, p. 105.

population was considered to be at or below this level.[11] Although these statistics refer not to consumption but income, we can try to approximate some things. In 1976 a family of four was considered poor if its income was 33.6 per cent or less of the median income of four-person families for the country as a whole.[12] The Soviet level of per capita consumption was 34 per cent of the American (Table 4.1), that is, the same as the poverty level in the US. Certainly, the first of these figures is in dollars and the second is calculated as a geometric mean, but recall also that the poverty level is based upon income. In 1976 the US population paid in taxes an amount equal to 14.5 per cent of what was spent on consumption and also set aside more than 6 per cent for investment,[13] but the poor pay little or nothing in income and property taxes and do not invest. Therefore, upon the basis of the authors' results, the level of consumption of the Soviet people in 1976 was lower than what was considered poor in the US.[14] And since I think that the authors have greatly overstated Soviet consumption . . .

5 Food

Now we will start looking more closely at the results of comparison for each group. As I already said, it is not easy to criticize this study and even more difficult to offer contrasting calculations. In this and the next six chapters, I try to give as broad a statistical picture of Soviet consumption in comparison with American as possible. Frequent references to and criticism of the authors' data help me to quantify many statements. I by no means strive to seek out and demonstrate everything that is, in my opinion, not quite correct in the authors' calculations. But using their results as a point of departure and modifying them, I can offer some quantitative estimates.

Alas, I am not Dumas père, and statistics, while mysterious, are much less intriguing than the adventures of the Count of Monte-Cristo. These seven chapters are difficult reading requiring concentrated attention and a desire to work through the tangle of prices, coefficients, various approaches, and conclusions. The reader is not obliged to believe me and I have tried to document as many assertions as possible with references to the literature; thus, the abundance of footnotes. I placed much additional material in them – for example, calculations of the Soviet lag in consumption of certain products. Still, the basic text is also overburdened with figures, calculations and explanations; it seemed necessary not only to give final results but to tell how they were obtained.

A few words on the methodology of my approach are needed here. First, in all cases where it is possible, I try to figure out the difference in the quantity of goods and services consumed in the two countries. Then, by comparing it with the geometric mean I get something like an estimate of the quality difference. Generally, using some additional material I consider this estimate and express my opinion on its correctness. Certainly my opinions are subjective. But first, to repeat, I at least try to illustrate my position with numbers, references and examples. Secondly, I do not pretend that my corrections are precise. Thirdly, the reader should not forget that, strictly speaking, the authors' position on quality differences is also subjective. Indeed, as I mentioned in Chapter 3, many goods were brought to the US and examined by experts who established some quality coefficients. But these coefficients were not checked by the real authority – the market. Besides, many perishable foods were not examined by the experts at all.

In Chapter 12 I address the question of quality comparisons and try to show that the expert estimates should by no means be thought perfect.

The importance of the issue of quality comparisons should not be overlooked. I do not have many questions (doubts) about the basic numbers that the authors used – total amounts of expenditures for consumption in both countries and the sums for groups and subgroups. But the results depend also on price ratios, and basically my criticism pertains to them. Ideally, a reviewer would be able to re-examine the ratios, to correct them if necessary and then to repeat the authors' calculations. I was constrained to use an alternative approach which, however, is no less legitimate. Although my approach may be indirect, in following this path I raise so many and such significant questions that they at least must be considered and answered.

The economic development of modern society is now manifested not in the growth of physical volumes of consumption. In my distant childhood, caricatures pictured the bourgeois as fat men with huge cigars; today's rich are lean, they jog and do not smoke. Differences in consumption are more and more frequently reflected in the quality of what is consumed. With respect to food, the process is all the more not reflected in increased quantities – quite the opposite, diets are fashionable – and in radical structural improvements: increased shares of high calorie products (although there are limits here), fruits and vegetables, in overcoming seasonality, attention to taste qualities, in degree of preparation, consumer convenience, and, of course, in variety.

Table 5.1   Food consumption, 1976, kg[a]

	USSR	US	USSR as percentage of US
Grain products	141	62	227
Potatoes	119	52[b]	229
Sugar	42	43	98
Meat	46	118	39
Fish	18	6[c]	300

[a][7]
[b]Plus 2.5 kg of sweet potatoes.
[c]See Chapter 6.

All the same, speaking of quantities, some of the authors' data are given in Table 5.1. We may add to them other comparisons in which Soviet per capita consumption calculated from official data are con-

trasted not only with American consumption but with so-called rational diet norms established by the Institute of Nutrition of the USSR
Academy of Medicine.[1]

As we see, the average Soviet soul is still far from the rational norms
of nutrition. But a comparison of the norms with actual consumption
in the US raises doubts about the norms themselves.

Table 5.2   Per capita consumption, kg[a]

	USSR According to rational norms	Actual, 1979	US Actual, 1979
Bread and bread products[b] (flour equivalent)	110	139	71
Potatoes	97	119	54
Sugar	40	43	42
Meats and fat	82	58	122
Milk and milk products	405	319	255
Eggs (number)	292	233	283
Vegetables and melons	146	95	106
Fruits and berries	113	38	113

[a]*Russia*, 1981, no. 3, p. 73.
[b]Including cereals (*krupy*) and legumes.

Differences between identically labelled indicators in Tables 5.1 and
5.2 are due not only to the fact that they are not for the same year; they
may depend upon differing definitions in the sources. Thus, the authors
compared the consumption of meat (Table 5.1) excluding 'subproducts'
and fats,[2] while in Table 5.2 Soviet data are taken as they are in official
statistics. We will speak of these data and their trustworthiness in more
detail in Chapter 6; for now, a little about the caloric content of food.
Table 5.3 shows that the quantities of calories are practically identical
in the two countries and that what is lacking in the USSR in meat, fish
and fats is made up in bread, cereals (*kasha*) and potatoes.

I am not a dietitian, and it is hard to judge definitely, but apparently
the average Soviet needs more calories. Many millions (several times
more than in America) are still employed at heavy physical labour, the
climate is more severe, people walk more, expend a lot of energy
standing in lines, riding in overcrowded public transportation with
transfers and long waits; and the American population is older.
Therefore, although more Americans engage in sports (see Chapter 10),
overall the caloric content of food in the USSR should be higher.[3] But,
as we see, it is a little less.

Table 5.3　Calories a day per person[a]

	USSR 1965	USSR 1976	US 1976
Total calories per day	3100	3330	3380[b]
Composition of diet, per cent			
Grain products and potatoes	54	46	22
Sugar[c]	11	12	17
Meat and fish	6	8	20
Fats and oils	9	11	18
Dairy and eggs	14	16	13
Other	6	7	10

[a][8]

[b]*AgSt-80*, p. 551, gives 3420 calories.

[c]Why the share of sugar in the US calories structure is almost one and a half times greater than the Soviet share even though their consumption figures are practically identical (Table 5.1) the authors did not tell. A significant share of sugar in the USSR goes for *samogon*, therefore life in the US is clearly sweeter, but the authors ignored *samogon* in their calculations.

The reader may be tired of figures, but Table 5.4 is most important and we will return to its indicators many times. It reflects not only the quantity of food and its caloric content but other qualitative characteristics. The significance of the comparison in Table 5.4, and especially the figures in the last column, should be fully understandable only to those 'laymen' who read Chapter 2 carefully. We will note several interesting points.

The main thing that follows from Table 5.4 is that in spite of the essential equality of the total amount of calories, the summary indicator of the total value of food consumption in the USSR is a bit less than half (49 per cent) of the US. The explanation lies in the differences of both structure of food consumption and product quality.

With respect to quality, recall that the authors reduced the prices of American products in order to take differences into account.[4] Presumably precisely for this reason, for example, the volume of consumption of potatoes in the USSR was 90 per cent of American consumption although in terms of weight American consumption was less than half (Table 5.1). In the opinion of American manufacturers the quality of almost all American products is higher. The only exceptions were dried split peas, for which the Soviet product was judged equal in quality to the American, and sugar cubes, which were rated better in quality than the American [34].

Table 5.4   Per capita consumption, 1976[a]

	USSR Rubles	%	US Dollars	%	USSR as percentage of US, geometric mean
Breads and cereals	60	11	110	10	96
Meat and poultry	101	18	282	25	34
Fish	17	3	48	4	67
Milk, eggs, cheese	63	12	116	10	59
Oils and fats	26	5	38	3	64
Vegetables	18	3	111	10	19
Fruit	20	4	61	5	20
Potatoes	16	3	13	1	90
Sugar and confectioneries	47	9	50	4	78
Other foods	14	2	39	4	39
Total food	382	70	868	76	49
Alcoholic beverages	138	25	133	12	119
Nonalcoholic beverages	11	2	54	5	37
Tobacco	15	3	75	7	18
Grand total	546	100	1130	100	53

[a][20]

Another reason for the difference noted above is that the share of the markup for public dining enterprises in all expenditures on food is much larger in the US – 12 per cent compared with only 4 per cent in the USSR. Its impact on the final results of calculations is not terribly important, but none the less, if we agree with the authors' estimate that the volume of Soviet food consumption is half of the American, the total amount of this markup in the US is six times larger than in the USSR.[5] It is quite possible that this figure rather correctly reflects the actual ratio of public dining in the two countries.[6]

Such a huge disparity in the shares and amounts of the markup on public dining makes one wonder whether it might influence the results of calculations. The concrete procedure used by the authors was the following. First, they determined the volume of consumption for each subgroup, listed in Table 5.4, without expenditures in public dining. Then the overall amount of expenditures on public dining (including both food and the markup) was distributed accordingly among subgroups. Thus, the amounts of expenditures for each subgroup and, correspondingly, the per capita figures fully include the markup for public dining. In itself, this is completely correct. However, in comparative analyses, particularly in comparisons of the quality of products, the amounts of these markups should be excluded.

Since the matter is by no means simple I will illustrate it using the same example with meat and poultry, but this time we will take actual figures. According to Table 5.1, Soviet per capita consumption of meat in physical terms is 39 per cent of that in the US, while according to Table 5.4, meat consumption based on the geometric mean is 34 per cent. What do these figures signify? They mean that the quality of Soviet meat is 15 per cent worse – precisely this determines the difference between the estimates in kilograms and according to the geometric mean. At the moment we will not discuss the question of whether these figures are correct, and in particular, just how much worse Soviet meat is: we will return to this in Chapter 6. But our conclusion was not quite right. The snag is that the summary indicators for meat on which the geometric mean estimate is based include the markups for public dining. If it were approximately equal in both countries, there would be no problem. But it differs sharply. Jumping ahead (see Table 5.5), I will say that in total expenditures for the 'meat and meat products' subgroup, this markup accounts for 20 per cent in the US and 5 per cent in the USSR. And this changes the conclusion that Soviet meat is worse. Indeed, the public dining markup has nothing to do with either the quantity of meat or its quality. And if we actually want to find out, on the basis of the indicators of meat quantity and the geometric estimate, what the quality of meat is in the CIA calculations, we must exclude these markups from the figures on the amount of consumption. Having done this, we reach the absurd conclusion that Soviet meat is 3.5 per cent better than American.[7]

To repeat, I am not ruling out the procedure for calculating the public dining markup that our authors used. Although, generally speaking, it could have been done differently, what the CIA economists did was not incorrect.[8] Indeed, the fact that the markup on public dining in America accounts for 12 per cent of all expenditures on food reflects a simple fact – the consumers want this and they are ready to pay this much. And if the consumer is ready to pay 20 per cent of his total expenditures on meat and meat products in 'eating and drinking places', by doing so he gives evidence that he is equating the expenditures, that for him 20 per cent is equivalent to an increase in the quantity of meat or an improvement of its quality. But the American consumer does not eat 20 per cent more meat and the Soviet consumer does not eat 5 per cent more. The reader should remember once again the sense of the basic procedure described in Chapters 2 and 3. The amount of the population's expenditures on each subgroup represents the total of the multiplication of the quantities of sample goods and

			US, billion dollars			The markup		USSR, markup, %
	Retail purchases of domestic production	Imports	Other consumption	Total	All consumption	Absolute	%	
	1	2	3	4	5	6	7	8
Bread and cereals	18.7	—	0.6	19.3	23.8	2.6	12	4
Meat and poultry	39.9	1.6	1.2	42.7	60.6	10.2	20	5
Fish	7.0	1.9	0.3	9.2	10.4	0.7	7	5
Dairy products and eggs	22.6	—	0.7	23.3	30.8	4.3	16	4
Oils and fats	4.2	—	0.1	4.3	5.7	0.8	16	11
Vegetables	18.7	0.4	0.6	19.7	23.8	2.3	11	4
Fruits	10.7	0.8	0.3	11.8	13.1	0.7	6	4
Potatoes	2.3	—	0.1	2.4	2.9	0.3	12	2
Sugar and confectioneries	4.8	1.2	0.2	6.2	7.6	0.8	12	4
Miscellaneous and Processed Food	4.4	3.1	0.2	7.7	8.3	0.3	4	4
Alcoholic Beverages	26.8	1.2	0.8	28.8	28.6	-0.1	—	2
Non-alcoholic Beverages	4.6	—	0.1	4.7	11.5	3.9	51	3
Tobacco	16.2	0.4	0.5	17.1	16.2	-0.5	—	0
Total	180.9	10.6	5.7	197.2	243.3	26.3	12	4

Sources:

Columns 1 and 5: [45]

Column 2: *StAb-78*, p. 883. The authors listed kinds of food imported but do not indicate fish, fats and tobacco. They cite the same yearbook but a different page (p. 880) where the data are less detailed. According to the source, total imports are less than in the authors' calculations by $1.1 billion, and I distributed the difference in column 3.

Column 3: Here the sums indicated by the authors – $1.3 billion for consumption in kind, $3.3 billion, for government purchases – and the difference in imports, $1.1 billion, are distributed among the subgroups proportionately to columns 1 and 2.

Column 4: Total of columns 1, 2 and 3.

Column 6: Column 5 minus column 4 multiplied by the coefficient calculated from the 1972 US input–output accounts (see note 5).

Column 7: Column 6 divided by the difference of columns 5 and 6. Certainly, the figures calculated are very rough, which is apparent from the fact that the markups for alcohol and tobacco are negative. Still these figures are satisfactory for our analytical purpose.

Column 8: The authors' data [44] which are also not ideal. For example, note that 2.5 per cent of the total was not distributed among the subgroups, and the rest is distributed according to data for Kazakhstan. Clearly wrong is the figure for fats; the markup for alcohol is ridiculously small. Still, these data as well are good enough for our purposes.

their prices; only under these conditions do comparisons based on price parities have a meaning. Including markups is equivalent to increasing the quantities of goods or improving their qualities.[9]

Therefore, in the analysis below in Chapters 6 and 7, I exclude the amount of public dining markups from the authors' figures for food consumption in both countries. For this, I calculated in Table 5.5 the percentage markups for each subgroup. Unfortunately, the authors' information is not exhaustive, and some things in their data are not entirely clear.[10] But all in all, the figures presented in Table 5.5 will serve our analytical purposes quite well.

We have digressed a little from our basic line of reasoning. In the next chapters I examine the authors' indicators for each individual subgroup and concretely, with facts and figures in hand, try to evaluate their reliability. However, already here I should say in the most decisive way: the authors' general conclusion that Soviet consumption of food is as much as one-half the American level is not correct. This may be said on the basis of very simple observations.

In the USSR, they are happy to have found some foods; they buy what the stores offer. Here, we buy what we want. There, food expenditures are a major part of family income; here, all including retirees and the unemployed eat well.[11] In plant and institute cafeterias there, meatballs are made almost entirely out of bread, and a home dinner consists of soup, breaded patties, and a large amount of potatoes (or macaroni); here, dinner is a good cut of meat with some small garnish. There, only a few people have eaten lobster, pineapple, or avocado in their entire lives. The quantities of juices, spices and various imported products cannot even be compared.

There, they eat tomatoes and fresh cucumbers from August through October, plums in September, and strawberries for two weeks at the beginning of summer; here, all these and much more is available year round. There, vegetables means cabbage, beets and carrots; here, there are dozens of types. There, apples are available in the fall; here, almost any fruit is eaten year round.

The appearance of the very best Moscow (Leningrad) food store (*gastronom*) cannot be compared visually with an ordinary supermarket in some out-of-the-way place in America.

There, the consumer carries his pickles home wrapped in *Pravda*; American packaging is carefully planned for convenience of storage and use.

Official Soviet propaganda admits that feeding the population is the basic problem of the current Five-Year Plan.[12] A special 'food programme' has been proclaimed with great fanfare.[13] There is a sharp difference in how well (poorly) people eat in different parts of the country; a large inequity exists between those with access to 'special supply' and the ordinary citizen. But in America the unemployed and millionaires buy food in the same stores.

And, of course, we should take into account American diversity, the availability of a literally uncountable number of food types and varieties.

In other words, these simple observations lead us to suspect that the results of the CIA comparison for food must contain some sort of fundamental error (or several errors). The difference should be substantially greater than the one found in the study.

As a preliminary general remark I must say that the authors in their calculations, and in particular in establishing price ratios, clearly did not take sufficient account of differences in the *quality* of food, all the more so since perishable products were not shipped to America and the experts could not compare them. I will talk below about the huge waste of potatoes, other vegetables, and fruits; a significant portion of them is lost after purchase, potatoes are sometimes frost-bitten, vegetables sold unwashed and unsorted, fruits half spoiled. American milk does not get sour in weeks; Soviet milk is sometimes spoiled already in the store (and still sold). American meat cooks much faster. In the USSR frozen meat is considered bad; here the process of freezing products has achieved a high degree of perfection. Practically all American food is enriched with vitamins, while in the USSR in 1974 only 15 per cent of bread and bakery products were enriched.[14]

The correspondence of products to norms and standards is also a part of quality. Not long ago a Soviet newspaper described in detail an inspection of the quality of beer, and standards were met at only 17 enterprises. The same story relates how 15 per cent of honey was rejected in a quality check.[15] Fish of 'second freshness' was talked about already by Bulgakov's Woland; the watering down of milk, beer, sour cream, *kvas*, etc. is an old tradition,[16] and it has in no way been curtailed. When things are scarce, consumers are not very 'picky' about quality (more about quality in Chapter 12).

The packaging of food is not comparable, as I already mentioned.[17] The degree of preparation of food for consumption is abolutely incomparable; there are hundreds of types of prepared foods in America, but in the USSR only one or two meat products.

Finally, the American food ration includes numerous products that have never been available in the USSR – countless spices, exotic fruits and vegetables, and those that are not so exotic for Western countries, and food of various ethnic groups (Chinese and other Oriental, Italian, Mexican, etc.).

The only thing that one might hold against American food is that it contains many more chemicals, but this factor was also not taken into account in the CIA study, and it is not clear how this should be done. On the other hand, the American consumer, first, knows from the labels that a given product contains 'non-natural components' and, second, he has a choice.

6 Food (Continued)

We will consider now each subgroup listed in Table 5.4 and examine concretely the results of comparisons. I will also present some data from the Soviet and American literature.

Regarding *bread and cereals*, we have little material for making a judgement. This group includes 'macaroni products', groats, dried beans, and all sorts of packaged cereals. In 1976 American per capita consumption of wheat flour was about 50, and rye flour less than 0.5 kg.[1] This would be (given a ratio for converting flour to bread of 1.35) 187 g of bread per person a day. Actually, of course, far from all flour was consumed as bread.

There are few interruptions in the bread supply in the USSR. However, 'the existing assortment of products does not fully satisfy the population's requirements. About 80 per cent is bread baked in special forms, 10 per cent is baked on the hearth, 8.5 per cent is pastries, and 2 per cent is rich bread. Not enough of the varieties of bakery products of different nationalities is baked'.[2] The fact that 12 per cent of bread in the USSR is still produced in home ovens[3] also can in no way be considered a positive factor.

Incomparability of the quality of bread greatly complicates the comparison. In the unanimous opinion of all Soviet emigrants and many other Europeans, the quality of bread in America is worse.[4] However, first, in Moscow, Leningrad, and other major centres it is significantly better than in provincial cities. Second, bread of 'European quality' can always be bought in American supermarkets; regardless of the foreigners' opinions, we eat the bread that we like. Third, in 1974 only 6 per cent of bread and bakery products in the USSR were baked from flour of the 'highest class (*vysshego sorta*)'.[5]

All the same, how much bread per capita is consumed in the USSR? In 1974 '32.8 million tons of bread and bakery goods were baked at industrial enterprises of all ministries and departments'. As we already saw above, this was 88 per cent of total production. Thus, we get 147.6 kg of bread (not flour!) per year or 404 g per person a day.[6] Although I have no data on bread in America, we can say with confidence that per capita consumption here is at most one-third to one-fourth of the Soviet level.

Also in 1974, Soviet per capita consumption of groats and dried beans was 13.6 kg: rice accounted for 23 per cent, buckwheat 10 per

43

cent, and millet 21 per cent.[7] Regarding macaroni products, a little less than 6 kg per person was produced in 1976.[8]

In America, millet is for birds; buckwheat is called 'kasha' and eaten very rarely. In 1976, 1.5 kg of oatmeal and 3.3 kg of rice were consumed per person here.[9]

Breakfast cereals are of significance in America. In 1976, 1.3 kg of wheat flour and several kg of corn were used in them per capita,[10] while they are hardly consumed in the USSR. Cereals should 'compensate' for the American 'lag' in baked bread.

As we saw in Table 5.1, the USSR is ahead of America in per capita consumption of grain products in kilograms by 127 per cent, while according to Table 5.4 the overall 'geometric' estimate of Soviet consumption was a little less than the American – 96 per cent. Thus, American 'quality' is 2.37 times higher. However, considering (Table 5.5) that in the compared amounts the markup on public dining is 12 per cent for the US and 4 per cent for the USSR, we establish that average 'quality' of American bread and cereals is approximately 2.27 times higher than Soviet. We have no grounds to dispute this, although I would like to see more concrete indicators for the various components of the comparison.

Meat. Here also at first glance we have no convincing material to support or refute the authors' conclusion that Soviet consumption amounted to one-third, 34 per cent of American. But we will not be hasty.

I already said that Soviet statisics apparently overstate total meat consumption in the country,[11] and the authors' calculations are fully based in them. Unfortunately, I cannot indicate the precise amount of overstatement, just as there was no way for the authors to do this.

The example with meat clearly shows the serious methodological problem already mentioned. Let us examine first concrete data on meat consumption by type (Table 6.1). Although I obtained these data for the USSR by indirect calculations, they more or less give the overall picture. Chicken is more expensive than beef in the USSR, while it is just the opposite in the US;[12] however the relative prices of fat and lean meat are reversed. The entire CIA study is based on the fundamental premise that the prices of goods are proportional to their consumer preferences (we have spoken of this as well). But one can hardly assume that the consumer characteristics of beef and chicken, of fat and lean meat, depend upon where they are eaten – in Tula or in Pittsburgh.[13] In other words, principles are principles, but in fact the study used prices that are proportional not so much to certain objective consumer

Table 6.1   Meat consumption, 1976

| | USSR[a] | | US[b] | |
	kg	per cent	kg	per cent
Beef and veal	22	49	60	51
Pork	15	32	27	23
Mutton and goat's meat	3	7	1	1
All poultry	5	10	24	20
Chicken			20	17
Turkey			4	3
Other[c]	1	2	6	5
Total	46	100	118	100

[a]Calculated on the basis of beef consumption in the CIA study, 46 kg, and the structure of meat production in 1976 'on all categories of farms', *Narkhoz-77*, p. 261. In 1975 and 1977, the shares of pork production were higher and of beef correspondingly lower.

According to the inexhaustible Lokshin, p. 106, beef accounted for 50 per cent, pork 17 per cent, poultry 13 per cent, and mutton 7 per cent of state and cooperative trade. Thirteen per cent remains, and Lokshin mentions rabbit. Actually, also included here are horsemeat, venison, and 'subproducts', which are distributed among all types of meat above. Lokshin says that these proportions were different in collective farm markets: one-third pork, one-third beef, less than one-fourth poultry, and 10 per cent mutton. *Narkhoz-77*, p. 192, gives the proportions of meat processing in industry, as well.

[b]*StAb-78*, p. 126. Meat is given here in 'carcass weight', i.e. the same as Soviet data, but poultry is given in 'ready-to-cook' weight. I calculated the total weight of poultry by summing chicken and turkey; little duck and goose is eaten in America.

Another source, *AgSt-80*, p. 554, gives total consumption of meat, excluding poultry, as 76.5 kg, i.e. a lot less than in *StAb-78*. It seems that the difference must be due to pork fat.

[c]For the USSR, this is rabbit, horsemeat, and apparently venison. For the US, it is the difference obtained between the total for all types and the sum of the figures in *StAb-78*. The figures also include wild game.

preferences as to relative costs. One may reply that there is no such thing as 'objective' consumer characteristics and that American consumers prefer to have 20 per cent of poultry in their meat ration while Soviets prefer only 10 per cent, or that in the USSR people love mutton and pork more than in the US. However, in fact relative prices are of decisive importance here; Americans 'love' chicken and turkey more because they are cheaper.[14]

This point is an example of the index number problem examined in

Chapters 2 and 3, and we will return to it in Chapter 12. However, surprisingly, the comparative estimates of meat and poultry consumption in the study, both in rubles and in dollars, given the quite different structures, came out exceedingly close to each other; they differ by less than a percentage point [20].

The figures presented characterise the total consumption of meat in all forms. In the USSR this includes 11 kg of sausage products, about 4 kg of prepared meats, and also about 4 standard cans of meat and 'meat-vegetable' canned goods (stuffed cabbage and the like) that contained 1 kg of meat.[15] In 1975, 0.4 kg per capita of hard smoked sausage and 0.9 kg of other smoked products were produced.[16]

I remind the reader that it was approximately at the time examined in the study that *The Washington Post* published a translation of secret Soviet instructions directing meat plants to reduce the meat content of sausage and frankfurters still further. None other than the USSR Minister of the Meat and Dairy Industry gave additional evidence of this. At enterprises subordinated to him, output in rubles per ton of processed raw materials increased by 11 per cent between 1965 and 1975,[17] which cannot be fully attributed to changes in product mix.

In 1975 the trade network accounted for 63 per cent of total sales of meat and poultry to the population and public dining for 37 per cent.[18] If this percentage is applied to 1976, given total meat production in industry of 8.4 m. tons, state and retail trade sold the population a little more than 20 kg per capita. Relating this to only the urban population, it amounts to 33.3 kg or 91 g per day. And this includes meat products, such as sausage, frankfurters and canned goods. The 1.5 million tons of meat sold in 1976 in collective farm markets don't change it dramatically.[19]

So, is the authors' estimate correct – Soviet per capita consumption of meat and meat products amounts to 34 per cent of American? No. First, as I already said, Soviet meat consumption indicators in kilograms are clearly exaggerated. It is difficult to say how much, but the overstatement could not be less than about 10 per cent.

Second, the authors' calculations substantially exaggerate the quality of meat in the USSR. This was also discussed in Chapter 5. If we fully accept all of the authors' data – that Soviet consumption amounted to 39 per cent of American in kilograms and 34 per cent according to the geometric mean – it follows that Soviet meat was worse by 14.7 per cent. This is inconsistent with the statement that for comparability American 'prices of fresh beef and pork beef generally were discounted 20 per cent, other fresh meats and poultry 15 per cent', and that processed meats, such as bacon and sausage, were discounted 5 to 10 per cent [34]. The only possible explanation of such a contradiction is that the poorer quality of meat was more than offset by 'structural advantages', but this is, as I said, only a formal advantage. In fact the situation is much worse. Recall that, taking this into account, the markup on public dining for the subgroup leads to the absurd conclusion that the quality of Soviet meat is somewhat better than American.

We come here to the crucial point of my entire overview. The poorer quality of Soviet meat is indisputable; such is also the opinion of the CIA economists. But how much worse? The problem is that the quality difference is difficult if not impossible to quantify; the estimate of the difference is unavoidably subjective. Strictly speaking, my subjective opinion is no more valuable than the subjective opinion of the CIA economists. In this particular case I have some arguments to substantiate my sharp disagreement with the CIA, but still I am forced to resort to a rather arbitrary estimate. I must say most decidedly that I fully recognise that many of my estimates are debatable. Lacking sufficient material, I often avoid numerical estimates (for example, in regard to publications – Chapter 8). For the same reason, I also make my final calculations (Chapter 13) in the form of a range of estimates. In most of the cases, my estimates do not pretend to be precise; they are to show the direction and the scale of my corrections to the CIA's calculations. Nevertheless, I believe that all the material presented in the overview is sufficient to substantiate my final conclusions.

Returning to our concrete case with meat I will say that here we do have the possibility of making a rough estimate. In the opinion of many emigrants the quality difference of Soviet and American meat can be likened to the difference between cheap and expensive meat in each of the two countries. In other words, average Soviet meat is as much worse than average American as cheap Soviet meat is worse than expensive. Roughly, expensive American meat costs twice as much as cheap (approximately the same correlation exists in the USSR), so we can deduce that the average quality of American meat is twice as good as the Soviet. To repeat, such a deduction and estimate are rough, but I think that this approach is right in principle and that we hit near the mark. This is supported also by a well-known fact: even when meat is available in Soviet stores, it is much more expensive (one and a half or two times) in collective farm markets – here quality is higher.

What has been said is quite enough to assert: the CIA estimate overstates the comparative level of Soviet consumption for this subgroup by at least a factor of two, and I take it below, in Table 7.1, as 17 per cent of the American level.[20]

The average per capita consumption of *fish and fish products* in kilograms was three times greater in the USSR according to Table 5.1, though total consumption in value terms according to table 5.4 was about 50 per cent greater in the US. A rather obvious explanation can be found, which apparently satisfied the authors. With respect to quantity, the USSR is quickly developing (more accurately, was developing)[21] large-scale ocean fishing, and many varieties of fish (including cod) are cheaper than meat, and were (!) more available. In Russia, traditionally, a lot of herring was eaten.[22] In the US comparably more crabs, oysters, shrimp, and lobster, which are light in weight but more expensive, are eaten, as well as expensive types of fish (in particular, salmon and trout), which leads to the overall preponderance for total consumption in the subgroup. Hence, it should turn out from the figures presented that the average quality of fish and fish products in America is 4.5 times higher.

We do not know if the authors reasoned thus or whether they tried at all to explain for themselves this difference in the results of comparisons in kilograms and in value terms. However, as is easily seen by examining American data in primary sources, average per capita consumption here is in 'edible weight'.[23] In itself this is quite logical; this is exactly how American statistics are constructed. But Soviet statistics are governed by their own logic and they count fish consumption according to 'live weight'.[24] And if you take data on the consumption of fish used for food in the US in live weight and sum them with the consumption of mollusks in edible weight, it turns out that in 1976 per capita consumption was not 6 but 15.6 kg[25] compared with 18 kg in the USSR. But then the 'quality' of American fish and fish products is only 1.7 times greater than in the USSR, and this cannot be right.

I already said that a lot of mollusks (shellfish) are eaten in the US. Concretely, in 1976, per capita consumption of fresh and frozen fish in edible weight was 2.5 kg, and mollusks were half of this quantity, 1.2 kg. In addition, consumption of smoked fish was 0.2 kg and canned fish, 2 kg.[26] Mollusks per unit of weight are much higher in 'quality' and more expensive than fish, and this should have a decisive influence on the ratio being examined, since they are practically not eaten in the USSR.[27] But this is not all. In America the share of better quality fish is unquestionably higher. This follows at least from the fact that in 1976 the catch of salmon in live weight was 625 g per capita (twice that of herring), and consumption of canned salmon (edible weight) was

200 g.[28] In the USSR salmon is now a very rare and expensive delicacy. Total per capita consumption of canned fish in 1976 was 2 kg in the US and 32 kg in the USSR.[29]

The authors' erroneous estimate of fish consumption in kilograms and the fact that their list of sample goods for the subgroup includes only three types of fish which are far from the most representative – fresh catfish, frozen codfish and tuna – are at the root of what I consider to be the unquestionable *overstatement* of the comparative volume of Soviet consumption for the subgroup.

As is apparent from Table 5.5, the share of the public dining markup for fish in the US is rather small,[30] although it is higher than in the USSR. In general, the 'correction for the markup' should not be significant here. On the basis, primarily, of the high share of expensive shellfish, and upon the fact that more high quality fish such as salmon and trout are eaten in the US, I consider that the authors have overstated the comparative volume of Soviet consumption for the subgroup by a factor of two.

I remind the reader of what was said at the end of Chapter 2. Quite probably, the authors' calculations were done by the 'indirect' method, which means that they did not use in their calculations the quantities of fish consumed. In such a case I can hardly talk about their mistakes in determining the quantities consumed. But if this is so, then my critique, as was also said in Chapter 2, pertains to the price ratios and price parities for the subgroup. What is important is not which particular method they used, but the results. And if we take into consideration the right quantities of fish and fish products consumed, then the ratio of qualities for this subgroup which follows from the authors' results does not look correct.

In regard to the size of my correction, all the material presented above shows, it seems to me, that the correction is minimal. Quite likely, the real Soviet lag in consumption of fish is even greater.

Now about *milk, eggs, and cheese*. In 1976 in the USSR the per capita consumption of eggs was 219, while in the US it was 274 or one-fourth more. The countryside gave the city 64.4 per cent of its total egg production,[31] although the portion of urban population was 61.5 per cent. Considering that part of the eggs went for incubation, we find that egg consumption in the city must have been higher than in the countryside.

Regarding milk, there are many riddles. First of all, the total volume of its production in the USSR is extremely suspicious. An elementary comparison shows an improbably large amount of milk relative to beef.[32] We estimated above (Table 6.1) that the US produces about three times more beef and veal than the USSR per capita, but the production of milk and milk products (converted to milk) in the USSR turns out to be 349 kg per capita compared with 254 kg.[33] In America, calves are raised specially for meat (which, incidentally, results in much better beef), but the difference is still too great, and we may suspect a significant overstatement of milk production in the USSR.[34] Attempts to investigate this encountered, to put it mildly, vagueness about its fat content. At a maximum it is 3.2 per cent, and in fact probably less,[35] while in the US in 1976 it was 3.66.[36]

Soviet data on the production of various milk products are fragmentary and incomplete, and whatever we can ascertain is not comparable to America statistics. For example, the latter do not distinguish sour cream and cream. Our authors did not demonstrate the details of their calculations, in particular of how much of which items was produced in the USSR and the US. I will try to fill out this picture somewhat.

With regard to the USSR, as the reader, of course, guessed, Lokshin has some data; he speaks of the percentage breakdown of basic milk products and it is easy to calculate that in 1974 industry produced 9.6 m tons of whole milk, 916 000 tons of sour cream, 592 000 tons of cottage cheese and related products, and 528 000 tons of cheese.[37] The yearbooks give the production of whole milk products – 23 m tons in 1974 and 23.4 in 1976 – and report that this includes 'milk, cream, sour cream, yogurt (*kefir, atsidofilin,* and *prostokvasha*), curds (*syrkovaya massa*), cottage cheese, and other whole milk products'. In 1974, 428 000 tons of ice cream were produced.[38] Using these and some other data (production of canned milk, etc.) and also norms of the use of milk, we can more or less calculate the output of other milk products by industry. But this is not enough: we have no data on the production of cottage cheese, butter, sour cream, etc. in the countryside, and this greatly muddies the entire picture. Things are no better with the sale of milk and milk products in *kolkhoz* markets. We know (as the statistics assert – Table 6.2) that their total in 1976 amounted to 2.3 per cent of all milk production in the country (4.5 per cent in 1960), but we do not even have a hint about the product structure of these sales. Evidently Soviet statisticians also do not know how much of various milk products is produced from private livestock holdings and how much is sold in kolkhoz bazars.

Undoubtedly, the authors were forced to resort to some sort of assumptions and estimates, but since they told us nothing we have no possibility of detailed discussion. However, there are enough data for one general remark. The authors determined the total per capita Soviet consumption for this subgroup to be R63.2 [20], which gives a total of R16.2 billion. Total retail sales in state and cooperative trade for these goods (milk and milk products, cheese and eggs) in 1976 were R10.6 billion, including R1.3 billion in cooperative trade.[39] If we assume that cooperative trade operates entirely in the countryside,[40] R9.3 billion remains for consumption in the cities, and total consumption in the countryside is R6.9 billion, i.e., per capita figures of R58.82 and R70.02, respectively. Or, in other figures, per capita consumption in the countryside is higher than in the city by about 20 per cent. This, of course, cannot be. Let us look at the figures in Table 6.2. Already in the 1960s workers and other employees consumed more milk and slightly fewer eggs than collective farmers. The overall trend for the period up to 1969, when these data were published, was generally toward the more rapid growth of food consumption by the urban population. Table 6.2 shows as well that the sales in collective farm markets as a share of total production were declining, and the share of state purchases was rising much faster than the urban share of population. As a result, if already in 1968 the city was significantly (by 8 per cent) ahead of the countryside in the per capita consumption of milk and only a bit behind (by 2 per cent) in the consumption of eggs, in 1976 the city should have moved farther ahead of the countryside in the consumption of milk and passed it in the consumption of eggs.

I add the following. First, the publication of the tables on consumption of workers and employees, and collective farmers was not accompanied by any sort of explanations, and one might suspect that the number of 'workers and employees' includes state farm workers. If this is so, the advantage of the city is even greater since state farm workers hardly drank more milk or ate more eggs then collective farmers.

Second, because of the absence of data for several years, I had to calculate the shares of state purchases and sales in collective farm markets as a percentage of production rather than consumption, relative to which the percentages would be higher.

Third, the comparison in Table 6.2 is made in physical units. The difference in favour of the city should be much greater in value terms. In fact, much more of such expensive products as ice cream, cheese, and curds is consumed in the city and the percentages of yogurt, etc. are much higher.

What else can be said about comparative indicators of consumption for this subgroup? In 1974 the per capita consumption of ice cream was 1.7 kg in the USSR and 8.2 kg in the US; in 1976 per capita cheese

52

Table 6.2 Consumption of milk and eggs

Year	Year-end urban share of %[a]	Milk				Eggs			
		Per cap. cons., kg		Share of tot. prod., %		Per cap. cons., no.		Share of tot. prod., %	
		Workers and employees	Collective farmers %	State purchases	Collective farm markets[b]	Workers and employees	Collective farmers %	State purchases	Collective farm markets[b]
1960	50	245	228 107.5	43	4.5	117	122 95.9	24	14.6
1965	53	257	234 109.8	53	3.0	124	123 100.8	36	11.7
1966	54	265	246 107.7	53	2.8	131	133 98.5	37	11.7
1967	55	279	260 107.3	53	2.8	137	141 97.2	35	14.5
1968	55	290	268 108.2	54	2.9	143	146 97.9	40	11.3
1970	57	—	—	55	2.8	—	—	44	9.8
1976	62	—	—	63	2.3	—	—	59	5.9

[a]Narkhoz-77, pp. 7, 208, 259, 263.
Narkhoz-68, pp. 322, 399, 403, 595.
Narkhoz-67, p. 697.

[b]Sales in collective farm markets were taken to be equal to the difference between the commodity output of agriculture and state purchases. Certainly the sales are overstated since it is not possible to separate out what state and collective farms sell to their own workers. But the error should not be great.

consumption was 2.4 kg in the USSR and 7.2 kg in the US.[41] I could not ascertain how much milk is drunk in the USSR. In the US in 1976 sales to consumers and consumption directly on farms in the form of milk and cream were 111.6 kg or 305 g per day.[42]

I repeat that it is not possible to judge the correctness of all the CIA calculations for this subgroup. We cannot even confidently compare the per capita quantities of milk in both countries. The most serious difficulty is the absence of exhaustive and comparable data on the consumption of various milk products – sour cream, yoghurt, cream, etc. – figures which the authors did not present. None the less, although in the USSR consumption of milk and milk products in 1976 was officially 316 kg and in the USSR 258 kg,[43] i.e., 18 per cent less, we can make the following correction for fat content. In the US it was 3.66 per cent and in the USSR a maximum of 3.2 per cent. Thus, Soviet per capita consumption at a fat content of 3.66 per cent is 276 kg or only 7 per cent more than in the US.

Even on the assumption that the CIA calculations regarding the urban population are correct, with respect to the rural population they are overstated – at least by about 15–20 per cent. The average per capita indicator for the country must similarly be overstated. Hence, here also the comparative estimate of Soviet consumption is exaggerated, and I correct the authors' data in Table 7.1 by 7 per cent.

One other point: although there is no doubt that the countryside has made a great leap forward from the hungry Stalin years, it is no less indisputable that the overall standard of living in the countryside continues to lag behind that of the city. The Soviet press admits this. But, in general, if people in the countyside dress more poorly, if, as the official statistics say, rural dwellers have far fewer televisions and washing machines (see Table 9.2), if rural life has few of the amenities of the city (if we can use this term at all for rural life in the USSR at the end of the twentieth century), it is thought that people in the countryside eat no worse than in the city. No special refinements, but it is still home cooking and plentiful. It turns out that even this is not so: the calculations presented above destroy this legend and prove beyond a doubt that even for such products as milk and eggs where the countryside was ahead, it now also lags significantly. It lags on the assumption that Soviet statistics are trustworthy, but it is precisely with respect to 'own' production of meat, milk and eggs that these data are most suspicious! There is no full account of the production of milk and eggs from private plots, and Soviet statistics are not very good at sample survey methods, even though there are much greater possibilities for all sorts of statistical tricks in using these methods.

Now, on *oils and fats*. In 1976 per capita consumption in the US was: butter, 2 kg; lard, 1.2 kg; margarine, 5.5 kg; shortening, 8.2 kg; and various vegetable oils, 10 kg.[44] These figures relate to direct food use of fats. Things are more difficult, of course, with Soviet data. We know only that the production of animal fats, including home production was 1.356 m tons, i.e., 5.3 kg per capita, and 'margarine products', 4.1 kg, while consumption of vegetable oils was 7.7 kg.[45] I could find no separate data on the consumption of lard. Thus, if we add in shortening, Americans consume more than twice as much vegetable oil as the average Soviet, but half as much butter. Based upon the correlation of these figures, the authors apparently concluded that Soviet consumption of fats was 64 per cent of American according to the geometric mean

This is all fine, but two things alarm me. One is that the authors use a price of butter of R2.41 per kg [41], which is incorrect.[46] The second is more fundamental, and we spoke of it in examining meat consumption. Americans, as we see, eat more margarine and less butter. Whose consumption is better (higher, greater)? According to the concept used in the study, the Soviet way of eating more butter than margarine is preferable, which follows directly from the relative price ratios – 0.846 for butter and 1.875 for margarine [41]. But is this right? Americans refuse to eat butter not because of its high price but because of cholesterol. And the taste of many types of American (not Soviet!) margarine can hardly be distinguished from that of butter. In 1976, the per capita consumption of butter in the US was 42 per cent lower than in 1960, while the consumption of margarine grew by 30 per cent, and that of vegetable oil almost by a factor of two.[47] Can we think that the volume of consumption of fats by some value measure thus declined? Of course not; such a structural change reflected the buyers' preferences; their demand for fats was no less satisfied.

I do not see any clear answer to the questions that arise in this connection, and therefore cannot criticise the authors' results. Within the framework of the method used, they are indeed completely logical. None the less, this question should be discussed further.

The authors consider the number of calories that Americans get in fats to be 1.63 times greater than in the USSR (Table 5.3), and this is the ratio of the volumes of consumption that they got for the subgroup (Table 5.4). But this must mean that the quality of fats in both countries (comparing one by one) is identical, which is obviously not so. It follows that here also Soviet consumption is unquestionably overstated in comparison with American, although apparently not by much.[48] In my further reasoning and computation (Table 7.1), I do not correct the authors' figures on fats, but I don't think that the figures are completely right.

Vegetables. Here the author's task was exceptionally difficult. The available data in the literature on Soviet consumption are very incomplete and contradictory. It is sufficient to say that the authors were forced to determine Soviet consumption of vegetables by type on the basis of data on the structure of retail sales in 1963 which, moreover, naturally do not include 'own' consumption. Unfortunately, American data are also far from ideal; figures in various sources are not always consistent and there is no information on 'own' consumption, which is not small – non commercial gardening is widespread. The Soviet consumer's expenditures on vegetables account for 3 per cent of total expenditures on food, and the American's 10 per cent (Table 5.4).

Table 6.3 presents some of my own calculations, and I must say immediately that far from everything in them is trustworthy. Regarding the data for the USSR, the point is not only that, because of the absence of other data, I distributed total consumption of vegetables by type proportionately to production on all types of farms excluding private plots. This is minor, all the more so since (according to official statistics!) only a little more than one-fourth of total production was on private plots. And the problem is not that, following Lokshin, I got an amazingly large amount of melons, but primarily that our totals are surely greatly overstated. The main thing, of course, is losses. If the reported per capitas consumption of vegetables (86 kg) is multiplied by the production and the resulting figure is subtracted from total production (25 m tons), we find losses to be only 11.7 per cent. But the Soviet literature is full of statements about significantly greater losses, which must at a minimum be two or three times greater.[49] We should also not forget that losses are considered to be only that which was not sold to the consumer; when he brings them home he throws away what is rotten and spoiled, which is not less than 10 per cent of the amount purchased (it is often mentioned in Soviet literature).

In other words, in examining the figures for the USSR in Table 6.3, the reader should in no case believe his eyes; both the total amount of consumption, and consumption of individual of vegetables, are overstated at a minimum by about 20 per cent.

Table 6.3 Per capita consumption of vegetables and melons, 1976, kg

| | USSR[a] | US | |
		Total[d]	Of which, canned and frozen[e]
Cabbage	32.2	5.2[e]	1.0
Carrots	6.5	4.1	
Beets	6.6	0.7	
Tomatoes	22.1	33.5[e]	27.7
Cucumbers	4.1	4.5[e]	2.8
Onions	5.3	7.4	
Total	76.8	55.4	
Watermelon	?	6.1[f]	
Other melons	?	3.7[g]	
Total	7.0[b]	9.8	
Garlic	?	0.2	
Beans	?	3.4	1.6
Green peas	?	5.0[e]	5.0
Sweet corn	?	12.7[e]	9.0
Head lettuce	?	11.4	
Spinach	?	0.9[e]	0.7
Asparagus	?	0.6[e]	
Broccoli and brussels sprouts	?	1.1	0.6
Green pepper	?	1.1	
Celery	?	3.6	
Other vegetables	?	7.4[h]	
Total	2.2[c]	47.4	
Grand total	86.0	112.6[i]	

[a]Calculations, except in noted instances, were made as follows. The gross harvest for all farms excluding private plots is taken from *Vestnik statistiki*, 1977, no. 9, p. 92. Calculated shares were applied to the entire gross harvest, which was then reduced for losses. The latter (11.7%) are the difference between the overall gross harvest reported (25 mil. tons) and reported consumption (per capita consumption of 86 kg multiplied by the population). Imports were ignored because they were insignificant. (The authors used a similar procedure, which distributed vegetables by type proportionally to retail sales in 1963.)

[b]The 1974 market volume (Lokshin, p. 135) multiplied by a coefficient of 1.5 to account for 'own' consumption.

[c]Differences between the total (86 kg, taken from *Narkhoz-77*, p. 430) and all 'identified' items.

[d]*StAb-78*, p. 722, except for noted items. Commercial production only, excluding own consumption on farms and that which was not grown by farmers.

[e]USDA, *Outlook and Situation, Vegetables*, July, 1981, p. 28.

[f]Ibid., p. 29.

[g]Ibid. and *StAb-78*, p. 722.

[h]Difference between totals.

[i]USDA, *Outlook . . .*, pp. 26, 29.

But the data for the US in the same Table 6.3 also suffer from major shortcomings, although in the opposite direction – here the totals are not exaggerated but understated.

The reader may ask: why do I present questionable figures which even I do not trust very much? There are no better data (or I could not come by them). Still, they give a certain rough orientation. And, of course, just these (or approximately these) data were the basis for the authors' calculations.[50]

Given these significant reservations, let us look at the structure of consumption of vegetables in both countries; it is radically different. In the USSR, three types – cabbage, carrots and beets – account for more than half of all vegetables (here and below references for now are to kilograms), and adding the three other most 'common' types – tomatoes, cucumbers and onions – the total is 93 per cent of all vegetables (without melons). In the US cabbage is far from dominating the vegetable diet and per capita consumption of beets is about one-tenth that in the USSR. If we exclude tomatoes from the six 'common' types of vegetables, the remaining five comprise only 19 per cent of total vegetable consumption in the US compared with 63 per cent in the USSR. Still, the main thing that should be given particular attention is that the consumption of all vegetables other than the 'common' ones and melons is 20 times greater in the US than in the USSR. Even if we exclude corn from the calculation, the US figure is still 15 times greater.

The fundamentally different structures, and the existence in the American diet of a large number of vegetables that are practically non-existent in the USSR (types which, in addition to everything else, are more expensive), led the authors to conclude that Soviet consumption for the subgroup amounted to 19 per cent of American (Table 5.4). Let us try to use our usual analytical procedure. In the entire study the authors do not give figures for the overall per capita consumption of vegetables in kilograms in either the US or the USSR. If we believe Soviet statistics, with correction for losses (20 per cent instead of 11.7 per cent), Soviet consumption of vegetables in kilograms was $(86 \times 1.117 \times 0.8) \div 112.6 = 68$ per cent of American.

According to Table 5.5 the markup on public dining for vegetables was 11 per cent for the US and 4 per cent for the USSR. By doing the remaining calculations, we find that the authors' overall estimate is correct if the 'quality' of Soviet vegetables is 3.3 times worse than American. From the data we have available there is no way to say whether this is correct or not. No doubt the Soviet vegetable diet is much worse than the American, but a quantitative estimate is possible only by using the procedure actually employed by the authors. I cannot fully reproduce it but in general we have no serious grounds for thinking that they are very mistaken here. However, taking the authors' results as they are, we will note at least the following.

First, there is a readily apparent inconsistency in their calculations. In 1976 the urban population bought R2.3 billion worth of vegetables in retail trade, i.e. R14.5 per capita. According to our favourite source, in 1974 collective farm markets sold 11 per cent of all vegetables in retail trade (including sales in the markets themselves).[51] This should relate only to cities, so we get another R2.2 per capita for a total of R16.7. The authors determined average per capita expenditures on vegetables for the entire population to be R18.25 [20]. We now remove the markup on public dining (4 per cent) and establish that vegetable consumption per rural dweller was a little higher than in the city – R19.25. In itself this does not seem incorrect. However, according to the authors' 'balance of vegetables' [109], own consumption was only 9 per cent of total vegetable consumption in the entire country. I have no desire to work out the details of all the relevant calculations here, but this fact alone is evidence that the authors greatly understated losses of vegetables and therefore overstated their total consumption in kilograms. I said above that the Soviet consumption shown in Table 6.3 is overstated by about 20 per cent, and I repeat that this is a minimum estimate,[52] especially since American consumption is understated.

Second, as the authors admit, they were not able to reflect in their calculations the fact that fresh vegetables are sold year round in the US and only in the fall in the USSR. In Table 6.5, I showed how much of various types of vegetables goes for canning and freezing in the US; as we see, quite a lot remains for consumption in fresh form. There are no corresponding data for the USSR, but they would not be very informative since the vegetables that are primarily consumed there – cabbage, onions, carrots and beets – are, so to speak, the least perishable (and this, incidentally, is one of the reasons that the production of other vegetables does not develop).

Third, the authors considered as sample goods only eight types of vegetables, of which six are common, that is, their calculations practically exclude those types which give basic advantage to American consumption.

Overall, without any hesitation, I will state here also the comparative volume of Soviet consumption is overstated by at least 20 per cent.

Alas, data on *fruits* are no better than those on vegetables, and this again relates not only to Soviet but also to American statistics. Table

6.4 presents those data that I was able to collect and calculate, and I warn again that they are only approximately correct. Regarding the Soviet data, they greatly understate losses – about 8 per cent of the total harvest – which contradicts everything that we know and that is directly stated in the literature.[53] We note also that the percentage of fruit production on private plots is significantly higher than for vegetables – 42 per cent,[54] – which sharply increases the possibilities for various manipulators of the statistics. A comparison of the estimated indicators for fruit consumption by type with the American data in Table 6.4 also raises serious doubts.[55] In sum, although I am forced to use reported Soviet data on fruits for our calculations, I think that they are overstated by 20 per cent at a minimum.

The American data are far from ideal. Our two basic statistical handbooks – *StAb* and *AgSt* – do not give a conversion of canned, frozen and dried fruit into an equivalent for fresh fruit. I found such data only in a special publication used as a basis for the calculation in Table 6.4. However, some data in it contradict the other handbooks, and the resulting picture is only approximate. It is clear that the figures could not be overstated; apparently they are too low.[56]

In spite of all this, the statistics presented in Table 6.4 are sufficient for our basic argument. We can compare the total production of fruit and also get an impression of its structure and basic correlations. Even with all our reservations, it unquestionably follows from Table 6.4 that not only did total American fruit consumption exceed the Soviet by more than 2.5 times, but the American structure of consumption was also much better. Attesting to this, above all, is the fact that the consumption of citrus fruits in the US was almost 27 times greater than in the USSR. Also evidence of this is the existence in the American diet of a significant quantity of such high-quality and genuinely exotic (for the USSR) fruits as pineapple, papaya and avocado, and a high percentage of fresh fruits in the US.[57]

In 1976 the Soviet per capita consumption of fruit juices was 4.5 kg, that is, less than half a glass a week. In the US in the same year 9.4 kg per capita of natural juices were drunk, of which 5.9 kg were citrus, 0.5 pineapple, 0.25 grape, etc. In addition, 16.1 kg of frozen juices (converted to natural weight) were consumed.[58] Thus, overall, the average American drank 4.5 times more juice than the average Soviet.

According to the geometric mean, Soviet consumption of fruits was 20 per cent of American (Table 5.4). Considering the differences in the totals in kilograms according to Table 6.4 and the difference in markups on public dining (Table 5.5), we find that the average quality

Table 6.4 Per capita consumption of fruits and berries, 1976, kg

	USSR[a]	US[i] Total	US[i] Of which, in fresh form
Fruits with seeds (*semyachkovyye*), total	28.2[b]	16.8[j]	9.7[j]
Apples	?	13.0	8.5
Pears	?	3.8[k]	1.2
Fruits with pits (*kostochkovyye*), total	6.2[c]	12.4[j]	4.3[j]
Cherries	?	1.1[k]	0.4
Plums	?	3.0[j]	0.6
Peaches and apricots	?	7.5[k]	2.8
Avocados	0	0.7[k]	0.4
Figs	?	0.1	0.1
Citrus, total	2.1[d]	56.1	13.2
Oranges	1.2[e]	} 45.0[k]	6.7
Mandarin oranges	} 0.9[f]		1.3
Lemons (and limes in US)		2.8[k]	1.0
Grapefruit	0	8.3[k]	4.2
Table grapes	2.3[g]	?	1.5[m]
Bananas	0.01[e]	?	8.7
Pineapples	0.02[e]	?	0.5
Papayas	0	?	0.1
Berries, total	?	?	0.8
Cranberries	0.15[h]	0.5[k]	0.1
Strawberries	?	1.2[k]	0.7
Other berries	?	?	0.05
Other fruits	0		0.1
Grand total	39.0	102.7	38.9

[a]Production according to *Vestnik statistiki*, 1977, no. 9, p. 92, imports from *VT-76*, p. 43. Adding all components gives a figure 3.1 kg greater than the official indicator – 39 kg (*Narkhoz-77*, p. 430). The difference was taken to be losses (8%), and was allocated to fruits with seeds (2.5) and fruits with pits (0.6), respectively.

[b]Production of 7530 000 tons and imports (apples) of 358 000 tons.

[c]Production of 1739 000 tons and imports (plums) of 6000 tons.

[d]Sum of the components. In 1974, retail sales were 1.6 kg (Lokshin, p. 129).

[e]Imports.

[f]Imports of lemons 88 000 tons, and of mandarin oranges, 7000 tons. Production (not broken down) of 128 000 tons.

[g]Imports of 43 000 tons and production of 5435 000 tons. The percentage of consumption in fresh form (10.9%) is taken as in 1973 (Lokshin, p. 132).

[h]State procurement in 1974 (Lokshin, p. 141).

[i]Unless otherwise noted, figures are from USDA, *Outlook and Situation. Fruit*, July 1981, pp. 31–3.

[j]Sum of components.

[k]*AgSt-80*, pp. 211–47.

[l]*StAb-78*, p. 722.

[m]According to *AgSt-80*, p. 231, 2.2 kg.

of American fruits was only 1.9 times better than Soviet. Keep in mind that the quantity of Soviet fruits is probably overstated and the American no less probably understated. Add to this the incomparably better assortment of American fruits. Add also the year-round availability of fresh fruits in the US. And also note that in physical units the Soviet lag is incomparably greater for fruits than for vegetables, while out authors calculated practically identical geometric means 19 per cent and 20 per cent for vegetables and for fruits. Thus, the CIA substantially exaggerated the Soviet level of consumption of fruits – at a minimum by one-fourth.[59]

With respect to *potatoes*, we note first of all that while average Soviet consumption for the population as a whole was 119 kg urban per capita consumption was 90 and rural 164 kg.[60] This is further confirmation of the fact that less meat and milk products are eaten in the countryside than in the city.

In this connection it is worth saying that in 1913 the Russian per capita consumption of potatoes was less than in 1976 – 114 kg,[61] in spite of a much lower urban share of population (18 per cent compared with 61 per cent in 1976) – a fact that gives cause for wondering about dietary progress in this country.

Moving now directly to the results the authors got, we note that Soviet consumption amounted to (including sweet potatoes in the US) 218 per cent of American in kilograms (Table 5.1), and 90 per cent according to the geometric mean (Table 5.4). Taking into account the markup in public dining (Table 5.5), we see that the quality of American potatoes was 2.2 times better than Soviet. That American potatoes are better is unquestionable. There are special varieties for boiling and baking. About 5 per cent of the total volume are sweet potatoes which are unknown in the USSR. The potatoes are carefully washed, sorted and packaged; frost-bitten potatoes are not sold (but there are very tasty specially-frozen potatoes). However, all this hardly leads to a difference of 2.2 times. Possibly (it is not stated anywhere) such a difference resulted from including in the subgroup various products from potatoes – in particular, potato chips.

We should not forget that potatoes are the mainstay of the Soviet diet. With the exception of people in southern regions, everyone eats potatoes every day and in large quantities. In America they are just one of many vegetables. Therefore, it could well be that the authors overestimated the difference in quality and thus underestimated the comparative volume of consumption for the subgroup. I would raise the comparative estimate of Soviet consumption by 10 per cent.

It is difficult to judge the consumption of *sugar and confectioneries* using general reasoning. None the less, two factors – the use of sugar in *samogon*, and the fact that many Americans limit their consumption of sugar – are so significant that total Soviet consumption for this subgroup might comprise not 78 per cent of US consumption (Table 5.4), but more than 100 per cent. However, again a definite conclusion is difficult since we have little comparable information.[62]

Talking about confectioneries, although this is very atypical, in my impression (and taste) Soviet cakes and pies, at least in Moscow, Leningrad and Kiev, are better than American, while candies, especially chocolate, are in no way worse.[63]

In the USSR about 72 per cent of all sugar in natural form (including the production of *samogon*), and 28 per cent as ingredients in food products;[64] in America this relation is apparently the opposite. Note also that in the US in 1976 (then, it had not yet been announced that it was carcinogenic), a lot of saccharin was consumed.

By our usual method (Tables 5.1, 5.4 and 5.5), we find that according to the authors' results, the 'quality' of Soviet sugar and confectioneries is 15 per cent worse than American, and I have no reason to dispute this. It would be interesting to estimate what would happen if we take into account sugar expended on *samogon*. the consumption of saccharin in the US, and also the difference in the shares of sugar consumed in food products. But I do not have the material for even rough estimates of this sort.

Other foods should include primarily various spices – pepper, mustard, salt, etc. – and also wild mushrooms, berries and nuts, honey, fish and game. A lot is unclear here – in particular, just how the authors calculated the total amount of Soviet expenditures on 'own' consumption of nuts, mushrooms, fish, game, home-grown tobacco (*makhorka*) etc. – R1434 m [47]. But it is really difficult – we have practically no Soviet data. Obviously, this is the reason why the list of prices for this subgroup includes only salt, and thus the price parity was calculated using it alone. In 1976 America produced (mushrooms are not gathered in forests, and it's too bad) and imported 874 g of mushrooms per capita. Honey consumption in that year was 0.56 kg per capita in the US and 0.7 kg in the USSR.[65] These are official data, but my personal impression is that per capita consumption of honey is not really greater in the USSR.

The American data for the subgroup need to be revised. Fish caught by sportsmen, as I already wrote, do not enter into statistics but game meat does. Of course, this is not substantial.

The main thing is that Americans consume an endless quantity of the most diverse seasonings, sauces (beginning with ketchup), and other spices, and the US lead over the USSR should be greater here than for any other subgroup.[66] However, the overall sum of per capita expenditures (including the exceptionally high markup on public dining) is rather small, and, therefore, I refrain from making any corrections to the results the authors obtained.

7 Food (Conclusion)

There are few direct data on alcohol in statistical sources. None the less, some estimates of its production and sales (taking into account imports) are possible, but even this can be said of *samogon* (moonshine).

First, about beer. Its production in the USSR was 592 m. decalitres in 1976,[1] i.e. more than 32 litres per capita. This seems a lot, all the more so since beer is in short supply in the countryside and even in the city it is often scarce. But note that beer production is growing very rapidly – in particular, by 2.5 times since 1969. Such a rapid rate of growth is due not only to great demand but also to the fact that the authorities would like to substitute beer for stronger drinks (as is often written in 'anti-alcohol' articles).[2]

In America, per capita beer consumption in 1976 was almost 82 litres.[3] If we assume that half of the population drinks beer, then the average Soviet drinker has almost a litre a week and the American more than three litres. As we see later, the average American gets most of his alcohol in beer.

With respect to wine, 'the growth rates of wine production in the USSR are the highest in the world. The Soviet Union now occupies fifth place in the world in the absolute level of production of grape wine and is led only by Italy, France, Spain, and Portugal'.[4]

The yearbook speaks of production in 1976 of 315 m. decalitres of grape wine,[5] but this is far from all: the production of fruit and berry wine and champagne is not included. Such data are available for 1975, when, in addition to 297 m. decalitres of grape wine, 116 m. decalitres of fruit and berry wine plus 9 m. decalitres (130.4 m. bottles) of champagne were produced[6] – that is, about 17 litres per capita. Also in 1975, 57 m. decalitres of grape wine and 28 m. litres of chateau wines were imported (assuming 0.7 litres per bottle), and exports were insignificant.[7] Thus, total per capita consumption of all sorts of wine, excluding home production, in 1975 was 19 litres, and as we just saw, production of grape wine grew by 18 m. decalitres in 1976. Regarding home production, in 1976 almost one-forth, 23 per cent of the total grape harvest was from private plots.[8]

In America per capita consumption of wine in 1976 was 6.7 litres (6.1 litres in 1975).[9] Thus, not taking into account home production, it was about one-third of the Soviet level.

Such a huge Soviet 'advantage' in wine drinking seems strange, but this is a relatively new phenomenon, and I cited a little above the statement about the highest growth rates of wine production between 1940 and 1976 in the USSR. It is revealing that the production of grape wine alone grew by a factor of almost 16, and on a per capita basis by a factor of 12 – while the gross grape harvest increased by less than 5 times during this period.[10]

There have been no direct Soviet data on vodka for 20 years. The last time the yearbook published the production indicator for 'vodka and vodka products' was for 1982 (182 m. decalitres), and in that year the production of ethyl alcohol was 204 m. decalitres.[11] The amounts of vodka per capita was 7.3 litres.[12] Data on the production of ethyl alcohol were last published for 1969 – 273 m. decalitres.[13] Taking the ratio of vodka to ethyl alcohol production in 1969 to be the same as in 1962, we get, considering population growth, 9 litres per capita in 1969.

The existing level of production of spirits at the end of the 1960s was considered insufficient, and 'during 1971–4 the actual increase in the capacity of plants producing spirits as a result of reconstruction and expansion of operating enterprises amounted to 29.64 m. decalitres', an increase of about 10 per cent. From this same book we learn that in the year of interest to us, 1976, the capacity of the 154 plants of the liquor-vodka industry, and 68 shops producing vodka products, was 266.3 m. decalitres.[14]

Now if we gradually assume that the capacity utilisation of all these plants and shops was only 90 per cent, we get per capita production in 1976, and hence consumption (the foreign trade balance for the year was about 1 m. decalitres), of 9.3 litres.

There are no direct data in Soviet statistics on the population's expenditures on alcohol, and we must use retail trade indicators on 'other food goods' for approximate data, for 1963, shows that it almost exclusively relates to alcohol. There are also some indirect data. Thus, in 1974 vodka and liquor-vodka products accounted for 24% of total turnover of consumer cooperatives for food products,[15] which gives R7.6 billion. Given the average annual rural population at that time of 100.8 m., we get R75.4 per person a year. 'Liquor-vodka products', of course, are not used in the countryside; they get by with vodka. Taking the price per bottle existing then to be R3.5 (excluding bottle deposit), we get a per capita figure of more than 10 litres a year. This is more than we just obtained on the average for the population as a whole, and there should be more *samogon* in the countryside though much less beer and wine. Thus, from this standpoint the figure of 9.3 litres of vodka a year per capita is more or less supported.

Consumption of all other strong drinks was about 400 g a year.[16] So the total is 9.7 litres of vodka and cognac per capita a year. In the US per capita consumption of whisky, gin, vodka and all other 'hard liquor' in the same year amounted to about 5.5 litres,[17] i.e. a little more than half.

A mass of evidence from the literature as well as indirect indications says that the figures that we got for the USSR are low. For example, in 1913, people drank only a little less than in 1976, which is difficult to believe. The very fact that first, data on the production of vodka, and then of ethyl alcohol, were removed from statistical publications clearly indicates a rapid growth of consumption. There is (among much other) evidence from a *Komsomol* journal that in one new town vodka consumption per capita was 50 litres, i.e. more than five times greater than the figure we got.[18] In a recent article in a mass-circulation newspaper, Academician A. G. Aganbegyan writes: 'In a year I visit 50 enterprises, and not only administration quarters but the shops. And with the utmost bitterness I note, for example, workers that are drunk on the job are encountered more and more often. At several enterprises special teams have even been created to hunt the very drunk (note this 'very') and not allow them to their machines so that an accident will not happen. They drink during working hours, they drink after work.[19] Another citation: 'a complete "sobering up" of work processes could provide about a 10 per cent increase in labor productivity.'[20] And it is well known even from the Soviet press how they drink on pay-days, weekends and village holidays.

Let us also try a crude estimate. We exclude from the calculation children and the elderly, and will also not count women. Roughly speaking, one-fourth of the population remains.[21] If only this fourth drinks, then each has 39 litres a year, i.e., 100 g a day, which is clearly low, even considering *samogon* and wine.

The following simple calculation also put us on guard. Take the alcohol content of vodka and other liquor to be 40 per cent, beer 6 per cent and wine 12 per cent. Then, basing out calculations upon the figures above, per capita consumption in the USSR is 7.3 litres of pure alcohol, and in the US it is more! – 7.9 litres.

How can this be? The largest part of American alcohol consumption, 62 per cent, is beer, and together with wine it is already 72 per cent, while in the USSR 53 per cent falls to vodka and cognac.[22] A substantial correction is also needed for *samogon*, on which only the crudest estimates are possible. In the opinion of a well-known econo-mist, the late Academician S. G. Strumilin, *samogon* consumption was the equivalent of at least half of vodka. In particular, he cited a rough calculation according to which, in 1960, for each resident of the Dmitrov region of Moscow *oblast*, there were 12.7 litres of vodka and 10.4 litres of *samogon*.[23] In addition to *samogon* itself (including *chacha*, another variant), a lot of grape wine, home liqueurs, and home-brewed beer is also made. But if we included *samogon* equal to 50 per cent of vodka and cognac in our calculations, the total number would be 9.2 litres of pure alcohol, i.e. still only 16 per cent more than in the US.

All this is very strange. I already presented citations from the Soviet press about the general drunkenness. As an old saying goes, 'the Russian national pastime is drinking'. Anyone who has had the opportunity to observe the real life of Soviet people and to compare it to American's will agree with me that the difference could not be 16 per cent; it must be much greater.[24]

Why then do we get such results? First of all, I apparently understate vodka consumption a little. As a check, I estimated whether the amounts of wine, beer, vodka and cognac consumption shown above fit in the retail trade figures for 'other food goods' mentioned pre-viously. Although the alcohol share of this total is not shown separa-tely, and there are many uncertainties regarding prices, overall we have enough room for a little larger consumption of vodka. We have no guarantee that the capacity utilisation of liquor-vodka plants was exactly 90 per cent and not more.[25] However, on the other hand, we must keep in mind that a large correction will not fit; we have an upper limit of the total expenditures of the population on 'other food goods'.

It is also possible that the actual consumption of *samogon* is much greater than Strumilin figured, all the more so since the prices of both vodka and cognac have risen greatly since the year he cited, 1960. The drinking of spirits stolen from factories and laboratories should also be of some significance. Finally, my estimate of the volume of alcohol is very rough; in particular, the small share of dry wines in the USSR (see note 5) tells us that the average alcohol content of wine should be higher than in the US. The comparison of beer by alcohol content should also be revised.[26]

In sum, the problem is not very simple. That the US is far from being the heaviest 'drinking' country among those with reliable statistics also enters into our thinking here. In 1969, per capita consumption in litres of pure alcohol was 5.9 in the US, 17.7 in France, 14.1 in Italy, 11.4 in West Germany, 9.9 in Austria, 6.2 in the United Kingdom, 5.7 in

Sweden, 4.4 in Finland, and 3.4 in Norway.[27] The important thing is not litres of pure alcohol ('proof litres') but the, so to speak, structure of drinking. As the well-known historian A. Kazhdan says, in the Byzantine Empire supper consisted of bread and wine but by no means were they considered to be wallowing in drunkenness. And in spite of the fact that the per capita number of 'proof litres' is three times greater in France than in the US, you cannot say that the French get drunk more than Americans. You also cannot say that the Germans are 'drunker' than the Swedes; beer makes the difference. Thus, the problem of Soviet drinking is not so much in the great quantity of alcohol but in the fact that more than half is in the form of 'strong' drinks, even excluding *samogon*.

Still, we cannot say that everything here is clear. Although the source of a possible error is not apparent, the results we obtained do not themselves look very convincing. The Soviets drink so heavily and so often, there are so many confirmed drunkards, and alcoholism has become such a serious problem that it is very difficult to reconcile all these facts that are widely known and openly admitted in the Soviet literature with the figures presented above.

Be that as it may, we must assume that the CIA used in their calculations approximately the same data that I presented (they are not in the work itself). The authors did not count *samogon*, and determined the volume of consumption of alcohol in the USSR to be 119 per cent of the figure for the US (Table 5.4). I have serious doubts about this. Indeed, as we saw, the US is a little ahead in litres of pure alcohol (the CIA, I repeat, did not consider *samogon*). Thus, for the figure 119 per cent to be correct, the 'quality' of Soviet alcoholic beverages must have been more than 20 per cent higher than American. To some extent this is consistent with the much greater consumption of wine in the USSR, the 'quality' of which is significantly higher than that of beer (which is seen from price comparisons). However, it is no less significant that, comparing beer with beer, wine with wine, and Soviet vodka with American vodka, gin, etc., the advantage must unquestionably be given to American beverages. The point is not the pretty American labels or that any American bottle can be closed while a Soviet bottle once opened must be emptied on the spot, but that American drinks are incomparably better in taste. A pedant will say that the US imports Soviet vodka, and it is expensive here. But the quality of the export and ordinary vodkas cannot be compared; vodka for export is produced separately and with much higher standards.

Here I must complain again about the lack in detail in the data presented in the study, without which it is difficult to make substantial criticisms. How this 119 per cent was specifically obtained is unclear. If it reflects that, in spite of all statistics, people drink more in the USSR, without even considering *samogon* (and with a discount for poorer quality), then I will not protest. But it well might be a mistake in the calculations.[28]

The study estimates of the amounts of the Soviet population's expenditures in rubles and the American in dollars are themselves apparently correct. The average Soviet spends on alcohol more than 25 per cent of all his outlays on food and more than 12 per cent of all consumption expenditures, while the American spends correspondingly 12 per cent and 2 per cent.[29] However, it is not clear how the authors of the study transformed these figures into an estimate of the volume of consumption using the procedure that we know. Although this estimate is debatable, I cannot offer a better one.

Moving now to *non-alcoholic beverages*, I will say immediately that the authors' estimate overstates the comparative volume of Soviet consumption, which, they assert, is 37 per cent of the American. It also amazes me that the price parities for this subgroup are almost identical [20]. Accidentally, of course, this may be, but it is not clear just how this accident happened. Supporting the authors somewhat, I must say that they faced a serious lack of . . . American statistics, which do not report exactly how much Pepsi, Coke, and Seven-Up in physical units were produced and consumed.

In 1975, Soviet mineral water consumption was 3.6 litres per capita a year, and other non-alcoholic beverages (*kvas, sitro,* etc.) 9.5 litres,[30] i.e a little more than a glass a week. These beverages are drunk primarily in the summer and then not everywhere.[31]

With regard to the US, in 1976, 122 000 people worked in the highly mechanised non-alcholoic beverages industry, and their output (in wholesale prices!) amounted to almost $42 per capita.[32] I repeat, we do not have data on the consumption of various beverages in physical units, but they are drunk year round and in incredible quantities. Add to this the incomparable quality, including packaging, and consider that these drinks are chilled year round, which requires a lot of energy. Americans consume also a large quantity of various prepared mixers for fixing cocktails, which (mixers or cocktails) do not exist in the USSR.

Regarding coffee, American consumption in 1976 was 32 times greater than Soviet[33] – 5.5 kg in the US and 173 g in the USSR per capita. For no other product is consumption this much smaller in the

USSR. The consumption of tea in the US in 1976 was 381 g per capita, and Soviet consumption in 1975 was 703 g.[34]

In sum, the relative volume of Soviet consumption is significantly overstated for this subgroup also, at a minimum by about one and a half times.

But the proportion of *tobacco and tobacco products* in the USSR is clearly understated – 18 per cent of the American level. In 1976, 1679 cigarettes and *papirosy* were smoked per capita in the USSR and 2852 cigarettes and 25 cigars in the US.[35] The difference, as we see, is in no way 5.56 times. True, in America smoking pipes, and also (though less so) chewing tobacco, are much more widespread, and there are many diverse knick-knacks for smokers and those who want to give them presents, but, on the other hand, 10 per cent of Soviet smokers use home-grown tobacco (*makhorka*).[36] For the authors' results to be correct, it must be assumed that the quality of Soviet cigarettes is more than three times worse than America. The concept of 'worse' here is itself rather arbitrary, but this correlation cannot be correct under any assumptions. In particular, the practice of chain smoking is less frequent in the USSR; in other words, Soviet cigarettes 'satisfy' better.

In sum, the CIA estimate for this subgroup must be changed in favour of the USSR, at a minimum by a factor of two.

Thus, we have examined all of the results of comparisons for food, and I presented quite a lot of corrections to the results the CIA got. Table 7.1 gives a summary of my corrections and a very rough estimate of their overall impact. In the first columns I give the CIA's geometric estimates for each subgroup, show my corrections in percent, and calculate a 'final' estimate. All together we examined 13 subgroups. For five of them I made no corrections. For two I considered the CIA estimate understated, that is, it appears to me that the level of Soviet consumption for these subgroups is higher than the CIA believes. For six subgroups, it seems that the CIA overstated the comparative level of Soviet consumption.

What is the aggregate of my corrections? To determine it precisely, a lot of calculations, particularly re-examining price ratios and parities, are needed. I limit myself to a rough estimate. In the second part of Table 7.1 I calculate what the figures of Soviet food consumption in rubles and American in dollars would be with my corrections. For example, since my correction for meat is 50 per cent, I decrease the CIA

Table 7.1 Correction of food consumption indicators

| Subgroup | USSR consumption as % of US | | | Amount of consumption | | | |
| | CIA estimate (geom. mean)[a] | My correction | 'Final' estimate | Soviet, rubles | | American, dollars | |
				CIA[a]	With correction	CIA[a]	With correction
Bread and cereals	96	0	96	60	60	110	110
Meat and poultry	34	− 50	17	101	51	282	564
Fish	67	− 50	34	17	8	48	96
Milk, eggs, cheese	59	− 7	55	63	59	116	125
Oils and fats	64	0	64	26	26	38	38
Vegetables	19	− 20	15	18	14	110	138
Fruit	20	− 25	15	20	15	61	81
Potatoes	90	+ 10	99	16	18	14	13
Sugar and confectioneries	78	0	78	47	47	50	50
Other foods	39	0	39	14	14	39	39
Alcoholic beverages	119	0	119	138	138	133	133
Non-alcoholic beverages	37	− 33	25	11	7	54	81
Tobacco	18	+ 100	36	15	30	75	38
Total	53		43	546	487	1130	1506

[a][20]

ruble estimate by this percentage and increase the dollar estimate by a factor of two. This method is suitable for a rough evaluation.

It turns out that the total of Soviet food consumption in rubles is 11 per cent less, and the total of American consumption in dollars is one-third more. This means that the geometric estimate of Soviet food consumption should be less by about 20 per cent. In other words, if the CIA asserts that Soviet food consumption is 53 per cent of American, according to my estimates it is no more than 43 per cent,[37] i.e. roughly about 20 per cent less.

I must say most clearly that no great faith should be placed in this estimate. Once again I remind the reader that, while persistently criticising the CIA figures, I was forced to base my calculations largely on them; in particular, I did not determine price ratios and parities myself. Many things could not be checked because not all details are given in the CIA report. Moreover, the extent of my corrections is arbitrary: they should give no more than an impression of the direction and scale of the corrections needed.

And, of course, my critique is far from over. As the reader will see in Chapter 12, there is still a whole series of comments that relate directly to calculations for food.

One of the first readers of the manuscript noted that my overall estimate does not very seriously change the CIA estimate, especially in rubles. If the present reader has formed the same opinion, it is mistaken. The point is not only that for individual subgroups the difference is great, but that, I repeat, not seeing many details, we may presume that there are other mistakes.

At the same time I should repeat once again – in no way do I pretend that my corrections are precise. My purpose is to ascertain their direction and scale. For example, in reducing the authors' estimate for Soviet consumption of meat and meat products by 50 per cent, I cannot guarantee that in fact it could not be 40 or 60 per cent. However, I assert that, first the estimate must be reduced, and secondly, that the reduction must be very significant.

In sum, considering the factors of which we will speak in Chapter 12, the overall CIA estimate for the group must be *substantially* corrected.

8 Soft Goods

Recall that by 'soft' goods we mean all consumer goods other than food and durables. Comparison is made difficult here, in addition to everything else, by different classifications in the statistics of the two countries.[1] In Table 8.1 (as in Table 9.1 in Chapter 9) I first present figures for goods for which the classifications coincide, and then try to place similar subgroups of goods close to each other. Remember (Table 4.1) that according to the authors' calculations, total Soviet per capita consumption as a percentage of American for this entire group is: in

Table 8.1 Per capita consumption of soft goods, 1976[a]

	USSR Rubles	%	US Dollars	%	Ruble–dollar price parity with American weights
Footwear	38	16	54	8	0.845
Drugs and medical supplies	4	2	48	7	0.499
Household soap and cleaners	4	2	64	10	0.956
School and stationery supplies	5	2	15	2	0.730
Publications	9	4	—	—	
Magazines and newspapers	—	—	38	6	0.206
Books	—	—	17	3	0.156
Sewn clothing	68	28	—	—	
Knitwear	35	15	—	—	
Fabrics	27	11	—	—	
Hosiery	9	4	—	—	
Women's and children's clothing	—	—	195[b]	30	1.554
Men's and boy's clothing	—	—	104[b]	16	1.531
Toilet soap and cosmetics	8	3	—	—	
Toilet paper	1	—	—	—	
Toilet articles	—	—	49	7	0.974
Haberdashery and notions	22	9	—	—	
Semidurable furnishings	—	—	42	7	1.164
Other goods	11	4	25	4	1.136
Total	241	100	651	100	1.136

[a]Calculated from figures in [62, 63], based on a population in the USSR of 256.7 million, and in the US 215.1 million. The CIA calculated the indicators for the USSR on the basis of the amount of state and cooperative trade sales (e.g., *Narkhoz-77*, pp. 458–9) and certain assumption about services, sales to organisations rather than the population (excluding servicemen), sales of used goods, and home knitting.
[b]To avoid misunderstanding, these figures mean that, on the average, expenditures for clothing amounted to $299 per capita.

73

rubles – 32 per cent, in dollars – 48 per cent, and by the geometric mean – 39 per cent. I recommend that the reader examine carefully the indicators for expenditures on various goods in Table 8.1 and compare them with each other: they are interesting in themselves.

Thus, analysing primarily the shares shown in Table 8.1, we see that the share of expenditures on *footwear* is twice as great in the USSR. According to the authors' calculations [20], the absolute levels of consumption of footwear in the USSR and the US are practically identical (98 per cent by the geometric mean) which is surely incorrect. Elsewhere [9], they state that the average Soviet buys 3.2 pairs of shoes a year,[2] and the American 1.9 pairs, which is no more correct.[3] The Soviets drive less and walk more, the harsher climate should have an effect, the durability of American shoes is higher (they are usually sturdier), and apparently the authors explained their results to themselves with these factors. However, there are others. Here, shoes are replaced more often, especially women's, and repairing shoes is much less common.[4]

Also of importance is the fact that according to the CIA data (see Table 8.1), the Soviet consumer's expenditures on shoes – R38 – amount to 3.5 per cent, while the American's $54 is less than 1 per cent of total annual consumer spending. The scarcity of shoes in the USSR must also have an effect. The Soviet consumption of shoes has not grown in recent years (see Table 13.5), and it has still not reached the so-called rational norm.[5] There can also be various opinions about aesthetics, but I leave this aside for lack of an objective measure.

Shoes provide a convenient example for explaining a point which is germane to our entire topic. Speaking only about 'need', we note that people are not tramping the streets barefoot in either the US or the USSR, and, as I already said, in the latter, shoes are worn out quicker. But consumption of shoes is determined not only by bare (an appropriate word here) necessity, rationality; they also have a social function. Precisely for this reason shoes are replaced before they have gaping holes. The comfort of footwear is also very important – how it fits, whether it rubs or is too tight, etc.[6] To a large extent the example of shoes can be likened to the situation with food. In general no one starves in the USSR, as no one goes barefoot, but this does not keep the total amount of food consumption in the US from being far ahead.

By taking these things into account, the authors would have examined their figures more carefully and would not have gotten caught in an elementary statistical trick. But trying to be just, I must say that several emigrants with whom I discussed these comparative figure saw nothing incredible in them.

I already said that Soviet statistics are rarely arbitrarily distorted, but it is always necessary to carefully keep an eye on the methodology and definitions. This applies fully to this concrete case. American statistics strictly differentiate between leather and non-leather shoes, and the statistical yearbooks have a special note that the figures are for leather footwear and that 'rubber and plastic footwear' is excluded.[7] Soviet statistics also speak of 'leather' footwear and give figures for 'rubber footwear' separately, but this is intended for the inattentive reader. In those sections of the yearbook that speak of the production and consumption of footwear, it is called 'leather', but the section on retail trade calls it 'leather, textile, and combined'.[8] The *CEMA* yearbook refers to the same figures as 'footwear from leather and leather substitutes (other than footwear from rubber)' and defines it as 'with uppers from natural leather, with textile uppers, with uppers from leather substitutes and combination uppers on any sole – leather sole, sole of leather substitute; ... dress, street, house, sports, and ortho-pedic footwear'.[9]

The wonderful Lokshin gives us some figures in this area also. Of all 'leather footwear' produced in 1974, 64 per cent had uppers of natural leather, and 30 per cent had leather soles. He says also that dress shoes amounted to only 12 per cent of total production of 'leather' footwear in 1973. He explains as well what is included in 'rubber footwear'. In 1973, 32 per cent of it was composed of galoshes, 30 per cent of women's full-length and half-length rubber boots,[10] and the rest must include men's rubber boots and sports shoes. In other words, an examination of data on 'rubber' footwear also shows that 'leather' footwear includes everything except galoshes, various rubber boots, and sports shoes.

What has been said is quite enough, but there are two more points. First, we have to pay attention to the fact that a direct division of expenditures in retail trade (R9060 m.) by consumption of 'leather' footwear (3.2 pairs per year) and by the population yields an average price per pair of shoes in 1976 of R11.03. For that money you cannot buy real leather shoes in the USSR (except children's). Second, the production of hard and soft leather in the USSR is growing much slower than the production of 'leather footwear'.[11]

Thus, it is clear that the actual consumption of leather footwear in the USSR amounted to at best half of reported consumption, i.e., a maximum of 1.6 pairs per capita a year against 1.9 pairs in the US. If we also take into account quality, the volume of consumption of Soviet leather (here without quotation marks) footwear was much less than American.

Data on the American consumption of footwear other than those in the usual statistical yearbooks are also readily available to us. From them it follows that 786.5 m. pairs of all sorts of footwear, including house slippers, plus 115.4 m. pairs with leather soles but vulcanised or textile uppers, were consumed (bought) in the US in 1976.[12] Not being a specialist on shoes, I will risk the assumption that the latter part is more or less equivalent to Soviet 'rubber' shoes. In other words, we must compare the official Soviet per capita consumption of 'leather' footwear of 3.2 pairs a year in 1976 not with 1.9, but 3.6 pairs a year actually consumed (bought) in the US.

In summary, we can say that the number of pairs of footwear consumed in the USSR per capita was not 1.7 times as big as in the US, but actually less. If this is so, the result of the CIA calculations – that Soviet consumption of footwear was 98 per cent of American consumption – should mean that the average quality of Soviet shoes was higher than American, which is, of course, absurd.

Once again, in pinpointing my disagreement with the estimates, I have no 'objective' basis for an alternative figure. But, hopefully, we can assume that the CIA estimate must be corrected by the extent of their error in quantities of shoes. In other words, the estimate must be reduced by 50 per cent, which means that Soviet per capita consumption of footwear was half of American.

The shares of expenditures on *clothing* in the two countries, including fabrics for the USSR, turn out to be quite close – 54 per cent in the USSR and 46 per cent in the US (Table 8.1). The volume of consumption for the USSR in this subgroup is calculated to be 40 per cent of the American [20]. I question this estimate as well.[13] The CIA experts could not peer into Soviet clothes wardrobes,[14] so I will try to help them.

The Soviet office worker wears the same suit to work day after day and, in addition, has a 'holiday' suit and a set of summer clothing. The American goes to work in his best clothes and must have many combinations. I already said at the beginning of this overview that the Moscow public does not dress poorly, but they have few changes of clothes. Moreover, the colossal difference in how Muscovites dress compared with people of provincial cities and especially the countryside is always apparent at a glance.[15]

We should also not forget that acquiring clothing in the USSR is not only a very difficult but an expensive business – buying a suit, dress, or even more so, a coat, is an appreciable blow to the family budget. A common expression is 'to build a winter coat'.

We will also take into account that the mass of Soviet people are employed in jobs where they need simple, inexpensive clothing, while in the US the share employed in such jobs is at most half as large. Of 106 m. employees in the USSR in 1976, 70 per cent were blue-collar workers. For the 15 million collective farmers, this percentage is higher. Regarding the US, out of 87 million wage and salary employees, 34 per cent were blue-collar workers; in addition, 14 per cent were service workers (most have to be well dressed!) and only a little more than 3 per cent were employed directly in agriculture.[16]

A passage from a mass circulation newspaper aptly characterises how Soviet people dress. The article, titled 'Nefertiti's wardrobe', says that some 'fashionable young women' have piles of smart dresses but sigh that they have nothing to wear. The author, a fashion designer, gives this advice: 'For the contemporary young woman, and especially the business woman, for going out it is sufficient to have a skirt, pants, two or three blouses, a sweater, and a couple of scarves'. To this the author adds a couple of dresses, but only 'if you have the free time to wash, iron, and go to the cleaners'.[17] This advice is more telling than any statistics.

And, of course, in no event should we forget about the quality of clothing; it is not without reason that Soviet consumers are eager to buy imported, but not domestic things. The Soviet press is constantly writing that the quality of domestic clothing is very low; an endless number of examples can be cited. Aesthetics aside,[18] it was always a riddle for me how Moscow ladies managed to look attractively dressed.

In sum, even from these elementary observations one can unquestionably conclude that the volume of Soviet consumption of clothing lags much farther behind the American than 40 per cent.

Undoubtedly the authors and some readers will exclaim: you cannot make such statements without objective computations; you must not only pronounce general impressions but indicate concrete disagreements with the calculations. Alas, this is too hard. The point is not only that the authors did not provide us with their basic information. Such a calculation itself is incredibly complex. Clothing, even in the USSR, is very diverse, and reducing it to one physical unit as, for example, with fruits, vegetables and shoes is impossible. In order to 'objectively' criticise the authors' calculation one must therefore duplicate it in all its details, but we do not have sufficient statistics.

Speaking of Soviet statistics, we note, above all, the amazing paucity of information on clothing in the yearbooks. There are data on the total production of sewn goods – about R77 per capita in 1976 in wholesale prices. There are also data on per capita sales in that year in retail prices: R75 for clothing and underwear, R3.3 for furs and fur goods, R1.3 for headgear, R37 for knitwear, and R8.4 for hosiery.[19] Not a lot considering how high prices are. Regarding production (or consumption) in physical units, the yearbooks are limited to hosiery and fur goods, underwear, and knitted outerwear (see the data in Table 8.3). Just the scantiness of these data tells the whole story: there can be only one reason not to publish figures on clothing production – it is disgracefully low.

We have one other indirect means (in addition to the cited data on expenditures) of judging. I already mentioned above the 'rational food norms'. There are also other no less (and no more) rational norms for clothing. They are given in Table 8.2 and refer not to total annual purchases but to what *should be* in the wardrobe. This is not the real state of the wardrobes of Soviet people, but their dream. In fact they are still very far from reaching even these rather meagre norms. That these rational norms have not been achieved is mentioned in the literature, and we can judge the extent of the lag – again, unfortunately, only indirectly – using the data in Table 8.3 where the actual consumption of fabrics and knitwear, for which data exist, are compared with the rational norms. The lag is more than one and a half times.

Table 8.2   Rational norms, number of items needed[a]

	Men	Women	Boys	Girls
Coats and raincoats	3	3	3	3
Jackets and sweaters	3	4	3	3
Suits	5	2	3	1
Pants	3	2	3	2
Dresses of all types	—	12	—	8
Shoes (pairs)	7	10	4	6

[a]V. F. Mayer, *Uroven'zhizni naseleniya SSSR*, M., 1977, p. 104. These norm are for the temperate climatic zone.

The attentive reader might ask about the share of fabrics from artificial fibres. In 1973 the share of true silk fabrics comprised only per cent of the production of 'silk' fabrics; only 16 per cent of 'woo fabrics were pure wool; and 45 per cent of cotton fabrics were produce with some artificial fibres.[20]

Table 8.3 Comparisons of actual per capita consumption
with rational norms

	Actual per capita consumption, 1976[a]	Rational norms per capita per year[b]
Fabrics, total, square metres including:	33.2	50.0
Cotton	22.5	28.4
Wool	2.8	3.8
Silk	6.1	9.1
Linen	1.8	4.5
Knitted outerwear, units	2.0	4.0
Knitted underwear, units	4.0	9.4
Hosiery, pairs	6.3	8.3

[a]*Narkhoz-77*, p. 431. The uses of fabrics in the production of industrial goods (automobile upholstery, furniture, etc.), about 9 square metres, are of course not included here.

[b]Mayer, *Uroven'* . . ., p. 105. The comparison may be a little inaccurate since the rational norms include some 'other' fabrics – 4.2 square metres.

As Lokshin says (p. 152), the norms existing in the 1970s (and given by Mayer) differ from the norms of the 1960s. Then, they were: fabrics 58 square metres, all knitwear 8.25 units, and hosiery 9 pairs.

Slightly different norms are given in the book, E. N. Voronova (ed.), *Razmeshcheniye proizvodstva neprodovol'stvennykh tovarov narodnogo potrebleniya v SSSR*, M., 1978, pp. 53, 68: wool fabrics, 4.6 and silk 10.8 square metres.

In examining the data on the consumption of fabrics in Table 8.3, the reader should keep in mind that they are for fabrics used not only in clothing, but also bed linens, tablecloths, curtains, etc. The reader should also note the miserly consumption of knitwear and hosiery.

Although, as I already said, the yearbook does not give other data on the production of clothes, Lokshin once again can help us.[21] He says how many sewn goods were produced by industry in 1973 (at the end of that year the population was 116 million males and 135 million females). These production figures are: 57 m. coats, 11 m. raincoats and cloaks, 75 m. suits, 219 m. dresses including sun-frocks and dressing gowns, 135 m. men's and women's pants, 165 m. men's and boy's shirts, and 12 m. skirts. Thus, each person could buy a coat once every four years, each male could buy a suit once in two years, the number of dresses including sun-frocks and bathrobes per female per year was 1.6 there was one pair of pants per male (if we ignore women's pants), and men and boys could buy a little more than one shirt per year. How many years a woman ought to wear a skirt I don't even want to guess.

Justifying the authors, I must say that there are many uncertainties with American figures also. The usual statistical yearbooks give few data, imports in physical units are not given, and even in special publications much information is lacking or difficult to extract. The more or less comparable data that I was able to find are the following. Consumption in the US in 1977 (taking into account exports and imports) was, in number of items, as shown in Table 8.4.

Table 8.4   Amount of clothing, USA[a]

	per male	per female
Underwear	7.6	7.6
Pajamas and nightgowns	0.4	2.3
Sweaters	0.7	2.0
Shirts	10.0	—
Dresses	—	2.3

[a]US Bureau of the Census, *C.I.R. Apparel*, 1977, MA-23A(77)-1, p. 16. The number of men (104.5 m.) and women (110.2 m.) are from *StAb-78*, p. 28.

Comparing these data with those presented above on Soviet consumption, we do not discover a big difference except for men's shirts, for which it is a factor of eight. By itself this very fact is surprising. I see no reason for consumption of shirts to be so different from consumption of other clothing.

Assuming that Soviet knitted underwear can be compared with American underwear, we see that the difference is only a little more than two times. (The difference is also small in dresses.) Why? It is hard to say; maybe a part of the explanation is that American women wear pants much more often. Also, American men wear longjohns much less.

Unfortunately, American data for other types of clothing relate primarily to production within the country, and without figures on exports and imports it is difficult to make comparisons (for example, in the data given above on sweaters, domestic production amounts to less than half). However, approximate estimates show that the numbers of men's suits, pants, etc., do not differ very greatly from the Soviet data.

In other words, the statistics at our disposal do not support my previous argument about the incredible advantage of the US over th

USSR in clothing. What is going on? The Soviet indicators presented above can hardly be extremely incorrect. The fact that the climate is much milder in the US has some effect; winter clothing is almost unnecessary in some of the most populated regions of the country. Many people dress very informally when going out for parties and other occasions. A large wardrobe does not mean that clothing correspondingly wears out more. On the other hand, underwear is clearly washed more often in the US, and people stop wearing old clothes much sooner and rarely wear them out.

None the less, the main point is that the quantities of clothing produced (bought) should not in itself be the only basis for an accurate comparison. The differences between the two countries are in the durability of clothing, in the frequency with which it is replaced, in the chance to have a big wardrobe, and finally in the very quality of clothing. But how can one get from such statements to figures?

As I already said, there is no other means of making comparisons for clothing than to repeat the same procedure that the authors used. I cannot do it, and instead will finish my discussion with two remarks about the results the CIA obtained. First, the Soviet lag for clothing is apparently greater than for food. This is also the authors' conclusion: the Soviet level *vis-à-vis* the US is about 50 per cent for food and 40 per cent for clothing. But I made some serious corrections to the indicators for food, and, in accordance with these, the Soviet lag for clothing is the same as for food. Apparently this is not so; hence, the figures for clothing also require correction.

Second, note the strange results of the following calculations. The authors assert – [20] and Table 4.2 – that in rubles the share of expenditures on footwear and clothing in the USSR is 17.2 per cent. By using price parities [20], we establish that in dollars the share was 12 per cent. The US share of footwear and clothing in dollars was 6 per cent (Table 4.2). According to Table 4.1, the total volume of Soviet per capita consumption calculated in dollars was only 43 per cent of American. Hence, the American consumption of footwear and clothing is $(6:12 \div 0.43) = 1.16$; that is, only 16 per cent more than Soviet, which is clearly absurd.

Let us try to draw an overall conclusion. Various reasoning and observations lead to the deduction that the Soviet lag for clothing is more significant than the CIA claims. Some analysis of the authors' data says this also, giving evidence that their estimate of the relative level of 39 per cent is clearly overstated. At the same time, this is not supported by the available stastitics. The questions must be studied further. It is necessary first of all to pay careful attention to the determination of the price ratios, and also, to the extent possible, to choose sample goods for the subgroup that are as representative as possible.

The authors placed at our disposal too little material to make definite judgements for other subgroups also. Note the larger share of *drugs and medical items* in America, which must obviously be explained by their high prices – the dollar–ruble price parity for the subgroup is 4.644 [62]. Although medical items have traditionally been very cheap in the USSR, many new medicines are notably more expensive. The selection of goods used to determine the price ratios and parities included only three medicines – iodine, multiple vitamins, and aspirin [58] and these items are hardly the most representative. Including such expensive items as penicillin and the newest medicines could have changed the results of the calculations substantially.[22] In sum, it is possible that the overall lag of the USSR for the subgroup is somewhat less than the authors found.

In the entire work the authors do not mention eyeglasses, which in the Soviet classification are included under medical items. The reason may be that there are no data on their quantity in American statistics. True, it is known that in 1986 per capita expenditures on eyeglasses, hearing aids, and certain prostheses was $8.90.[23] But only making several crude assumptions enables us to arrive at the quantity of eyeglasses from this. If we presume that spending for eyeglasses composed 80 per cent of this amount, and that the average cost of a pair was $25, we get 61 million pairs of them. In the USSR, 20 million pairs of glasses were sold in 1976;[24] i.e. on a per capita basis, the USSR lagged here by a factor of more than three. In fact the real lag must be much greater. More or less attractive glasses were and continue to be extremely scarce in the USSR. Not long ago a newspaper wrote: 'it is well known that to buy fashionable and pretty frames for eyeglasses is not easy'.[25] Other newspapers also write on the suffering of people with defective vision who cannot get even unfashionable but appropriate glasses. In America glasses play a much larger social function; they are replaced with changes in fashion. And the quality of eyeglasses is incomparable. Contact lenses are much more widespread in the US. Soviet frames are ugly and uncomfortable. The glass has many defects and only a small share of eyeglasses is made with glass imported from the GDR that is fully comparable with American glass.

There are many legends that people read a lot in the USSR, while in America they almost never read. This is not so – very many *newspapers* and *magazines* are read in America, and a mass of paperback *books* (I don't discuss their content) are sold.

The results of the authors' calculations were greatly affected by the high price of American books in hard covers. On the other hand, they in no way considered that the prices of periodicals in the US are greatly understated because of advertisements. In general I decisively refuse to agree with the authors' assertion that Soviet 'consumption of books, magazines, and newspapers is more than nine-tenths of that in the United States' [9]. This, once again, is without a doubt a great exaggeration of the Soviet level.

Here are a few figures. In 1976 in the USSR 47 147 books and brochures were printed. How many of these were brochures is not stated, and this in itself says that there were a lot. Of these, 8000 were fiction (including 2000 children's books). Production and technical literature (manuals and exchanging experience on advanced techniques), instruction books, official norms, and other official literature accounted for 14 000 titles, and mass political literature for over 4000. In the same year, 35 141 books were published in the US, but this does not include government publications, subscription publications (except encyclopedias), and pamphlets up to 49 pages. Fiction, poetry, drama and biographies numbered almost 6500 titles, plus 2200 'youth' literature, 500 on tourism, and 1200 on sports and recreation.[26] The USSR is significantly ahead in the total number of titles, but I presented the breakdown of these totals for a reason. It is clear, in particular, that for comparability the normative and official literature must be removed from the Soviet figure, and brochures make up a large part of the remaining figure.[27]

It appears that the Soviet intelligentsia and the Soviet population in general read more fiction – in particular, classics.[28] However, if we could somehow calculate the quantity of pages read per capita, then, taking into account newspapers and magazines, America should be far ahead.[29]

Unfortunately, measurements are extremely difficult here. How, for example, can one estimate how many persons read a given copy of a book or a magazine? American statistics do not give the number of books (not titles) printed or the total number of pages in them. However, one handbook has a table showing how many books were published per capita in 1976 in various countries. In the lead was Switzerland with 1.57 books per capita followed by Denmark with 1.34; the list ends with Chile at 0.05 and India with 0.03. Regarding our two countries, this indicator was 0.33 for the USSR and 0.39, or 20 per cent greater, for the US. But this comparison is not quite legitimate – all publications are included for the USSR, and far from all for the US. To this we may add that according to the results of a survey in 1977 in the US, 15 per cent of all free time was spent reading, and 62 per cent of those interviewed read a newspaper every day.[30]

And, of course, the quality of American printed products is much better. The following story is appropriate. Because of some oversight, the remarkable anti-Soviet book *Tynyanov* by A. Belinkov was published in the USSR, although in a very small number of copies. A perfectly exact copy of it was manufactured abroad, one of which I have – it is impossible to tell them apart. (Since the books looked exactly like the original, a lot of copies were squeezed through the rusting curtain.) As I was told, there was only one difficulty – to find the sort of poor quality paper on which the book had been printed in the USSR.

The large share of cleaning preparations in the US includes the various pastes and aerosols that so simplify the life of the American home-maker. Since we have arrived at *household goods*, I will note that the Soviet set includes no tools (according to the Soviet classification they are included in durables, see Table 9.1). I try to avoid criticising the American data in the CIA report, but the share of expenditures on tools and 'other goods', which should include materials for do-it-yourself projects and hobbies, is too low. A visitor to the corresponding section of an American department or specialised store would agree with me. In addition to everything else, 'other goods' should include photographic materials, seeds, and seedlings (in 1976 the average American spent $18 on flowers, seeds and house plants),[31] fertilizer, and a multiplicity of the most diverse things that American stores are full of and that do not exist in the USSR.[32]

I cannot say anything substantive about other subgroups mentioned in Table 8.1, primarily due to the lack of information and the incomparability of the Soviet and American classifications. But it is worth noting the incomparability of the cosmetics available to Soviet and American citizens in quality, diversity, and quantity.

And overall, although there are some doubts about medical goods and possibly clothing, the results of comparisons for footwear, publications, tools and household goods lead to the certain conclusion that here again, for soft goods as a whole, the level of Soviet consumption is substantially further behind the American than the 39 per cent in the CIA calculations. Unfortunately, I cannot offer a more accurate estimate of my own.

9 Durable Goods

While in the USSR the consumption of soft goods is twice as large as of durables, in the US significantly more is spent on the latter than on the former (see Table 4.1). Unfortunately the CIA work gives only a limited presentation and a very meagre analysis of its results of comparison for this component of consumption. It is unfortunate because, as other basic components – food, clothing, and housing – are increasingly satisfied, the growth of the standard of living and significant qualitative changes in it are manifested in durables.[1]

Determining price ratios and parities for this group is hampered by the fact that many goods are not comparable, and very far from all exist in the USSR. In the opinion of experts [4], a typical contemporary Soviet sewing machine is similar to one used in the US 60 years ago. The standard Soviet one-door refrigerator is not produced in the US now. There are essentially no fully automatic washing machines, electric (or gas) clothes dryers, toasters, or air conditioners in the USSR.[2] The authors did what they could but there is no iron-clad certainty that the price parities they got are indeed accurate.

Let us look at Table 9.1. The reader should remember that, as shown in Table 4.1, the total volume of consumption of durables in the USSR is only about one-eighth of that in America. And it is apparent from the table that this huge difference is due not only to cars.

Overall, as we see, Soviet consumption of durables is concentrated in the most needed goods – furniture, utensils, radios and TV sets. In America the shares of these groups are smaller (though the absolute volumes are much greater) and, correspondingly, the shares of sports equipment, recreational goods, and everything connected with cars are much higher.

A figure that stands out is the twice as large share of consumption of *watches and jewellery* in the USSR. In 1976 the average Soviet spent R7.61 on jewellery and R3.7 on watches.[3] Certainly, jewellery is used by the rich of America no less than in the USSR: it is much easier to buy, gold and jewellery are comparably much cheaper, and in the USSR not everyone would wear them in public. A more careful look reveals that there are no prices for jewellery in the study, and nothing is said about how they were weighted. I mentioned the poor representativeness of the selection of watches in Chapter 3. On the other hand, gold jewellery is

Table 9.1   Per capita consumption of durables, 1976[a]

	USSR Rubles	%	US Dollars	%	Ruble-dollar price parity with American weights
Watches and jewellery	10	10	33	5	1.855
Furniture and rugs	20	20	93	12	1.164
Kitchen utensils and tableware	10	10	30	4	1.336
Household appliances	9	9	52	7	1.347
New cars[b]	18	17	183	25	1.679
Automotive spare parts	2	2	39	5	1.937
Used cars	—	—	64	9	1.801
Other household appliances	—	—	46	6	
Sewing machines	0.5	—	—	—	
Household tools	4	4	—	—	
Sports, recreation, and bikes	—	—	93	12	0.841
Other motor vehicles	—	—	39	5	0.352
Sports equipment	3	3	—	—	
Bikes and motor bikes	5	5	—	—	
Photographic supplies	1	1	—	—	
Toys	4	4	—	—	
Radio, TV, musical instruments and records	—	—	77	10	1.294
Radios and TV sets	12	11	—	—	
Musical instruments	1	1	—	—	
Other	3	3	—	—	
Total	102.5	100	749	100	1.376

[a]Calculated from data in [62, 64].
[b]For the USSR, this includes resales in commission stores.

becoming more and more popular in the USSR.[4] In general, I have no grounds to agree with or reject the result on this subgroup.

It would seem that the substantially larger share of expenditures on *furniture and rugs* in the USSR can be fully explained by the significantly smaller amount of total expenditures for the entire group, but this is not exactly so. The volume of Soviet consumption for the subgroup amounted to 27 per cent of the American [9]. As in many other cases, a variety of explanations may be offered – the correlation of living space is about the same (see Chapter 10), there are many built-in closets in America, the American house is not as overloaded with furniture as the tight Soviet apartment, etc. But there are factors acting in the other direction. We may directly compare only rugs and it turns out that in the US there are 22 times more rugs per capita.[5] On the basis of some other figures[6] and personal observation, I would assert that the authors significantly overstated the comparative Soviet estimate of consumption for this subgroup.

This example will serve to examine a significantly more general point. Throughout the work the authors consider annual expenditures on consumption, which overall is correct, but with respect to durables it leads to unpleasant paradoxes. Assume John has three chairs and Ivan not even one. This year each bought one chair. Their expenditures in this year were equal, but John's real level of consumption is in fact four times higher – he and his guests sit on four chairs rather than one.

I understand why the authors measured durables using annual expenditures on them – the basic goal of the entire study was to determine the amount of annual production of consumer goods and services for GNP accounts (see Chapter 14). But Americans *already have* a huge amount of durables and buy new items primarily to replace what has worn out or gone out of style. The Soviet people are at a significantly lower absolute level of consumption of durables and the rate (not absolute amount!) of their purchases is higher. Therefore, judging volume of consumption of durables on the basis of the amount of purchases during the year substantially distorts the results of the comparison in favour of the USSR.[7]

In other words, even on the assumption that the authors determined the price ratios and the amounts of purchases of furniture and rugs entirely accurately, the level of the Soviet standard of living has still been overstated.

Regarding *kitchen utensils and tableware*, I did not find American data; the Soviet data are as follows. In 1975 per capita production of all sorts of plates was 2.4, and less than one cup and saucer per person was produced. So little of all other types of china and glazed earthenware dishes was produced that we must speak of them in different terms. In other words, one teapot was produced for every 14 people, one tea or coffee service for 52, and one dinner service for 390 people.[8] The reader is invited to calculate for himself how many dishes Soviet people can break, and how many decades it would take for the majority of families to acquire a set of dishes on the assumption that the old ones are not broken.

In sum, saying nothing about quality, the Soviet lag is also very great here, certainly greater than our authors determined.

There is no doubt that the authors also underestimated the difference in the use of various *household appliances*.[9] At the end of 1976, only two-thirds of Soviet families had refrigerators, sewing machines, and washing machines, and one-fifth had vacuum cleaners.[10] There were also a miserly number of coffee grinders, food processors, coffee makers, pressure cookers, etc. In America practically all families have refrigerators (some have two), the majority have washing machines and dryers, toasters, can openers and sharpeners, sewing machines, dish-washers, mixers, blenders, garbage disposals or compressors, electrical knives – you cannot list them all. Those that have been named are, of course, standard – the ordinary family, and not only the rich, has practically all of them (see below).

The difference in the quality of equipment is colossal. The freezing compartment of Soviet refrigerators is small and there are no automatic ice-cube makers. American washing machines operate automatically and on different cycles, while Soviet machines merely spin the clothes – the difference is like that between silent movies in the 1920s and modern cinema. The authors (although not in such decisive terms) note this difference and mention obsoleteness of sewing machines, but the price ratios [60] and parities [62] are not convincing. For example, the price of a Soviet refrigerator is taken as R348 and an American $233, which one can more or less agree with. But it is harder to accept the relation of prices for washing machines – R135 and $104. And it is no easier to agree with the comparative prices of sewing machines – R67 and $60.[11]

The price parity for the subgroup of home appliances is 0.913 with Soviet weights (0.938 for sewing machines) and 1.347 with American weights [62]. Without a special calculation all this is difficult to refute, but to me these parities understate the difference in quality,[12] i.e. they correspondingly overstate the Soviet level of consumption.

The phenomenon that we considered a little above in discussing furniture applies to an even greater degree to household appliances. The authors, governed by their methodology, considered annual expenditures on new acquisitions and not the real consumption of property in 1976. But just at this time a relatively large number of various home appliances were being newly acquired in the USSR, while in America the 'initial accumulation' had been essentially completed long ago and a process of replacing worn out and obsolete things was underway.[13] Therefore, even if we fully agree with the authors' calculations, for this reason alone the results substantially overstate the Soviet standard of living.

Speaking of other durables, we may note that in 1976 there were 223 TV sets per thousand residents in the USSR and 571 in the US (Table 4.3). Their differing quality is more or less taken into account in the study (see also Chapter 12), but not reflected is the fact that Muscovites can watch only three channels (two in 1976) and Washingtonians can watch seven, two of which are free of commercials. Even six years after 1976 only every tenth Soviet TV is a colour set, and colour broadcasts can still not be received on one-fifth of the country's territory;[14] 13 per cent of the populace cannot receive TV signals, and 31 per cent can get only one channel. Furthermore, Soviet television operates for a much smaller number of hours a day.

In 1976, 8.5 m. radio receivers were produced in the USSR, of which 3 m. were tube type; 1.5 m. were exported. In the US, production and imports totalled 44.1 m. radio receivers.[15] The difference per capita is almost eight times, not considering quality – tube type radio apparatus has not been produced in America for a long time.

From the statistics we also know that in 1976 the USSR produced 104 000 home movie cameras, 2.6 m. tape recorders, 175 000 pianos,[16] and 53 000 stringed and 81 000 wind instruments. There is no American data for precise comparison. There are also no data on typewriters, but it is well known that Soviet typewriters are incredibly poor. Imports in 1976 amounted to 121 000, including 71 000 from the GDR,[17] and the largest part of these must have gone to institutions. In typewriters the USSR lags dozens of times behind the US.

That there are very many *cars* in America and very few in the USSR is not news. There were 98 m. passenger cars in the US in 1976 and about 5 m. in the USSR in personal use.[18] In the same year 10.1 m. passenger cars were sold in America, i.e., about one-tenth of their total number. Sales in the USSR amounted to 1.02 m.,[19] of which according to the authors' estimate [9] only 80 per cent were new. In other words, sales amounted to about 16 per cent of cars in use. Thus, other things being equal, Soviet consumption of cars is overstated in the calculations by 60 per cent. Correspondingly, although the study calculates that Soviet consumption for this group was (by the geometric mean) 5 per cent of American [9],[20] in fact, it was, other things being equal, only 3 per cent.

The reader should pay careful attention to this. Even after the sharp increase in gasoline prices, owning his own 'wheels' is the fondest dream of the average Soviet, but the lag here is the most dramatic. The opinion of various people about the advantages of public transportation are of little significance. In examining the standard of living and comparing it, we must first pay attention to the population's desires, to how their requirements could be satisfied, even if it seems that these requirements are 'incorrect'.

It would be an illusion to think that the lag for automobiles is being noticeably reduced. True, 1970–76 was a period of rapid growth in passenger car production in the USSR from 123 000 to 1 021 000 (mainly after a Fiat plant had been bought), but sales barely increased in 1977 and since have stabilised at 1.1–1.2 m. In order to increase sales to the population it would be necessary to buy new auto plants abroad. In the US, although for other reasons, sales have also stabilised, and new cars are primarily replacing old ones: during 1965–76 per capita retail sales grew by 2.2 per cent.[21] In further comparisons, we must consider that the mass replacement of old cars has hardly begun in the USSR, and it is unavoidable.[22]

Table 9.2   Number of various durables in the USSR, 1976[a], units

	Per 100 families			Per 1000 persons		
	Total	City	Country	Total	City	Country
Watches[b]	470	519	381	1362	1567	1030
Radios[c]	81	86	71	235	261	192
Televisions[d]	77	84	64	223	253	174
Cameras	27	36	13	78	110	35
Refrigerators	67	82	39	194	248	106
Washing machines	67	78	49	195	234	131
Vacuum cleaners	20	26	9	58	79	23
Motorcycles and motor-scooters	9	6	15	26	17	40
Bicycles and mopeds	53	42	71	153	128	193
Sewing machines	62	60	66	181	182	179
Tape recorders	13	?	?	39	?	?
Cars	6	?	?	18	?	?

[a]Data (for the end of the year) from *Narkhoz-77*, pp. 431–2; tape recorders from Ya. L. Orlov, *Torgovlya i proizvodstvo*, M., 1977, p. 159; cars estimated.
[b]This, of course, is not only wrist watches but also alarm clocks, grandfather clocks, etc. In 1976, 58% of all watches produced were wrist watches (*Narkhoz-77*, p. 189). Judging from this correlation for other years also (e.g., 63% in 1960, *Narkhoz-60*, p. 237), there were no more than 800 wrist watches per thousand persons in 1976 and probably many fewer (not everything is clear with exports).
[c]In 1976 only a little less than two-thirds of total production was made with semiconductors (*Narkhoz-77*, p. 189); we must assume the rest were tube-type.
[d]Not more than 5–6% of them were colour sets.

In Table 9.2 I present some figures on the extent to which the Soviet population's demands are satisfied. At first glance, this does not look bad. With the exception of cars, tape recorders, vacuum cleaners, and cameras, it would seem that their needs are almost filled. And fragmentary data in the literature on the population's demand for these goods would also seem to give evidence of a relative lowering of the demand for them. There are even cases of gluts of sewing machines, TVs, certain brands of refrigerators, etc. However, there is no doubt, and the Soviet press speaks of this, that surpluses accumulate primarily for goods of obsolete brands or of unsatisfactory quality.

Unfortunately, we can compare Soviet and American data on durables owned by the populations only for certain goods. It turns out that per thousand persons in 1975 in the US there were 1882 radio receivers and 571 televisions,[23] i.e., 8.2 times more radios and 2.66 times more TVs than at the end of that year in the USSR. And we should not forget quality here.

Regarding other durables, the percentages of the total number of American homes (households) equipped with various electric durable goods in 1976 were:[24]

Air conditioners (by number of rooms)	54.4
Dishwashers	39.6
Frying pans	63.6
Steam and steam/spray irons	97.7
Can openers	56.4
Coffeemakers	99.4
Food waste disposers	40.7
Microwave ovens	5.1
Mixers	91.1
Refrigerators	99.8
Home freezers	44.4
Televisions	99.9
of which, colour	77.7
Washing machines	72.5
Clothes dryer (including gas)	58.6
Vacuum cleaners	99.5

In addition to everything else, reliable comparisons for durables are made very difficult by the fact that in the US there are many types of them that do not exist in the USSR: personal airplanes, numerous different kinds of yachts, video tape recorders and TV cameras, telephone answering devices, home computers, and much, much more.

And, finally, still one more time: quality. I am almost ready to apologise for this example, but when the celebrated Moscow Palace of Congresses was built in the Kremlin, what impressed us most of all was the imported urinals. Nowhere else in the USSR had I seen such magnificent urinals, but in America they are everywhere, even in camping grounds.

I will refrain from making an overall evaluation of the results for the entire durables group. The geometric mean of 13 per cent (Table 4.1) emphasises the colossal lag of the USSR in this area. To all appearances, the real lag is greater, but an estimate would require detailed additional calculations and checking the correctness of the price ratios. A greater gap than that found by the authors follows from the fact already discussed above – the CIA made comparisons on the basis of purchases and not quantities consumed.

Finally, a conclusion that follows directly from the preceding analysis. That Soviet agriculture functions poorly is not news, and the lag for food is an obvious consequence of this fact. However, it has been, and still is, thought that Soviet industry works much better and, therefore, it would seem that the people should have the industrial goods that they need. It is frequently said that the production of industrial consumer goods has been growing rather fast, especially since the end of the 1950s. Indeed, their production, especially those that do not require agricultural raw materials, has grown rather fast; the supply of these goods to the population has changed radically in recent decades. At the same time, it turns out that the Soviet lag in personal consumption for industrial goods, especially durables, is much more significant than for food. The reasons are clear. Although the supply of these goods to the Soviet populations is indeed growing rather quickly, in Western countries it is growing in any event no slower. And the conclusion is also clear – the blame should not be put only on agriculture; Soviet industry is also in no condition to supply the elementary needs of the population. The lag for durables, which is in fact much more than eight times (!) affirms this most eloquently.

10 Household Services

It is quite clear that mankind's material progress is expressed not only in the physical growth of the absolute volume of consumption, but in improvements in the quality of goods and the appearance of new ones. No less characteristic for our century is the rapid growth of the service industry. What used to be done at home with one's hands is now done outside the home and by machines.

The results of the CIA's calculations on this are given in Table 10.1. As we saw in Table 4.1, overall Soviet consumption for this group is: about one-seventh in rubles, a little over one-fifth in dollars, and 18 per cent according to the geometric mean. Only for durables is the Soviet lag greater.

While the lag for the entire group is so tremendous, the share of *housing and utilities* (heat, light, water and gas) in this total is much lower in the USSR than in the US – 30 per cent versus 50 per cent – i.e., the lag is even greater for these two subgroups than for service as a whole. Note in this connection that expenditurés on utilities in the USSR are greater than on housing itself, while in the US they are substantially less. This is not becuase utilities in the USSR lag behind those in the US less than does housing (just the opposite assertion is

Table 10.1 Per capita consumption of services, 1976[a]

| | USSR | | US | | Ruble–dollar price parity with American weights |
	Rubles	%	Dollars	%	
Housing: rent and repair	17[b]	14	743	38	0.160
Utilities	19	16	235	12	0.451
Public transportation	31	27	39	2	0.266
Communications	7	6	98	5	0.346
Repair and personal care	28	24	137	7	0.505
Recreation	11[b]	9	98	5	0.381
Automotive services	3	2	313	16	0.944
Miscellaneous	–	–	293	15	0.536
Total	116	100	1956	100	0.420

[a] As in many other cases, I had to regroup the data from the study [6, 73] and to calculate some figures.
[b] Excluding state subsidies.

more likely to be true),[1] but because Soviet expenditures on housing are artificially and very greatly understated.[2]

Using data on total consumption in both countries from Chapter 4 (R1153 and $5583), we find that expenditures on housing and utilities in the USSR (excluding subsides!) amount to 3.1 per cent of total consumption, and in the US – 17.5 per cent. Overall, the authors [20] take the level of Soviet consumption of housing (including subsidies) to be 15.2 per cent of the American (there is only one sample good in this subgroup, so the estimates in rubles and dollars coincide with each other and with the geometric mean). The level for heating and lighting is 23 per cent, and for housing and utilities together, 17 per cent (geometric mean). It is difficult to judge the accuracy of this comparison, all the more so since the authors consider it the 'least satisfactory' [2]. The price parity for housing was determined by comparing the rent for a 'typical urban apartment in the USSR' with that for a two-room (not two bedroom!) apartment in the US located in a poor region and of 'deteriorating quality'.[3] The authors, quite correctly form a methodological standpoint, make the comparison not on the basis of the value of housing but according to annual expenditures on it (rent payments or capitalised rent payments for owners plus annual repair expenditures).

Let us examine now the available statistical data. The authors say [10] that in 1976 there were 12 square metres of living space for the average Soviet and 44 in the US, a difference of almost four times. Naturally, it is not said what sort of space they have in mind; such a question does not come up in the West. Under Soviet conditions, a sharp distinction is made between total (it is also called 'useful') housing area and 'living' area.[4] Living area includes the rooms themselves, and total (useful) area also includes everything else in the apartment – halls, lavatories, bathrooms, kitchens and wall closets. All these auxiliary areas amount to about a third of total area in Soviet conditions, which means that there were about 8 square meters of living area itself.

The authors do not indicate the source of these data on the USSR (and for the US they say it is an estimate). The Soviet yearbook publishes data on the annual amount of useful area put into use[5] (but not on the amount withdrawn) and on the existing urban housing stocks. There are no data on the rural housing stock. With respect to urban housing, at the end of 1976 its total area was 12.1 square metres per capita.[6] We have no reason to doubt these data.[7]

We should note that the authors compare the entire American

housing stock with the urban stock in the USSR. It is difficult to judge the significance of this, primarily due to the continuing outflow of the population from the countryside; the rural population declined by 8 m. during 1960–76. One other difficulty is that rural population is distributed very unevenly among regions, and calculations of the overall total would include the area of abandoned houses. Probably the average person in the country has a little bit more space than in the city, but average figures mean very little here.

A quarter of the entire urban housing stock in 1976 was 'the private property of citizens',[8] and this does not include cooperative apartments. The authors cite Henry W. Morton's estimate that one-third of the urban population lives in dormitories and communal apartments.[9] Given that the Soviet population was 119 per cent of the American, the number of individual apartments and houses in the USSR according to the authors' estimated data was 87 per cent of that in the US. They also say [10] that the ratio of the number of families to the number of apartments and houses is equal to 1.23 in the USSR and 0.97 in the US. Consider here that in the Soviet countryside practically every family lives in a separate house; thus, the ratio of *urban* families *vis-à-vis* the number of urban apartments and houses must be substantially higher than 1.23.[10]

I did not discover data on the number of *dachas* in the USSR. They are primarily around the major cities – Moscow, Leningrad, Kiev, Riga. At most they number in the hundreds of thousands. True, collective gardening and orchard tending is well developed. In 1978, 2.6 m. people were involved in the latter and another 5.7 m. in the former.[11] Presumably the difference is that the latter have small houses on their plots (according to the existing rules, a fireplace is not allowed, and modern heating equipment is not available; i.e., they can live there only in the summer), while the former do not.

Now we will turn to the basic statistics on housing in the US[12] of which not all my fellow Americans have a good impression. There were a total of 80.9 m. housing units in 1976. Each 'unit' was one of several rooms intended and used for housing. The occupants of the unit (the definition carefully avoids the term 'family', and not by accident) do not live or eat (in Soviet terminology, do not maintain a common household) with anyone from other units. The unit must have a separate entrance from the street or hallway and must be equipped with a full kitchen for the exclusive use of those living in the unit. In sum, a unit is a separate house or a separate apartment. I will note immediately just what is considered a 'room' in American housing statistics. It includes bedrooms, the living room, dining room and kitchen. The bathroom, pantry, halls, foyer, garage, furnace rooms, laundry rooms and workshops are not considered 'rooms'.

All together in 1976 there were 72.9 m. families and unrelated singles including 14.8 m. of the latter.[13] Of the total of 80.9 m. housing units, 5.3 m., or about 7 per cent were vacant during the entire year. If we assume that each single person lived separately (and not with a friend) then 2.3 m. families and singles, i.e. 3 per cent occupied two units, say, an urban apartment and a summer home. Only 1.6 m. out of the total number of housing units were not suitable for year-round use.

Of the total number of occupied housing units in 1976, 65 per cent were owner-occupied and the remaining 35 per cent were rented.

The largest part of the population lives in detached houses. In 1976 such houses accounted for 68 per cent of all 'housing units', and another 4 per cent were trailers. In addition, 13 per cent of housing units were in buildings with 2–4 units and, thus, only 15 per cent of all housing units were in multiple-apartment buildings with five or more units that one may relate to the urban European type.[14]

I did not discover data on the housing area, but there are data on the number of rooms. The average housing unit had 5.1 rooms. Units with 1–3 rooms made up 15 per cent of the total, units with 4 rooms accounted for 20 per cent, and those with 7 or more rooms another 20 per cent. The first of these figures caught my attention – there seem to be a very large number of housing units with 1–3 rooms. More detailed data show 1.3 m. housing units with one room ('efficiencies'), i.e. less than 1.7 per cent of the total number of housing units. The number of units with two rooms was a little larger – 2.2 m. (presumably these are apartments with a kitchen and one other room), and all other housing units, i.e. 96.7 per cent, had at least three rooms. Recall also that the number of single persons numbered more than 14.8 m., i.e. noticeably exceeded the total number of housing units with 1–3 rooms.

From the data given – the total number of housing units and the number vacant – it is easy to calculate that on the average there were 1.8 rooms per person. The statistics also indicate the number of housing units in which there were one to one and a half persons per room – this, for example, could be a husband, wife and child occupying a two-room apartment. There were 2.7 m. units of this type, of which 1.5 m. were owner-occupied and 1.2 m. rented. I will add that in many states the law forbids renting an apartment (house) if it would require children of different sexes over a certain age to share a bedroom.

And the last thing. In one of my comments above, I noted that in the

USSR you can be 'put in line' for housing (which gives you the hope of getting something after many years) if you do not have more than 5 square metres of living area per person. The American norm for living space in cells for prisoners is larger – 5.6 square metres.[15]

The statistics presented can be expressive, but housing differences are not determined only by square metres (feet). Although I have seen apartments in America that are no better than those in Moscow and in 'deteriorating condition', they are in no way typical and do not give the overall picture. In general, American housing is not only much larger but much more comfortable.

None of the figures reflect that the ordinary average American home has succeeded in combining the advantages of urban life – comfort, convenience of transportation – with the advantages of life outside the city. In the USSR, only the highest bosses and those 'free artists' who are paid very well can live year round in a *dacha*. Here, this is the lot of the majority of the population: people still live in cities only by choice.

It is impossible to express in figures that five-storey buildings have no elevators, that low ceilings are not compensated for as in American apartments by large area and air conditioning, that the almost ideal sound conductivity of floors and walls, is again, not offset by the amount of space or by (obligatory in such cases in America) thick carpeting.

I already said that a quarter of the entire Soviet urban housing stock consists of private houses. Specifically these houses largely account for the fact that on 1 January 1977 16 per cent of the entire urban housing stock of the RSFSR was not connected to a sewer system, i.e. every sixth urban (!) resident goes outside for all purposes. Half of all urban housing stock was without hot water, 28 per cent did not have gas or a bathtub (shower), and 14 per cent did not even have running water.[16] The RSFSR Council of Ministers announced not long ago that 'the state of the water supply of many (!) cities and workers' settlements cannot be considered satisfactory ... The quality of piped-in water leaves much to be desired, especially in small cities and towns.[17] Although we do not have precise figures on this, there is no doubt that practically all private homes and also quite a lot of one-storey buildings are heated only with fireplaces.

Only 69 per cent of the urban housing stock was supplied with gas at the end of 1976,[18] and there were very few electric stoves (1.2 m. in 1975[19]), i.e., approximately 60 m. urban residents cooked their food with kerosene, a primus-stove, or a primitive electric hotplate.

In spite of how poor – disgraceful for a superpower – living conditions are for the majority or the urban population, they are incomparably worse in the Soviet countryside. Here, heating is only with fireplaces, food is cooked on wood stoves or in wood-fired ovens, the toilet is in the back yard (in the Russian climate!) water is from a well, and there is no hot water.[20]

The characterization of living conditions in the countryside would not be complete without mentioning the eternal Russian lack of roads, the absence of stores and personal services enterprises in rural areas, and the fact that children often have to go (walk) many miles to school (don't forget about Russian winters).

I did not say just for effect that the difference in comfort cannot be reflected in any figures. The authors operated with the usual procedure. They established the price ratio for the 'sample apartment', and the differences in the quality of other housing were supposed to be automatically taken into account by the differences in the prices for it. Here we see a typical example of transferring American impressions to Soviet reality. For American housing the premise adopted is correct – if the quality is different, so is the price – although here also many apartments are subsidised and rent control in many cities keeps rent artificially low. But this premise does not work at all in the Soviet economy, which is especially evident in this case.

Because of the tremendous understatement of rents, their relation to the prices of gas, electricity, etc., reflects nothing. More important is the fact that rents are practically identical for different types of housing and depend only on floor space – whether you live in a 'communal basement', or in separate apartment next to the subway stop with all conveniencies, and enjoy a beautiful view.[21] Perhaps for this reason the authors set only one and not several price ratios, but there is no proof that the American and Soviet sample apartments that they used can be indeed of average quality. It would have been much more correct to establish not one but several ratios – for example, for some average urban apartment, a separate urban house, and also a house in the suburbs and in the country. The authors' basic error, which here also significantly overstates the comparative level of Soviet consumption, is that the single 'sample' urban apartments that they used are more or less comparable, but the differences for individual houses both in the city and in the countryside is much greater, and in favour of the US.[22]

Without a detailed scrupulous check of all the initial data and calculations, one cannot say how accurate is the authors' conclusion of a Soviet lag in housing and utilities by a factor of six [20]. However, what we know – the four-fold lag in floor space, the sharp lag in the comfort of urban, and especially rural, housing – suggests that this estimate greatly overstates the volume of Soviet consumption for these two subgroups. This follows most obviously from a fact already mentioned – the authors used only one 'sample apartment' in their calculations and for the USSR this kind is the best. Not less importantly, the authors' calculations do not reflect the basic fact – the largest part of the American population lives in separate houses, and this is incomparably better than the Soviet type of housing arrangements. It is worth noting that the cost of American housing accounts for more than 30 per cent of the national wealth of such a remarkably rich country as the US, while in the USSR, the amount of fixed capital in housing with communal services is less than one-fifth of all capital.[23] It is also worth saying that Soviet lag in housing is apparently the most fundamental[24] and the most difficult to overcome.

Let's dream a little. Imagine that on the vast expanse of that great and unlucky country a democratic regime comes to power. The arms race, which has been sucking the life-blood from the country, is ended. A means of sensibly organising the economy is found and implemented. Even under such ideal conditions people will have to wait for long, long *decades* before they approach the conditions that we already enjoy.

Perhaps the authors should have adjusted the methodology a little bit and put great emphasis not on a comparison of square metres and utilizers, but on what this all costs, i.e. how many trillions of rubles the Soviet housing sector would need to overtake America.[25] Certainly, the calculation would require using several sample apartments/houses.

Although the overstatement of the Soviet volume of consumption for housing and utilities appears indisputable, I cannot indicate its precise extent.

Let us now turn to *transportation*. In public transportation the USSR is far ahead of the US – 2.5 times [20]. Its lead is not due to the good life but to poverty: they cannot and will not be able to produce as many cars as the population wants. As we saw in Chapter 9, the Soviet lag in private transportation is more than a factor of 30.

In Table 10.2 I present various indicators from both the CIA study and other sources.[26] We see much that is curious. I did not expect that almost half of the Soviet population's expenditures on public transportation would be on buses and that railroad transportation has slipped to 16 per cent.[27] I also did not expect such a large share of expenditure on taxis.

The authors' laconic explanation makes it impossible to understand how much of total expenditure on passenger transportation they related to business trips, which, naturally, are not a part of personal consumption. There are no statistics on this and it is necessary to resort to crude estimates. In my opinion, more than half of all Soviet airplane flights relate to business trips,[28] but what particular share the authors used is not clear.

Table 10.2   Public transportation, 1976

Type of Transportation	USSR Billions of passenger-kilometres[a]	USSR Expenditures[c] Rubles, m.	USSR %	US Expenditures[d] Dollars, m.	US %
Railroad	315	1270	16	505	6
of which local urban	91			224	
Ocean ships	2.4	90	1		
River ships	6	83	1		
Air	131	1058	13	4206	50
Bus, urban	156	1284	16	1346[e]	16
Bus, intercity and suburban	169	2679	33	608	7
Streetcar	8343[b]	233	3	—	
Trolley bus	8345[b]	311	4	—	
Subway	3229[b]	150	2	599	7
Taxi	1778[b]	915	11	1112	14
Total	—	8073	100	8376[f]	100

[a]*Narkhoz-77*, pp. 306, 309, 325–7.
[b]Number of passengers (m. trips).
[c]Data are from the study [80] and do not include expenditures on business trips, which, incidentally, are – in my opinion – understated.
[d]Data from [85].
[e]Together with trolley buses.
[f]In addition, there were $209 m. of expenditures on 'other' forms of transportation and $841 m. of tolls for bridges, roads, and tunnels.

A much more serious point against the authors is that they did not take into account the difference in the quality of transportation service. With regard to urban transportation, we will let a well-known Soviet specialist speak: 'The problem of creating normal conditions for passengers in suburban and urban transportation has become extremely acute ... According to our data, the loading of buses at rush hour has in some instances reached 11–12 persons per square metre of free space in the salon, which, of course, is impermissible.'[29] The press keeps complaining about the overloading of urban transportation at rush hour, and there is much evidence that in recent years it has gotten even tighter in Moscow subways, trolley buses, and buses. Note also that in America the distance between stops on subways and buses is shorter and that public transportation is adapted for use by the handicapped.[30]

The situation is much worse with inter-city transportation. The problem begins with buying a ticket; this requires a lot of time, special trips to the station, standing in long queues for hours, knowing the right people, etc. You must arrive at the airport long before departure. I used to fly from Moscow to Novosibirsk, and the time for this long flight (about the same length as coast-to-coast in America) was less than all the 'preliminary and final operations'. On trains, it is stuffy in the summer and cold in the winter.[31] On long trips in regular cars, the picture is something inconceivable to a civilised person – 60 people sleep in one area, a third of them on so-called side benches, which I simply have difficulty in describing to someone who does not know what this is.[32] Trains, buses, and planes are often late.[33] It is incredibly difficult to change flights, and there is a very high penalty for missing a flight – up to 25 per cent of the price of the ticket if not more.[34]

One must also ponder a simple fact: in America, the greatest number of inter-city trips are by automobile, and in the vastness of the USSR, Soviet people travel little – in particular, because of the inconvenience of transportation, transfers, the bother of getting tickets and, of course, because of the lack of roads. To this day, 'one-fifth of regional centres and a third of central farmsteads in the RSFSR still do not have road connections [hard surface roads] with oblast cities'.[35]

The figures for travel in the USSR are in Table 10.3. In examining these data, several things must be kept in mind. First, it is thought that Americans travel a long distance to work. In 1976 the average (median) distance to work was 13 km for home owners (average time was 21 minutes each way) and 8 km for renters (19 minutes).[36] Therefore, inter-city trips to work and back should not significantly affect the figures in Table 10.3.

Second, the size of the territory of the US is much smaller than the USSR, and we are comparing not the number of trips but their distance.

Third, for both countries I took figures relating to all trips, including business. It is difficult to say where the share of business trips is higher, but if we had these figures, the picture could look different.

Fourth, the mileage per car in America is, naturally, greater, but not many times greater. The average run of an American passenger car in 1976 was over 15 000 km, and according to relatively old data, the average use of Soviet private cars was 8000 km.[37]

Concluding the discussion of transportation, it is pertinent to present data on automobile roads. The yearbook says that at the end of 1976 there were a total of 689 700 km of automobile roads 'with hard surfaces' in the USSR, of which 315 100 km were 'improved (with cement, asphalt, and black-top)'. However, the CEMA handbook gives only 642 000 km of roads with hard surfaces;[38] apparently, the definition agreed to by CEMA countries is stricter than that used in Soviet statistics. I will use the latter figure below.

Table 10.3   Inter-city trips per capita, 1976, km

	USSR[a]	US[c]	USSR as % of US
Automobile	156[b]	9247	2
Bus	658	187[d]	352
Rail	1227	82	1497
Air	510	1234	41[e]
Water (river, lake, sea)	33	30	110
Total	2584	10 780	24

[a]Calculated from Table 10.2. American data on intercity travel include suburban trips; therefore, for comparability I took suburban trips for the USSR.
[b]Estimate. Conveyance of passengers in individually owned passenger cars in 1976 amounted to 5 325 000 trips (*Narkhoz-76*, p. 410). If we assume that 15% of all trips were suburban and intercity, and that the average trip distance was 50 km, we get 40 billion passenger-kilometres.
  Another method yields approximately the same figure. We assume that the average annual number of cars in private use was 4.8 m., they travelled an average of 2800 km per year on intercity and suburban trips, and there were three passengers per trip.
[c]Calculated from *StAb-78*, p. 639 (inter-city travel).
[d]Excluding school buses.
[e]Within the country only. It seemed that the difference for air travel was greater. We may note that the distance of an average flight is only a little greater in the USSR than in the US. But not long ago I read somewhere that half of all Americans have never flown.

In the US at the end of the same year there were 6.208 m. km of roads; 1.127 m. km of them were not surfaced.[39] Although I have been in 25 American states and travelled many tens of thousands of miles, I have not seen any Russian-style dirt roads, impassable in bad weather. But we will believe the handbook and accept that there are 5.081 m. km of roads with hard surfaces. Then, per thousand citizens in the USSR there are 2.5 km and in the US 23.6 km of such roads. It is much more complicated to take into account the quality of roads. As we saw, only half of Soviet hard surface roads are covered with cement or asphalt; the rest, presumably, are gravel or cobble-stone.[40]

In America there are 658 000 km of multi-lane highways alone, while in the USSR there are still almost no such roads. And in addition to all else we should not forget that the territory of the USSR is more than twice as great as the US. Therefore, incidentally, per thousand square kilometres of territory there are 29 km of hard surface roads in the USSR and 543 in the US, i.e. almost 19 times more.[41]

Roads are one of the main components of the US national wealth. Our possibility of driving to any house year round is an unrealisable dream for the Soviet countryside. Precisely because of the roads we are able to live outside the city permanently, to reach public centres easily, and to travel a lot. Roads in fact are one of the basic components of the quality of American life. Though my comparison can be discussed (for example, possibly one should exclude from it the Soviet North-East and Alaska), still, in the foreseeable future, the USSR simply cannot catch up to America in roads.[42]

In sum, according to the authors, the USSR is ahead in public transport by two and a half times, but the Soviet personal transport is only 3.9 per cent of American. The substantial mistake in personal cars is discussed in Chapter 9. In regard to public transport, there are difficult aspects of the comparison. Certainly, the number of passenger–kilometres per capita is much much larger in the USSR; though the quality of American transport service is much higher. Possibly here we have a rare case when the authors underestimated Soviet consumption.

I can say only a little about *communications*. The authors write [81] that their data are based on overall expenditures for the economy and an arbitrary estimate of the population's share of expenditures. The results of their calculations are given in Table 10.4.

Applying the price parity we find that, in dollars, the USSR lags behind the US in postal services by only 50 per cent, which has nothing to do with reality. As a matter of fact, this conclusion by the authors contradicts figures that they themselves used. In 1976, 9.028 billion pieces of mail were delivered in the USSR and 89.768 billion in the US,[43] i.e. the difference per capita is not 2 but 12 times. Several years ago when an American postal workers' strike threatened, troops were prepared to deliver the mail. In the USSR if the mail stops, life will not change much.

The official data on the number of letters in the USSR look very strange. If we believe them, it turns out that there were 35 letters per capita during the year, which is a fantastically large amount. The authors assumed that 55 per cent were personal mailings, but even in this case we get 19 cards and letters per capita, or 70 per family, again an unbelievable figure (the Soviets don't pay bills by mail). If, following the authors, we take the number of personal mailings as 19, the average turns out to be 19.3 kopecks – another absurdity, even taking into account packages, since their total number amounted to only 2.5 per cent of all mailings.[44]

Table 10.4   Per capita expenditures on communications, 1976[a]

	USSR Rubles	%	US Dollars	%	Ruble–dollar price parity with American weights
Postal services	3.47	49	12.70	12	0.615
Telegraph	0.78	11	2.26	2	0.217
Telephone	2.58	37	88.10	86	0.310
Radio-TV broadcasting[b]	0.23	3	—		
Total	7.06	100	103.1	100	0.346

[a]Calculated from the authors' data [81, 85].
[b]Although there was already cable TV in the US in 1976 (about 1 m. subscribers, *StAb-78*, p. 592), the authors did not consider these expenditures.

What exactly is going on with the official data I do not understand. The idea suggests itself that periodicals are included in the total amount of correspondence sent, but the annual number of copies of newspapers alone is 38.5 billion. It could be that only magazines were included in mailings; their annual total number of copies was 3.1 billion.[45] We note that the cost of a periodical in Soviet statistics is entered fully in retail sales and not in postal expenditures.[46]

Regarding telegraph communications, according to the authors' calculations the volume of Soviet consumption in dollars is more than one and a half times greater than American. In 1976, 1.8 telegrams per capita were sent in the USSR and 0.3 in the US,[47] which is easily explained. In America, long distance telephone has supplanted telegraph, and since 1950 the number of telegrams sent within the country has fallen by 75 per cent. The share of personal telegrams is not known for either country, but it is quite probable that the authors understated the comparative volume of Soviet consumption here.

For telephone services the Soviet lag is a factor of ten, which almost exactly corresponds to the ratio of the number of telephones shown in Table 4.3.[48] In other words, if we believe these data, there is practically no difference in the quality of telephone service, i.e. everything is determined only by the number of telephones. Trying to work all this out, let us look first at the number of telephones.

Both Soviet and American statistics give the number of telephone instruments, not of telephone numbers (lines), and we will return to this shortly. Of course, we need not the total number of telephones but only those that are used in personal consumption. In the US at the end of 1976 there were 114 m. residential telephones, 529 per 1000 population. In the USSR at the end of the same year the 'total number of telephones' was 20.9 m., but how many of them were in personal use is unknown. I discovered such data only for the end of 1970, when out of a total number of 11 m., only 3.8 m. were in apartments.[49] Even if we assume that the total increase in 'telephones in the general telephone network' in 1970–76 were apartment phones, at the end of 1976 the total number of apartment phones would have been 11.2 m. or only 44 per 1000 population. Thus, the difference in the number of telephones per capita in private use is 12 and not 10 times, but even this greatly exaggerates the Soviet level. The authors themselves cite a source which says that in 1974 only 31.1 per cent of urban telephones were in private use,[50] while in the countryside there were practically no telephones in private use and there still are not.[51] Very generously we may assume that in 1976, 30 per cent of all telephones in the city and the country were in private use, which gives 24 telphones per 1000 population, i.e. 22 times fewer than in the US.

Thus, the number of telephones shown in Table 4.3 is obviously incorrect, and the authors' calculations were apparently based precisely on them. Of course, it is necessary to compare not the number of telephones, but of telephone numbers (lines); however there are no statistics, and the authors did not do this sort of comparison. According to my rather broad personal impression, the total number of additional telephones in personal use in the USSR is rather small. Even for the US it was surprisingly difficult to determine this number, but at last I discovered that at the end of 1976, given a total of 114 m. residential telephones, there were 70.2 m. telephone numbers, i.e. for each basic phone there were 0.6 additional phones.[52] Thus, if we compare not telephones but telephone numbers, the Soviet lag may be less than 22 times, but I repeat that we probably overstated the number of phones in private use in the USSR.

Now about the quality. I will begin with what we have just been discussing – the large number of additional phones in the US greatly improves it. We may add that a significant number of telephones in the USSR were not automatic.[53] Add that even now there are still no push-button phones in the USSR. Add the fact that party lines are used in the USSR, especially in the countryside, and they are forced on people. Add the many forms of additional service that are unknown in the USSR. And add the fact that on a per capita basis the USSR lags in the number of public telephone booths by many times.[54]

Long distance telephone service deserves separate discussion. In the USSR there were 3.4 long distance calls per capita in 1976, and, of course, the majority of them were business calls. In the US there were so many that the handbook gives the number per day. Converted to three-minute calls, in 1976 there were 45 m. per day.[55] On an annual basis, this is 76 conversations per capita, i.e. 22 times more than in the USSR.

Regarding the quality of long distance conversations, getting through to another Soviet city always was, and remains, a bothersome problem that tries one's nerves. It would seem that with the introduction of automatic dialling this should have become easier, but several times in recent years *Literaturnaya gazeta* has complained bitterly and explained in detail the suffering invloved.[56]

And, finally, audibility of both local and long distance calls is incomparably better in the US. Also, while in the US audibility is identical throughout the country, in the USSR it is sharply poorer in cities other than Moscow, Kiev and Leningrad, and still worse in rural areas.

The only thing in which the USSR is possibly ahead is the number and length of local phone conversations by those lucky enough to own a phone, but we must also not underestimate the talkativeness of Americans. In 1976 in the US there were about three local calls per capita a day.[57] For the USSR there are no such data.

Summing up, we may confidently assert that the CIA estimate – that Soviet consumption of telephone services lags behind American by ten times – overstates Soviet consumption by at least a factor of two and apparently by much more.[58] Soviet consumption is also significantly overstated relative to American for the entire subgroup, even though the authors take it to be rather modest – 17.5 per cent of American.

Regarding the next subgroup – various *repairs, personal services*, etc. – I have few comments. One should not think that the significantly larger share of this subgroup (24 per cent compared with 7 per cent, Table 10.1) speaks of the development of these services in the USSR.

This, of course, is not so, although the CIA study contains too little evidence in this area.

Furthermore, even the information they give, derived from Soviet sources, is far from the most characteristic. With due respect to the authors, I cannot take seriously their scrupulous calculation showing private laundry service for the country as a whole to be R11 m., and private furniture repair of R14 m. [82]; here the authors' sense of humour has failed them: just the size of these figures clearly shows that determining them is not possible. They did not invent these figures but conscientiously used fragments of information from the literature. For other services they took data from the most solid source – the *Narkhoz* yearbooks.[59] But I cannot believe, for example, that total barber services amounted to less than R2 pre capita for the year.[60] Apparently the largest part of the receipts of Soviet barbers miss the cash register, and the accounts. In 1976 the average American spent $21 in barber shops and beauty salons – also, incidentally, not very much.[61]

The authors refer approvingly to Soviet laundry services, but it turns out that 'of 29 kilograms of laundry per resident, washed, on the average, in a year, a little more than a kilogram passes through laundry plants'. And, at that, capacity is underutilized; for example, in the RSFSR it is only three-quarters used. Why? Because 'many have serious complaints about the quality with which orders are fulfilled'.[62] Considering the quality of home washing machines, we are unavoidably led to the sad conclusion on how much the Soviet woman must wash and iron.

It is appropriate to say that in the words of the *Pravda* article just mentioned, 'housework takes Soviet citizens 275 billion man-hours a year', which on a per capita basis is more than 1000 hours or 130 full working days.[63] And this includes every single person in the calculation. It is easy to figure that such a quantity of man-hours is equal to a full year's work for more than 100 m. persons, i.e., exactly as many as there are state employees (excluding collective farmers).

With no pretensions of paradox, I will note that the indicators of the standard of living for the subgroup also include expenditures on funerals. There are absolutely no Soviet statistics on this, and I would not have tried to work out price parity for such a service.[64]

The figures for *recreation* are only a little more abundant and accurate, and the authors themselves admit that the comparison here is no better than for housing [2]. The data are given in Table 10.5. Analysing these data is not easy. In particular, they do not consider the direct expenditures of labour union organisations, sports socieities, and enterprises on resorts and sport, which in 1976 amounted to R2.3 billion [14]. The authors, as we see, did not succeed in distinguishing expenditures on trips abroad.[65] And not everything in their calculations is clear to me.[66]

Table 10.5   Expenditures on recreation, 1976[a]

	USSR, m. rubles	US m. dollars
Movies	850	2987
Other performances	514	2484
Musical performances	?	929[b]
Spectator sports	?	1555[b]
Commercial participant amusement	0	3895
Hotel–motel	83	3818
Net foreign travel	?	3374
Vacation resorts, sports	1328	—
Miscellaneous	—	5028
Total	2775	21 586

[a]Data from [81, 86].
[b]According to *StAb-78*, p. 245, $907 m. was spent in the US in 1976 on theatres, operas, and performances organised by non-profist organisations, and this sum presumably includes musical performances. Spending for spectator sports was $1704 m.

None the less, let us turn our attention to several things. Taking into account the cost of tickets, we see that people go to the movies more in the USSR than in the US, which is as least partially connected with the fact that television is less widespread.[67] On the other hand, in the US, expenditures on 'commercial games' (including automatic games but not 'one-armed' bandits or amusement parks) are high – $18 per capita.[68] Although I have no comparative data, there must be more theatres in the USSR, but total attendance is apparently equal in the two countries.[69]

In the USSR 0.8 records per capita were produced in 1976;[70] I found no information for the US. Here, though, tape cassettes are incomparably more prevalent.

Some Soviet critics of my book will say that Americans spend more on spectator sports than on theatres, opera and serious music, and that the youth listen to more Beatles, rock and jazz. I will not argue with people who look down on sports fans. But this is irrelevant. The point is that in America, people themselves decide what, how, where, and how often to attend, on what to spend their idle time. Whether we like it or not, Soviet souls prefer soccer and hockey to opera; the order at concerts by native and foreign singers is maintained by mounted militia, but classical music concerts in the provinces play to half empty halls.

A little about museums. In 1976 there were 1323 museums in the USSR, including 220 revolutionary-historical and historical, 279 memorial, 564 museums of local lore, and only 36 scientific and 187 are museums. The total number of visitors was 133 m. plus 10 m. to the Moscow National Economy exhibition. Things are a little worse with data for the US; we have none for 1976. In 1979, there were 4408 museums including 2204 historical, 800 scientific, 609 art, etc. According to the same source for another year, there were 1821 museums in 1972, and it is difficult to believe such rapid growth in seven years. Attendence was 308 m.[71]

So, there are clearly more museums in the US and they are better attended. Again, we must say at least a few words about 'quality'. The reference is not to picture galleries, although in the opinion of people who know, American galleries are richer. I remember well how the museum of natural history in Vienna on our road to America amazed us: both the richer exposition and the more well-done exhibits. The same, incidentally, relates to zoos. One of the explanations is that museum workers in the USSR are paid pennies. The better quality of American museums is proved best of all by the figures presented above; as we saw, on a per capita basis attendence at American meuseums is 2.5 times greater.

In order to get an impression about the scope of involvement in sports in America, in Table 10.6 I present some data on the number of participants by type of sport. The handbook shows separately the number of those who participated in the corresponding sport more than five times in the year. There are data only for 1977 (average population during this year was 216.8 m.).

One of the American statistical yearbooks published a table showing the percentage of the population 20 years and older that participated in various physical exercises in 1975, including only those who exercised on a regular basis no less than once a week. This percentage was 48.6, i.e. almost half the adult population including the elderly. Only a third of this number engaged in walking and only 4.8 per cent in jogging. The majority were involved in swimming, gymnastics, etc.[72]

We have essentially nothing to compare with these impressive indicators; Soviet statistics on sports are rather modest as the activities

Table 10.6   The US: participants in physical activity,[a] m.

	Total	Of which, not less than 5 times per year
Camping		
Developed areas	51.8	21.0
Undeveloped areas	36.0	15.0
Hunting	32.6	24.5
Fishing	91.0	61.9
Hiking, backpacking	48.1	28.1
Other walking, jogging	116.1	96.7
Horseback riding	25.2	13.5
Water skiing	26.8	13.1
Sailing	19.1	7.8
Canoeing, kayaking	26.9	9.0
Other boating	57.3	34.3
Swimming		
in pools[b]	107.4	83.5
other	77.9	59.5
Scuba diving	0.2	0.2
Golf	27.1	18.9
Tennis, outdoors	55.7	40.9
Skiing, downhill	11.9	7.3
Ice skating, outdoor	27.8	15.7
Snowmobiling	13.8	7.8
Parachute jumping	0.2	0.2
Total	852.9	558.9

[a]*StAb-78*, p. 241. I did not include in the table riding off-road vehicles, bicycling, 'other games or sports', picnicking, sightseeing, visiting zoos, parks, fairs, etc., for which the figures are no less impressive.
[b]Including those who are just getting a suntan.

themselves are. The yearbook informs us that in 1976, 52.4 m. were involved in physical activities, i.e. one-fifth of the entire population, but it does not say exactly what activities this includes. Undoubtedly, it is the number of those who paid a few kopecks in membership dues to a 'voluntary sports society' and not those who were actually regularly engaged in sports. In the same year 17.6 m. people were given the Soviet rating of so-called 'third-rank athlete', but real athletes – those given first rank and higher – numbered only somewhat over 200 000. A large percentage of these were chess and checkers players. They tell us that there were 98 000 soccer fields and also 371 000 volleyball, basketball and tennis courts.[71] But surely this untruth includes the most primitive 'fields' and 'courts'. I guarantee that there were not even about 100 000 specially equipped and surfaced soccer fields in the country and that any place where a net could be hung between two poles was considered a volleyball court. With respect to tennis courts, I must say that at the end of the same year there were only 211 in all of Moscow, and not many more throughout the rest of the country.[74]

There are now 3 m. 'small size' boats in personal use in the USSR, and only 40 per cent of the population's boats in the RSFSR had motors. Among the boat motors in use, 'motors with 11–30 horsepower predominate', and the rest have up to 10 horsepower. In the US in 1976 there were 7.7 m. boat motors in use, and 468 000 motor boats with an average motor of 42.1 horsepower were sold.[75]

No 'health clubs', so numerous in the US, exist in the USSR, although the Soviets have quite a number of 'health groups' – the difference, and very substantial, is in equipment. In my impression, the sports complexes of American universities have no equal in the USSR. The sports fields and gymnasiums of an ordinary American school are usually better than at Soviet higher educational institutions.

In 1976 in the US 656 000 specially equipped recreational vehicles were sold (85 per cent self-propelled), and in addition, 100 000 vans with minimal equipment including a sleeping area.[76] In the USSR neither the former nor the latter exist.

There is a special network of resorts and 'recreation houses' in the USSR, but we should in no way exaggerate their real significance. A total of 32 m. people visited such places in 1976, including 4.5 m. at resorts, 5.2 m. at recreation houses and boarding houses, 2.6 m. at rest facilities, and 16.6 m. at tourist camps.[77] In other words, all of these forms of recreation, including tourist camps, provided service for 12 per cent of the population, while only 3.8 per cent of the population visited resorts or recreation homes and less than 2 per cent were in resorts alone. Thus, the average Soviet person could be in a 'recreation institution' once every eight years and in resort once in his life.

Several times above I made calculations of how many decades it would take for the USSR to catch up to the US in particular types of consumption. Here is what a Soviet author says: 'Extrapolating ... current rates of growth .. shows that the full satisfaction of requirements for the services of vacation resorts will be achieved sometime in the middle of the twenty-first century.'[78]

The reader must also have a clear picture of what a Soviet recreation house or resort is. In the large majority of them, people sleep in rooms with four or more persons, and practically no such institution is designed for families. The author just cited asserts: 'Let us assume that a sleeping room with 1–2 places, fully equipped with sanitary facilities, and with an area of 7–9 square meters per person, meets the requirements of contemporary workers. Today less than 15 per cent of all labour union resorts meet these requirements.'

In 1976, 21 m. 'children and youth spent part of their summer at Pioneer and school camps, at excursion-tourist camps, or went to a childrens' institution in the countryside during the summer period.'[77] A remarkable achievement, but, first, this is much less than a third of all children and youth, and, second, the phrase 'school-camps' in the above citation troubles me; I am afraid that these are so-called urban camps, whose name speaks for itself. But we will be fair – the US has many fewer country camps for children than the USSR.

Also absent in the US is a developed system of recreation homes and resorts, but the many hotels, motels, rentable apartments and restaurants in resort areas more than make up for this.

It is not easy to compare hotels. The authors say [11] that there are hotel accomodations for 33 400 people in Moscow[80] and for 200 000 in New York alone. We have no other evidence about Soviet hotels, but it must be said that Moscow is an absolute exception both in the overall number of places in hotels and in their number on a per capita basis. Incomparably fewer hotels in all other cities, to say nothing of towns and villages. In practice hotels are completely inaccessible to the population; they are intended for those on business trips and for foreigners. Thus, even the modest amount of expenditures by the population on hotels – R83 m., or 32 kopecks per capita a year [80] – is greatly overstated. I noted above that the authors overstated the price of hotels, but on this scale it makes little difference.

Regarding the US, the situation with hotels is much better than with the statistics on them. The Census Bureau publishes complete data on hotels that are independent, but if, for example, a restaurant has several rooms it is not included in the statistics. Also not included in the statistics are small 'rest homes' that serve one family, hotels occupied more or less continuously by their residents, some tourist camps, rooms owned by clubs, etc. Knowing that the statistics given below are understated, we will examine them none the less for lack of others. In 1977 there were 12 500 hotels and 39 000 motels. The latest data on the number of rooms are for 1972. Then, there were 755 000 rooms in 10 800 hotels and 1.24 m. rooms in 30 000 motels. Using the same correlation for 1977 we get 2.5 m. rooms. The occupancy ratio for 1977 was 68 per cent.[81] We will assume that there were 1.5 persons in each room. I base this on the fact that American couples often travel together (even on business trips) and quite frequently with children. The result is that in 1977 the average American spent 4.3 nights in a hotel or motel.

Although this figure is many times greater than in the USSR, it does not reflect the number of nights that Americans spent in other recreational spots. We must add to it the figures from Table 10.6 on nights spent in campgrounds, consider the cited figure on the number of recreational vehicles, and also the larger number of apartments and houses that can be rented in resort areas. On the other hand, we must subtract the number of nights spent on business trips, but how many they are I do not know.

A huge American advantage is the extremely long coastline of beautiful natural beaches. According to data for 1971, a total of 5500 km of publicly owned coastline and 9400 km of privately owned coast was used for recreation.[82] In the USSR things are much worse in this respect also. The coastlines of the Black Sea, the Sea of Azov, Caspian Sea, and the Baltic Sea that are suitable for swimming are much shorter; many rivers and lakes are poisoned. Many American natural waterways are also polluted, but 90 per cent of the coast line noted above is along oceans.

Overall the authors consider the volume of Soviet consumption for the recreation subgroup to be 22 per cent of the American level in rubles, 40 per cent in dollars, and 30 per cent by the geometric mean [20]. Considering that for this entire subgroup the USSR has the advantage only in movies, that there are no commercial games there, that the lag in sports is huge and for hotels monstrous, etc., here also the Soviet level is overstated relative to the American, although again I must avoid any sort of quantitative estimate. The CIA estimate that the geometric mean of Soviet consumption considering state subsidies is 44 per cent of the American level [11] is all the more so in error.

It is hardly worth it to expand on *automotive services*; the difference here is colossal. The Soviet volume is 1 per cent of the American, which more or less corresponds to the difference in the number of cars and the levels of service for them. Expenditures under this item include not only repair but also expenditures on gasoline.[83] Still, I have to say that the authors' price parity for the group (Table 3.1) is grossly overstated.

The group includes, as a special subgroup, a large amount of *miscellaneous services*, primarily financial – banking, insurance, credit cards, etc. Having lived since 1974 in America, I am more and more of the conviction that these services primarily raise the cost but do not improve the standard of living. This is one of few instances in which, in my opinion, the CIA overstated American consumption with Soviet.

The overall volume of 'miscellaneous' services is rather great – the average American spent $293 during the year (Table 10.1), i.e. 5 per cent of all consumption expenditures. More is spent on them than on utilities, almost as much as on automotive service or on clothing, and a little more than on meat products. And given such a huge volume of expenditures, someone's personal opinion (including my own) makes no difference: the fact that so much is spent on these purposes, and not just by particular groups but almost all Americans, means that the population as a whole wants these services and is willing to pay for them.

Concluding my analysis of the comparison of services in the CIA study, I once again avoid an overall quantitative estimate. Although from everything we saw above it is clear that the authors significantly overstated the comparative volume of Soviet consumption for this group also, a quantitative estimate is very difficult to make.

11 Education and Health Care

In describing in Chapters 2 and 3 the methods used in the CIA study, I did not say a word about education and medicine, but they were not compared in the same way as all other components of consumption. Here the authors' task was exceptionally difficult.

The main problem is the absence of a measure of 'output'. True, some sort of ersatz for education might be devised (for example, years of learning), but the fact that different levels of education cannot be reduced to a single unit of 'output' makes it hardly possible to use. And for health even such an ersatz is not apparent.

The fact that education and medicine in the USSR are practically fully paid for by the state[1] also creates impediments; however, ultimately the total amount of expenditures and not the distribution among payers is important.[2]

With regard to health, the authors of the CIA study identified nine categories of medical personnel – doctor, dentist, nurse, radiologist, pharmacist, etc. – and for each category calculated an average wage for both countries.[3] Further, following the principle 'a doctor is a doctor', they calculated price ratios, which in this case reflect the ratio of the earnings of a Soviet doctor in rubles to those of an American doctor in dollars. If all expenditures on medicine were limited only to wages, the results of the comparison would be entirely determined by the difference in the numbers of personnel in the two countries and the differing structures of these totals – roughly speaking, by the shares of doctors. But, of course, there are other expenditures, and the calculation included material expenditures on health, which are easily classified into our very familiar 'soft goods', durables and food (in hospitals). The price parities for material expenditures were taken from other sections of the study.

For education a procedure similar in principle was adopted. It was divided into 'elementary, including kindergarten, and secondary' and 'higher education'. Soviet specialised secondary schools (*tekhnikum*) were arbitrarily divided in half with one half allocated to elementary and secondary and the other to higher education. The comparison was then made on the basis of the number of workers in the two categories of education. As with medicine, material expenditures were also taken into account.

Critically examining this method, we note first of all that it is based on expenditures and not on their effects, results, which in principle contradict the normal Western approach. Incidentally, this is not the only example of this sort, and we will speak of this in Chapter 12.

Let us now look more concretely at the CIA's method of calculations for *education*. What determines their results? Three factors: the number of workers in schools and colleges in both countries, the ratio of wages in schools and colleges, and the ratio of earnings to material expenditures. Let us examine each of these three factors in turn. The total number of workers in schools and colleges in the two countries is approximately equal – 6.4 m. in the USSR and 5.8 m. in the US [95]. This would seem to give the advantage to the USSR, although not per capita. But that total includes 1.3 m. workers in Soviet kindergartens, while for the US they seemingly are not considered. The existence of kindergartens in itself benefits society, but it must also be shown to what extent they benefit education. Precisely because a kindergarten is not a school or college the ratio of the number of workers in it to the number of 'students' is completely different than in schools. And, of course, it must be kept in mind that a Soviet kindergarten has not only an older group that can more or less be equated with the first grade of an American school but also a younger group including three-year-olds. Thus, at a minimum a serious revision for this factor is needed.

Regarding the second factor, the ratio of the number of people employed in elementary and secondary education to the number in higher education is 6:1 for the USSR and 2.8:1 for the US.[4] If everything else in the comparison were identical, this alone would have produced a much better overall result for America. The sense of these proportions is that many more people work in American colleges. Why? One reason is the different structure of education, and a significant part of what is considered higher education in America I would include in secondary (see below). Another reason is that the majority of American scientists are concentrated in higher educational institutions and not in specialised research organisations as in the USSR. The resulting undercount gives the US a large advantage. None the less, this proportion is primarily determined by the fact that there are more professors and other teachers per student in American colleges than in the USSR. This in itself is wonderful, but I object to the assumption adopted in the study that the volume of education is, so to say, proportional to the quantity of teachers. In the USSR teaching a course with 3–5 students as in America is impossible (Soviet supervision of graduate students is not in the nature of class work), and it is a great delusion to think that the 'quantity of education' received by a student in such a group is ten times greater than by a student in a group of 30–50. Moreover, the advantage of small groups is appreciably compensated for by the much larger number of hours of class work in the USSR. It is also clear that such a student–teacher ratio is largely caused by the fact that students in American universities can choose their courses and teachers; this, again, is in itself not bad but the growth of expenditures here is hardly proportional to the growth of the effect.

Of course the results of the calculation depend not so much upon the ratio of the number of teachers in schools and colleges as on the amounts of their earnings. The ratio that the authors took – workers in Soviet higher educational institutions get 1.7 times more than workers in schools, and in the US 1.2[5] – generally speaking weakens the negative impact on the results of the comparison of the correlation in the numbers of personnel just examined. However, the correlation of earnings in no way corresponds to the actual difference in qualifications, in so to say 'useful return'. In other words, in no way should it be thought that the personnel in Soviet higher educational institutions are precisely 1.7 times more qualified than the personnel in Soviet schools. In fact this difference in salary developed historically (the sharp raise in pay given to 'degreed' personnel just after the war still has an effect today), and is at best a statistical surrogate for the real ratio of qualifications.[6] There are more grounds to think that the difference in pay of school and college personnel in the US is 'more justified' – this reflects 'market reality', the market 'value' of a professor and a school teacher, but this correlation only emphasises the chancey nature of the Soviet correlation. Indeed, who would dare to assert that the difference in qualifications of a professor and a school teacher is almost one-third lower in the US than in the USSR?!

In sum, the premises the authors adopted for this factor are at a minimum questionable, but they exerted a decisive influence on the results of their calculations.

Speaking of the third factor, I note that while the cost of materials was included in the calculation, the cost of buildings and equipment was not, and it is precisely here that the difference between the two countries is most striking.[7] The authors say [4] that they ignored this factor in the calculations for both education and health, but later [18] note that an adjustment of 7 per cent was made in certain calculations for health. This is clearly insufficient. The consequences for the comparison of education are less than for health but also very substantial. A stroll on a university campus and a half hour in a swimming pool in themselves do not add to the quality of education, but campuses, in addition to everything else, save students a lot of time and effort. Another relevant issue of no small importance here is educational equipment, in which America is far ahead, as well.

At the same time, all this is not so simple, and even including the cost of materials might be questioned. The example I just mentioned, auditoriums, is of some relevance for the cultural events held in them, but again this has little effect on the quality of education itself. The authors include expenditures on school lunches in the calculations. And though it is said that a hungry stomach is deaf to studies, this also in itself only clouds the overall comparative picture of education.[8] (In one version of calculations [118], lunches were excluded.)

I might add other critical comments, but what has been said should be enough – the method the authors used is not too convincing. Things are no better with the comparisons for *health*. Here, to be sure, there is no collision of secondary and higher schools, but the problems are no less. The results are largely distorted by an entirely 'objective' factor – the absurdly higher wages of American doctors. The simple fact that in 1976 doctors on the average earned $53 000 and nurses $9000–$12 000 a year,[9] i.e. one-fifth as much, clearly says that the method the authors used is unsuitable. It is precisely because this difference is so large in America, while in the USSR a doctor earns only about twice as much as a nurse, that the results of the comparison for health in dollars and in rubles differ so greatly from each other (see Table 11.1). One might object that such is American 'market reality', that consumers pay and that's it. But the high earnings of doctors are shameful; they are the direct result of the monopoly of the American Medical Association and, real as they are, these earnings in no way reflect the actual effect of their labour.

It is also regrettable that the authors did not sufficiently consider fixed capital in health. The actual difference in the health care of the two countries is determined primarily and most decisively by the fact that the American doctor is incredibly better 'equipped' than his (her) Soviet colleague. The most varied and perfect machines and devices, primarily for analysis, but not individual art, underlie the unquestionable qualitative advantage of American medicine. This fundamental difference should be captured by indicators of fixed capital, but the authors did not make such a comparison.

I have full respect for the difficult investigation that the authors

Table 11.1 Expenditures on health and education

	Education[a]	Health[a]
Per capita expenditures		
USSR, rubles	69.84	45.47
US, dollars	472.13	646.63
Ruble–dollar price parities		
With Soviet weights	0.153	0.117
With American weights	0.225	0.4
USSR as percent of US		
Comparison in rubles	65.7	17.6
Comparison in dollars	96.7	60.1
Geometric mean	79.7	32.5

[a][20]

carried out in these two spheres of consumption and, alas, I probably could not have done it better myself. None the less, the circumstances cited make us rate the method they used unsatisfactory. The authors believe that among all the results they obtained, the worst were for housing and recreation. But it seems that even worse were their calculations for medicine and education.

After my remarks concerning methods, the reader is right to expect harsh criticism of these results, a sharp disagreement with them. But such expectations, if they are there, are in vain. While criticising the method the authors used, I find it difficult to propose or apply a better one myself, to give my own alternative estimate.

None the less, it is useful to give below the available statistical material, (and to indicate the existing difficulties), and attempt on this basis to arrive at some qualitative, non-quantified evaluations.

Education. Here, no criteria for comparative evaluation are evident. In both countries all children go to school and the majority of them finish, but the quality of education must also be considered. How? There is no doubt that American children like their schools much more than Soviet children like theirs, but in the unanimous opinion of emigrants – parents and teachers – the American school overall gives less knowledge than the Soviet. I fully agree with this, all the more so since this opinion is also shared by native 'enlighteners'.[10] The Soviet school takes 10 years and the American 12, but this is not a criterion, all the more so since Soviet school children go six and not five days a week, the school year is longer and students have much more homework. In the first grades American school children play, and they study hardly more than in Soviet kindergarten. In Soviet schools they begin algebra now in almost the first grade.[11]

But there are also factors complicating the calculation, like the dissimilarity in the levels of teaching in different schools in the USSR and the US (urban and suburban, and also private and public schools in the US; urban and rural, and also 'special' schools in the USSR) and the level of instruction in different subjects, the emphasis in the USSR on memorisation,[12] and in the US on the existence of differing points of view, the transition to new programmes in the USSR, etc.

No fewer are the problems with the comparison of higher education and advanced degrees, which in principle can be only approximate. We will begin at the 'end'. In the US there is no equivalent for the Soviet doctor of science degree. Roughly speaking, this is something like a 'full professor researcher'. The American doctor of philosophy (Ph.D.) is entirely equivalent to the Soviet candidate's degree. Some sovietologists (!) do not agree with me, but such is the practice in American universities, to say nothing of European. Decisive in this comparison, of course, is the simple fact that each of these degrees attests to the capability and qualifications of its holder to do independent scientific work and to teach courses in universities.[13]

Correspondingly, in the majority of cases the equivalent of Soviet higher education is the American master's degree. This is proved by a comparison of the difference between these degrees and the candidate of sciences and doctor of philosophy degrees. This is unquestionably also proved by the fact that doctors and lawyers graduate from 'regular' institutes. Somewhat less certain statements can be made about the comparison for technical specialties, but as the emigre engineers working quite successfully in American firms demonstrate, Soviet engineering education, if not exactly equal to a master's degree (the majority think just this) is at least closer to it than to a bachelor's degree.[14]

From this I conclude that the American bachelor's degree must be likened to the Soviet *tekhnikum*. American nurses have a bachelor's degree (very few, a master's); it seems to me correct to compare teachers who have finished college (i.e., having received a bachelor's in education) with graduates of Soviet specialised secondary schools but not institutes. It is also entirely correct to compare graduates of Soviet engineering technical colleges with bachelors in technical specialities.[15]

My opinion may be disputed, but there is no doubt that equating all American bachelors to those who receive a higher education in the

USSR is incorrect. The authors of the study do not understand this,[16] but Soviet statisticians also, to the misfortune of their propaganda, overlook this point.[17]

If we speak of the quality of higher education, it is known that former Soviet engineers easily find work in their specialities in America and handle their jobs with no problem. Former Soviet mathematicians teach at the best universities in America. Soviet physicians rather quickly overcome obstacles in taking examinations (see below). Those in the humanities have it much worse, but here the language barrier and the generally unfavourable situation with these professions in America have an effect.

I have run into cases where an attempt was made to compare higher education on the basis of the number of class hours. This, of course, is nonsense – Soviet higher educational institutions are far ahead in class hours, although American students work much more outside class. They say that a large part of Soviet students' time is spent on 'fundamentals of Marxism–Leninism', 'scientific communism', and the like. But in America there are broad religious programmes, to say nothing of the fact that there are plenty of Marxists.

The quality of education in Soviet evening and correspondence colleges leaves a lot to be desired, but the comparative levels of education at Harvard and some college in Oklahoma are also far from identical.

It is not clear how to show in the estimate the American student's possibility of choosing subjects beginning with the ninth grade, and for college students not only the subject but the teacher. Of huge significance also is the fact that in America it is possible to receive all three degrees – bachelor, master, doctor – in different specialities; in the USSR a graduate of a financial *tekhnikum* will not be taken in a Physics Institute, and from it for graduate study in 'theaterology'.[18]

Let us now compare a few figures. At the end of 1976 there were 3.2 m. children in day nurseries in the USSR, i.e. 23 per cent of those born during the previous three years. There were 8.9 m. children in kindergartens, or 51 per cent of those born in 1970–73. There are corresponding data for the US only on children three years and older. In 1976 there were 1.5 m. of these in day nurseries, and the number in kindergartens was 3.5 m.[19] Remember that children begin school at age six in the US and seven in the USSR.

Regarding elementary school, in the USSR in 1976/7 school year there were 159 000 schools that were attended by 46.5 m. children. There were 144 700 daytime general education schools with 41.5 m.

pupils. In grades 1–8 there were 35.6 m. students (of which 0.8 m. in evening schools) and in grades 9–10 (and 11 where it exists, in particular in Estonia) 10.9 m., including 4.6 m. or almost half in evening schools.[20]

Since there are no detailed data in Soviet statistics on population by age cohorts,[21] it is difficult to determine directly what percentage of children went to school. None the less, there is every reason to believe that practically all children finish the eighth grade.[22] Regarding later grades (a complete secondary education), for 30 years now they have been talking about the transition to universal secondary education,[23] but the transition is still taking place. According to the yearbook, 'in 1976, 97 per cent of eighth grade graduates continued their studies in secondary school and in other educational institutions giving a secondary education'.[24] 'Other educational institutions' here means so-called secondary professional–technical specialised schools in which young people learn an occupation in addition to getting a general education. This form is growing rapidly. There were 615 of them in the 1970/1 school year with 180 000 students, and in 1976/7 almost 1.5 m. young people attended 3087 specialised secondary schools.[25]

In the US in 1976 there were 77 200 elementary schools, including 1200 with one teacher, and 14 000 private schools. There were 29 000 secondary schools. A total of 47 m. students attended all schools, of which 34 per cent were in grades 9–12.[26] Thus, American schools are significantly, one and a half times, larger. And for the US as well it is hard to directly compare the number of students with the number of children of the corresponding ages. But, roughly speaking, all children went to school.

In sum, the figures presented say that in both countries practically all children now finish school of one level or another. Although the attainment of universal education in the USSR, as we see, is to a large extent ensured by the organisation of professional-technical specialised secondary schools, I would not consider this a shortcoming. In addition to all else, in the majority of American public schools students in higher grades also have the option of getting some training in certain occupations.

A concrete comparison of higher education is much more complicated, primarily due to the dissimilarity of the systems of education and degrees discussed above. In the USSR at the beginning of the 1976/7 academic year there were 4303 secondary specialised educational institutions (*tekhnikums*, including 1.8 m. in evening and corresponding divisions, and there were 5 m. students in higher educational institu-

tions, including 2.7 m. evening and correspondence students. A total of
1.4 m. students were accepted in *tekhnikums* and 1 m. in higher educational institutions in 1976.[27] What percentage of school graduates
continue their education? Eighteen years before 1976, in 1958, 5.2 m.
children were born.[28] Some of them did not live to age 18 and some
went to *tekhnikums* after the eighth grade. On the other hand, some of
the graduates of *tekhnikums* entered higher educational institutions,
many of those entering evening and correspondence divisions were not
18-year-olds, and many get into higher educational institutions only on
the second or third try or after service in the army. Given all this we can
confidently say that significantly fewer than half of the young people of
the corresponding age go to higher educational institutions and *tekhnikums*, and significantly less than 20 per cent go to higher educational
institutions.

In 1976, 735 000 students completed higher educational institutions
and 1.1 m. completed *tekhnikums*.[29]

Let us turn now to the US. In 1976 there were 11 m. students in
universities and colleges (including 179 000 foreign students), i.e. 14 per
cent more than in Soviet higher educational institutions and *tekhnikums* in spite of a total population 16 per cent smaller. Of this total,
3.9 m. students attended two-year colleges. Of all high school graduates
20–24 years old in 1976, 27 per cent had attended a college or
university. In 1976, 1 799 000 persons completed colleges and universities, including 448 000 from two-year colleges, 998 000 with a bachelor's
degree, and 313 000 with master's degress.[30]

If you agree with me that a bachelor's degree (and even more so
completing a two-year college) is equivalent to graduation from a
tekhnikum and consider the difference in population, it turns out that in
the US the output of *tekhnikums* was one and a half times higher than
in the USSR, and the output of higher educational institutions was
only half as great. This means that the US is ahead in, so to speak,
secondary-technical education but lags sharply in higher education.
The reader should keep in mind that both American and Soviet sources
believe that the USSR is lagging in higher education.

Regarding candidates of science and Ph.D.s, the Soviet handbook
gives only the number who completed the required course work and
examinations, but who did not necessarily present or defend a dissertation. These persons who 'completed graduate training during the year'
numbered 23 600 in 1976.[31]

In the US in 1976, 34 100[32] Ph.D. degrees were awarded – more than
in the USSR by any measure, especially on a per capita basis.

As we see, an overall evaluation is far from easy. The USSR has a clear advantage in day nurseries and kindergartens, and there is approximate equality in elementary–secondary education. The US is far ahead in 'bachelors', but even further behind in 'masters', although ahead in Ph.D.s. It is still more difficult to introduce the comparative quality of education at various levels into the overall evaluation. In general, the advantage of Soviet elementary and secondary schools is indisputable, but regarding secondary-technical and higher education I find it hard to make an overall evaluation. The social advantage of the fact that in the US a significantly larger percentage of young people can continue their education after secondary school needs no proof, but many professors complain that at the end of the 1960s when this was achieved, the 'quality' of students quickly declined, which had an immediate impact on the quality of education. It is of great significance that most American students stop after receiving a bachelor's degree.

My short analysis of the situation is clearly insufficient for any sort of general conclusions, but the authors' conclusion – that the volume of consumption per capita for education in the USSR is 80 per cent of the US level by the geometric mean (Table 11.1) – is also not very well founded. Intuitively, I would sooner be inclined to think that by and large the US has a certain advantage in education over the USSR in the sense that specialists are better prepared for their future work, but I repeat this is no more than intuition. Also intuitively, I think that so to speak non-professional education in the USSR is at least no worse than in the US.

It is by no means easier to compare *health*. Soviet comparisons concentrate on the number of doctors and hospital beds, and by these indicators the USSR is clearly ahead. In 1976 the USSR far outdistanced the US in the number of doctors per 1000 residents – 3.35 *vis-à-vis* 2.1 in the US; and even more in hospital beds – 11.9 per cent per 1000 souls *vis-à-vis* 6.7.[33]

As was already said, a comparison of the number of doctors underlies the CIA comparison of levels of consumption for health. None the less, these figures in themselves tell us little. Soviet doctors spend a lot of time visiting the sick at home, while American doctors receive patients only in their offices. Of course, it is convenient when doctors come to the sick but, strictly speaking, the quality of care in a clinic should be better.[34] People often go to Soviet doctors not for treatment but for sick-leave certificates. The fact that treatment is 'free' means that people go to the doctor with a runny nose or even without any clear necessity. The Soviet doctor does much of what is done by a nurse in America, but in spite of this, while a doctor in a clinic is supposed to spend an average of 12 minutes with a patient according to the norm, the actual time is less than 5 minutes,[35] which is hardly sufficient. It is very significant that analysis with the aid of excellent equipment quickly gives the American doctor a much clearer picture of the patient's condition. Finally, by my observations, the American doctor works a greater number of hours.

Two more remarks on this subject. The authors, on the one hand, as we know, build the entire comparison on the number of doctors and equate an American doctor to a Soviet one. However, in doing so they decisively declare [4] that emigre doctors from the USSR must go through 'radical' retraining in order to practise medicine in the West. This, to put it mildly, is not quite so. Soviet medical degrees are recognised in West Germany and Israel, and 'retraining' in America involves primarily refreshing one's memory about institute courses, becoming familiar with equipment and drugs, and mastering the language. In sum, the authors contradict themselves here.[36]

It is also worth noting that if indeed the US lags in the number of doctors, in the number of pharmacists per capita they are ahead of the USSR by 2.3 times.[37] It is hard to say why this is so. Generally speaking, American medicines are more diverse and, let us hope, more effective. Here, moreover, there are no interruptions in the supply of medicines, which the Soviet press is increasingly complaining about. Possibly such a large difference in the number of pharmacists is due to the fact that many more medicines require a prescription in the US, and prepackaging of medicines is less frequent.

The reasoning about the number of hospital beds is analogous to the arguments about doctors. Not only are there more beds in the USSR, but they are used more 'intensively'. However, this in itself is by no means necessarily a positive factor. The point is not only that the length of a patient's stay in the hospital is connected with the effectiveness (ineffectiveness) of treatment, but primarily that Soviet people in general, and including when they land in the hospital, are less healthy.

The difficulty with health, as is well known, is that a large amount of medical services is not necessarily positive; quite the opposite – in principle it would be wonderful if mankind had fewer doctors and hospital beds, needing all of them much less. And better health depends only in part upon medicine; it is to a large extent determined by the standard of living.

As we see, from a methodological standpoint the comparison for health is even more difficult than for education, primarily due to the absence of a measure of 'output of health care'. 'Average life expectancy' could, generally speaking, be a sort of distant surrogate for it. Soviet statistics have not published figures on this for almost 10 years, simply repeating in all yearbooks data for 1971–2: 70 years.[38] This unquestionably says that the figure is getting worse. While in 1971 life expectancy was 64.8 years for men and 74.7 for women, calculations based upon indirect data indicate that in 1976 it was 63.1 and 73.9 years. The average for the population as a whole was 68.9 years.[39] In the US the average was 72.8 years (69 for men and 76.7 for women). One might think that this is not a big difference, but in the US life expectancy was the same as the 1976 figure for the USSR over 30 years ago – in 1950.[40]

A necessary reservation that is directly relevant to the problem we are examining is that life expectancy is far from only dependent upon medicine. In the US its increase is related not only to the successful struggle with heart disease and other medical successes but to improved diet, a sharp decline in smoking, a jump in involvement in sports and other physical activity, etc. None the less, even if we did not have these data, we could from the life expectancy indicator speak of better medicine in the US, in spite of the smaller number of doctors.

Keeping all this in mind, let us examine the results. Aggregate data are given in Table 4.1. Here, in Table 11.1, I give more detailed data (slight differences from Table 4.1 are due to differing classifications).

What do these data mean? If we take them as they are, it turns out that for education, measuring in dollars, the USSR is almost at the level of the US. When measured in rubles the Soviet lag, relative to its lag in other components of consumption, is not great – only 1.5 times. By the geometric mean the USSR comes closer to the US in education than in any other group of consumption. Things are much worse with health. Here the lag by the geometric mean is about the same as for consumption as a whole. However, pay attention to the huge difference in the sizes of the lags measured in rubles and in dollars.

There are also some other data. The yearbook for 1974 published for the last time (in later editions it disappeared) a table from which we learn that in that year industrial workers missed work 13.5 days due to illness and giving birth. This is only 0.4 days less than in 1940. Furthermore, this reference is to days paid from social insurance funds,[41] so the actual absences for these reasons were higher. Regarding the US, in the same year, 1974, the number of days of restricted activity to illness or injury was 16.8 per capita. The per capita number of bed-disability days was 6.6, and lost working time (related, of course, not to the entire population but to the number working – 93.2 m.) was **4.4** days.[42] This is so low that one might think that people went to work sick, but lost school days by children of ages 6–16 were not much greater.[43] It stands to reason that the data are not entirely comparable, primarily because we are comparing Soviet blue-collar workers with all workers and employees in the US. But in spite of all reservations[44] it is clear that in the USSR people are sick 2–2.5 times more. In a report at the last congress of Soviet labour unions, it was said that 'losses of working time due to temporary inability to work continue to remain high' and that in the last five-year plan period payments for medically excused sick leave grew by 20 per cent.[45]

Let us move on now to treatment. For the USSR in this case we have rather more complete data for 1974:[46]

	Doctor visits per resident	
	Urban	Rural
Total	11.12	4.04
of which:		
in clinics, out-patient clinics, etc.	9.92	3.88
care at home	0.79	0.1
emergency care	0.41	0.05
air rescue	0	0.01
In addition, visits of nurses (medical assistants)	3.20	4.14

Beginning with 1977, the *Narkhoz* yearbook publishes the number of 'visits to doctors (including doctor's house calls)' in out-patient clinic institutions, which in that year numbered 9.6 visits per capita.[47]

In the United States the number of visits is much smaller. In 1976 the per capita number of visits to the doctor was 4.9 plus about 1.6 visits to the dentist. Among the total number of visits was: 69 per cent in doctors' offices, 12 per cent consultations by telephone, and 13 per cent emergency service, and so on.[48]

These data are not very comparable. A doctor's aid by telephone is a form unknown in the USSR, although there is such a form as false requests to summon emergency aid.[49] I already mentioned trips to the doctor not for treatment but for a medical excuse. In spite of all this I repeat that the average Soviet sees a doctor not less than twice as often as an American does.

In regard to data on hospitals, in 1974, 215 people were hospitalised per 1000 residents in the USSR, i.e. about one-fifth (the urban figure was 212 and rural 215). The per capita number of days spent in the hospital for each urban resident was 3.5 days and for rural residents about 3.7 days. And one other figure: the average length of stay for each urban patient was 15.2 days and for each rural patient 13.4 days.[50]

In America these figures are lower. In 1976 for each 1000 residents 173 landed in the hospital. The per capita number of days spent in the hospital during the year was 1.9, and the average length of a hospital stay was 8.5 days (excluding psychiatric and tuberculosis hospitals).[51]

Thus, there are many more doctors and places in hospitals in the USSR than in the US. The sick and well visit doctors more often, and in addition it is possible to call the doctor to your home. Being ill more often, the average Soviet gets correspondingly more medical care, including in hospitals. And automatically doubts arise – can we really speak of the lag of Soviet medicine, and especially one of three times as our authors assert? After all, the fact that Soviet people get sick more often and for a longer time does not, generally speaking, necessarily relate precisely to the quality of treatment – this is a consequence of poor living conditions, long times spent standing in queues, a poor diet, alcoholism, heavy work, etc.

From the figures presented above we see that the average Soviet receives twice as much medical care. This also follows from figures on 'doctors' visits' and those on the per capita number of days spent in hospitals. But if that is so and if we accept the authors' conclusion about the USSR lag in medicine by three times, it turns out that the 'quality' of medical care in the USSR is six times worse than in America. And this, I repeat, is given that the authors themselves in their calculations equated a Soviet doctor to an American. From this alone the fundamental incorrectness of the authors' calculations and conclusions on health is indisputable. It goes without saying that the quality of medical care in the USSR is much worse, but 'much' is not a difference of 6 times!

To emphasise once again the difficulty of this problem and to vindicate the authors somewhat, a few words about another social problem – the security of citizens. Where is it higher? In which country, the USSR or the US, are citizens protected against various forms of crime (we will leave aside political crime)? We might, for example, say that since there are many fewer prisoners in the US,[52] American citizens are much less protected than Soviets from crime. Or security might be measured by the number of police per capita. I will go no deeper into this question, but it emphasises that in similar problems it is not easy to find criteria and, therefore, quantitative estimates are very difficult.

So what are we to do now? Over and over in examining the problem of comparing education and health we are again and again shut off by the need to designate 'output', which is somewhat easier in education but practically hopeless in medicine. Precisely for this reason the price parities calculated by the authors for these groups of consumption are in essence meaningless. It is impossible to rationally explain just what they mean. In any event they in no way show what they are supposed to show – how a ruble is to be equated with a dollar (or the opposite) in this type of consumption. However, in themselves the amounts of expenditures in each country, for example that per capita spending on medicine is R45.47 in the USSR and $646.63 in the US, reflect certain realities. Theoretically speaking, the Soviet people could refuse medicine and spend these R45.47 on other types of consumption, increasing their consumption for other components by this amount.

The following approach suggests itself. Since we have no grounds for establishing price ratios (parities) for medicine and education, it makes sense to give up entirely on making what we know will be unsuccessful attempts at calculating them. Instead of calculating special parities for these groups we should use average parities for all other groups of consumption. The justification is elementary – in allocating certain resources for medicine and education, society, although not directly, measures the effect of these expenditures against the effect of their consumption for other purposes. However, as is obvious, by accepting this approach we, in fact, give up the comparisons of consumption in these two groups. Indeed, using the same price parities we will get the same results for consumption as a whole with and without medicine and education.[53]

As is apparent from Table 11.1 and Chapter 4, the parities the authors used for medicine and education are much lower than the average parities for consumption as a whole. This means that implementing the proposal would increase the comparative estimate of Soviet consumption for these two groups and, much less significantly, for consumption as a whole. Well, maybe that's the way it is; the varied statistical material I presented above confirms that the authors clearly exaggerated the Soviet lag in medicine and, possibly, for education. In Chapter 12 I attempt to correct these exaggerations in my final estimates.

12 Additional Methodological Discussion

It is time to consider several complex methodological problems. The authors themselves frankly list certain insurmountable difficulties but reduce them primarily to statistics [3]. While unquestionably agreeing with the authors that for decisive improvement of such calculations much better (and available) statistics are absolutely necessary, I permit myself to say that the methods also need improvement; they are far from blameless.

In drawing attention to a number of methodological issues in this chapter, I make no pretensions to the absolute truth of the points I consider, but only hope to have them discussed. Alas, I am not sure that everything here will be clear to the non-specialist. And I hasten to note: the matter does not end with a discussion of methodology (theory); entirely practical conclusions relating to concrete figures from the arguments to be made.[1]

A) Most important, of course, are prices. The question is not how accurately Soviet prices were recorded or average American prices calculated (we have dealt with that) but what, precisely, do prices reflect (express, measure) and correspondingly, what do the results of calculations based on them characterise?

There are at least two opposing approaches to price formation. According to contemporary Western theories, a price 'formed in the market' reflects the consumer qualities of a good (service) and is proportional to them. Simplifying, this means that if the price of a movie ticket is $5, a kilogram of potatoes $1, and a pair of pants $20, the, so to speak, aggregate of the consumer qualities of a pair of pants is equal to four movie tickets and 20 kg of potatoes.[2] This premise is fundamental. Without it the calculation in the study and any other value measurements of consumption have no substantive meaning.

According to the Soviet (Marxist) concept, price is determined not by the consumer qualities of a good but by expenditures on its production. Again simplifying, this means that the price of a pair of pants is equal to the price of four movie tickets not because this is the correlation of their consumer qualities but because this is the ratio of their production costs. This conception in principle rejects the possibility of equating the consumer qualities of goods, and also of reflecting supply limitations and shortages of goods in price.[3]

Real prices in real life do not follow conceptions – either in the USSR or the US. There are state subsidies (for example, to agriculture and urban transportation); some Western prices are deformed by taxes (gasoline, alcohol, tobacco), and others are altered by monopolies (medical services in America). None the less, the American 'market' price correspond much more to 'their' principle than the prices centrally established by the Soviet state correspond to their principle of accordance with expenditures on production. You cannot name a good the price of which has not been distorted by turnover tax, subsidies, enterprise losses, other forms of financial relations of an enterprise with the state budget,[4] and raw materials prices. All of this pertains less to intermediate goods for productive use, but with respect to consumer goods it is absolutely clear – prices for housing, alcohol, children's clothing and shoes, theatre tickets, meat, etc., are established not on the basis of production cost and even less so by some measurement of their consumer qualities, but on quite varied, including accidental, bases. Therefore, you just cannot say what they are proportional to.

The simple fact that prices are rarely revised in itself says that they differ from production costs. It is funny that Soviet economists for about thirty years have debated,[5] what in general should be considered production expenditures and what principle should be used in calculating them in setting prices? and at the same time they continue to speak about the accordance of prices with production costs that have not been defined.

All this is not news. Our authors briefly mention it and, following A. Bergson, state that the Soviet prices they use do not reflect real resource costs but should be called 'existing' (or 'prevailing') prices. They specially calculate [14] what the structure of consumption would be if the two most significant factors distorting prices did not exist – turnover taxes and subsidies. It turns out that the structure of consumption would be approximately the same, and with that the matter is ended. A pity.[6]

Although it would have presented certain difficulties, the correction in the 'basic' calculation would be worthwhile; the difference amounts to several percentage points.[7] It is also a pity that the CIA did not repeat what was already done once in calculating the gross national product for 1970 – there, they equalised the profit ratios for various branches;[8] here, they do not even mention this.

Even if the authors had corrected Soviet prices so that they would approximate actual costs, the results of calculations for the two compared countries would have differed sharply: American consumption would have been determined at prices reflecting preferences of the consumer. However, at least we would have known what the basis for Soviet prices was. But, as it is, Soviet consumption was measured in prices that exist ('prevail'), and what precisely they reflect (express) is absolutely unclear.

This fact is of cardinal importance. It is small consolation that Soviet consumers make their expenditures, pay for goods at the same prices that were used in the study (and that in this sense the volume of Soviet consumption accounted for in these prices fully reflects their expenditures). Other points are important. First, the amount of consumption in no way reflects society's actual expenditures for it. Since, as is well known (this is shown, in particular, in the cited book by Belkin), prices are set lower on means-of-production and higher on consumption goods, the amount of consumption determined by the authors is overstated. Second, the fact that prices are not proportional to consumer qualities cheapens (no pun intended) the comparison or consumption in rubles. Indeed, the structure of consumption is distorted, which strongly affects the entire comparison with the US. Third, this is the very time to speak of one more circumstance.

One of the basic differences of a Western economy from a Soviet-type economy is that the former is a, so to speak, economy of surpluses, while the latter is an economy of shortages.[9] The Western consumer has freedom in his market actions, constrained only by income (the amount he designates for consumption). In spite of all examples of the 'distortion' of Western prices, he makes his purchases in accordance with his own impression of the relative worth of the consumer qualities of various goods. In general and overall in a Western economy, the buyer (consumer) forms the structure of consumption.

The situation, as we all know, is the opposite in the Soviet economy. The consumer's own decisions are sharply restricted, and the structure of consumption is formed by his desires to only a small extent. Enormous savings in banks and 'under mattresses'[10] and universal queues give evidence of this best of all.[11] Assume the improbable: the Soviet consumer, given the same prices and the same level of income, is provided with the Western possibility of acquiring exactly what and exactly as much as he wants (and, certainly, can afford). The structure of consumption would change immediately, and even its level would change.[11] What follows from this?

This calls into question in the Soviet case the use of the authors' second fundamental premise – taking into account the differing structures of consumption and solving the index number problem with simultaneous calculations in both rubles and dollars, and determining the geometric mean as a comparative measure of the level of consumption in the two countries. Let us ponder once again the meaning of the estimate of Soviet consumption in dollars – 43 per cent of the American level (Table 4.1). The sense of this indicator (assuming all our authors' calculations are correct) is that in order to live 'Soviet-style' it would be sufficient for the American to spend (and for the economy to produce) 43 per cent of the actual American level. Although we must ignore here the 'income elasticity of consumption', this interpretation should raise no objections. But the mirror-image assertion – since in rubles Soviet consumption amounts to 28 per cent of American, it is sufficient for the average Soviet to spend almost four times as many rubles to reach the American standard of consumption — is incorrect; under the specific conditions of the Soviet economy, an economy of shortages, this is not so.[13] Why?

Recall that the cause of the index number problem is the different correlation of prices for various goods in the compared countries and the natural desire of consumers to buy what is cheaper.[14] Both of these elements are here – the structure of prices in the USSR differs greatly from that in the US, and consumers prefer cheaper goods.[15] However, the cardinal difference of the Soviet economy, as is well known, is precisely that people are not free in their choices; they cannot acquire what is cheaper. A very obvious example is housing – it is indeed cheap, but you cannot move into a new apartment. The prices of fruits in state trade are practically identical year round, but you cannot buy them in winter. Hotels and theatre tickets are not expensive, but consumption cannot deviate in that direction. The large percentage of potatoes and bread in the food ration is due not so much to the fact that they are cheap as to the impossibility of buying (finding) goods that, though more expensive, are more desirable. In an economy of shortages a large money income in itself does not ensure a correspondingly high level of consumption, and in order to achieve the American standard of living in the USSR it is not enough to spend a correspondingly larger amount of rubles. Besides, you couldn't.

The average Soviet, precisely like the consumer of any Western country, tends to purchase the cheaper goods, but has few possibilities for this. The structure of Soviet consumption reflects not the preferences of Soviet purchasers but decisions of the Soviet chiefs. And to 'equate' it with the structure of American consumption is not legitimate.

As far as I can see, this very phenomenon is ignored by authors of other works. In the most well-known of them, in which 10 countries including 'non-market' Hungary were compared, cheap housing in Hungary is mentioned but it is considered as one of the cases of government subsidies. The difference between market prices and prices based on production cost is also mentioned here. However, it seems to me that the problem is not analysed enough.[16]

One more point. Speaking of the index number problem and of 'deviations', we imply a deviation precisely from the geometric mean. However, this is entirely correct (other things being equal) only on the assumption of the relative equivalence of the compared volumes. The volumes of Soviet and American consumption are of such different size (this is evident irrespective of the method of measurement and point of view) that the mean inevitably twists the result in favour of the country with the smaller volume. To avoid this, special calculating methods are needed.[17]

I am far from the idea that it is not at all necessary to study Soviet prices of consumer goods, that it was not necessary to send an expedition to Moscow and to make complicated recalculations; this huge effort served a certain purpose. In particular, calculations at Soviet prices are necessary for the calculation of the size of the national product according to the Soviet concept (Chapter 14). Determining the volume and structure of consumption at existing prices is unquestionably of interest. And in general it is absurd to study the Soviet economy without Soviet prices. However, the authors mistakenly considered equal the calculations in dollars and rubles; because of the distortions mentioned above, their results should not be equated, so the mean calculated from them is not very 'legitimate'.

Introducing into the basic calculation turnover tax and subsidies, and calculating coefficients showing the branch deviation of prices from the Soviet principle of pricing (of the type in the CIA calculations for 1970 mentioned above) would have corrected things somewhat, but not by much. I have much more faith in the estimates in dollars than in rubles; in spite of all their shortcomings, the former are based on 'market' conditions, on prices reflecting market reality and not the arbitrary decisions of the USSR State Committee on Prices.

Here my position, at first glance, is close to that of the USSR Central

Statistical Administration (TsSU). Soviet statistics make international comparisons ignoring the index number problem, and calculations are made not in rubles but in dollars: 'The USSR TsSU compares the levels of economic development of the USSR and the US by recalculating Soviet value indicators from rubles into dollars. This is done so that, using prices of the United States, statistical indicators of the USSR TsSU can be compared with value aggregates that are identical in their economic content not only for the US but not for other capitalist countries.' The author of this statement is the head of the TsSU Division for the Statistics of Foreign Countries, and he should know perfectly well that the main reason for this methodology is quite different. In fact, he names this himself, 'comparison of the levels of economic development of the USSR and the US based on United States prices gives higher results than calculations at prices of the USSR'.[18]

One cannot disagree with this. We saw already in Table 4.1 that the difference between estimates in dollars and rubles is very great: the percentage ratio of the levels of consumption in the two countries calculated in dollars is one and a half times higher than the same ratio in rubles. Therefore, in repeating that the calculations in dollars can be trusted but those in rubles cannot, I am none the less not suggesting that we should agree with the TsSU and limit ourselves to measurements in dollars. The sense of my remarks is in fact as follows. First, it must be clearly understood that due to the existing system of Soviet prices, and to the peculiarities of the Soviet economy, all calculations in rubles are inevitably inaccurate, and the extent of this inaccuracy is not small. Therefore, we must at a minimum keep this in mind and not overstate the geometric mean. Second, the problem deserves further careful study. We must especially consider in which direction the specifics of Soviet prices influence the results of comparisons. If the study of concrete material (how great the index number problem is in comparison with other countries, how much the results of comparisons in dollars and rubles change in different periods, for which groups and subgroups of consumption the impact of the index number problem is greatest, etc.) helps in this, then we may succeed in arriving at some useful conclusions. Third, in all this, the reader should not understand what has been said to mean that the real Soviet lag is closer to the figure in dollars (43 per cent) than in rubles (28 per cent). It might well be that if we could make a 'correct' calculation in rubles its difference from a 'correct' calculation in dollars would be still greater; I simply do not know.[19]

In sum, while clearly recognizing the imperfection of calculations in rubles, I cannot propose an appropriate alternative. And this is one of the reasons why I give in Chapter 13 only very rough summary estimates of the actual lag of Soviet consumption. We must hope that future researchers will find some new approaches here.[20]

B)   One of the cornerstones of the entire CIA study was the comparison of specific goods in both countries, and determining differences in their qualitative characteristics. While giving the authors their due for their efforts, it is regrettable that the overwhelming part of the expedition's purchases were made in Moscow, Leningrad and Kiev, where the correspondence of goods to standard is incomparably better than in ordinary cities, and especially in the countryside. Listen to a well-known specialist on trade: 'In 1979 the RSFSR State Trade Inspectorate made about 99 000 checks of the quality of food and nonfood goods, and in 61.8 per cent of the cases the goods were rejected or classified as lower quality ... the percentage of rejects and reductions in quality exceeded 50 per cent of the quantity of goods checked.'[21]

The point here is not that the functional characteristics of Soviet goods are worse than American – these differences should have been taken care of in establishing price ratios (see also (C) below) – but that, as we just saw, at least half (!) of Soviet goods do not correspond to the standards set for them. This point, which was not even mentioned by the authors, should reduce the comparative estimate of Soviet consumption. By how much? It is hard to say. In America a customer quickly returns a good that does not meet standards, while in the USSR this is not always possible; because of a shortage the buyer often resigns himself to goods with obvious defects. In America a deviation from standards affects a firm's reputation and reduces prices. But in the USSR prices do not depend upon the reputation of the producer and have absolutely no relation to deviations from standards (if they are not noticed by inspection). Smokers, for example, know well that Moscow 'Yava' cigarettes are better than those made in Dnepropetrovsk and Rostov factories, although some prefer the Leningrad Uritskiy factory. However, prices for cigarettes that are identically named but, I repeat, very different in quality, i.e., deviating from standards, are the same.[22] And given identical prices, one cannot objectively estimate the extent of such deviations and appropriately reflect them in the scale of consumption.

My subjective estimate, considering the widespread extent of non-observance of standards, is that the overall estimate of comparative Soviet consumption (including services, where standards are also not observed) should be reduced by a minimum of 5–10 per cent.

C)   But the deviation from standards is a trifle compared with the quality standards themselves. Reflecting on the reasons why the CIA estimate overstates the level of Soviet consumption so greatly, I would confidently put in first place the mistakenness of price ratios. It is precisely due to these errors that Soviet consumption of food, clothing, footwear, and many other components is overstated.

The disgusting quality of Soviet goods is widely known, and appropriate examples abound in the Soviet press. Here, for example, is what the USSR Deputy Minister of Trade writes: 'Many goods significantly lag behind foreign analogues in their technical specifications and appearance; the share of shipments of electric appliances with the state Quality Emblem is still insignificant.'[23]

In Chapter 3 I talked about the authors' comparison of the quality of televisions. Here is some evidence from the head of a special Inspectorate For The Quality of Goods. He says that several years ago (meaning in 1976 also), colour televisions required technical service 6–7 times a year, but now this figure has been reduced by two-thirds, i.e. a Soviet colour television is still in need of repair twice a year.[24] And 'statistics show that about 20 per cent are in need of repair soon after purchase'.[25]

It should not be thought that low quality is the only characteristic of various 'complex' goods. Very low coefficients for the comparative quality of footwear were used in the study. But 'for the first category of fashionable shoes, the state standard permits up to 39 defects in the material for uppers, lowers, and trim, and up to 50 defects for second category'.[26] I have not observed a practice of varying goods by quality category in the US.

Here is another example from *Literaturnaya gazeta*, which published a reader's letter that a factory was producing primarily small shirts, thereby 'saving' material. The newspaper received 500 letters, all agreeing with this. The readers unanimously presented examples of labels overstating the sizes of clothing and footwear (the price varies with size!) and the lack of seams. One reader reported that a blanket cover (in short supply) that she had bought shrank so much after the first washing that she had to fold the blanket in by 8–10 cm.[27]

All these examples, as the reader sees, are from the official literature and there are a lot of them.[28] When I speak in American auditoriums about the quality of Soviet goods, I usually use two examples. First,

Soviet dustpans do not have a special jut (or bump) that keeps the swept-up dust from spilling out. And second, in 1906 an old Russian encyclopedic dictionary wrote: 'a large number of iron shovels are shipped in from abroad, but lately they have begun to make them pretty well in Russia too'. Many decades have passed by now and they make them pretty poorly – in particular, the tube into which the handle fits is too short, and the handle often breaks off. Of course, I will be told that the very method the authors used, and specifically the setting of price ratios on identical goods with a correction for quality, should have taken these differences into account. Theoretically speaking, this is right, but in practice the authors' results suggest that not everything is in order here. In no way doubting the authors' good intentions and their conscientiousness, I none the less think this question must be examined more attentively. Unfortunately, the authors gave too little material for a detailed and concrete analysis. In particular, they did not report the size of the adjustments for quality they used, and therefore, we are limited to examples and speculative reasoning.

First, the question of specially selecting sample goods with regard to the need to compare quality deserves particular attention. The point is that the authors should have taken the trouble to select sample goods that would reflect some average quality for their subgroup. They did not say a word about this, and, seemingly, no attention was paid to this factor in the selection. True, it could work 'in either direction'. Supposing that a sampling was accidental from this standpoint, the average quality of the goods in the sample could be rather representative. But this could happen only accidentally. Moreover, the Americans buying the goods were supposed to judge automatically the representativeness of goods on the basis of their American experience, which could not help causing distortions.

This is especially important for the Soviet economy. In a Western economy where price relations (ratios) are determined by consumer preferences, theoretically speaking, it is not so crucial which goods were sampled – one may hope that to a substantial degree each good of mass consumption is representative enough for its subgroup. But Soviet prices have little to do with consumer preferences, and at least the availablity of good to consumers must be taken into account in sampling. Somewhere above I mentioned that the authors had sampled digital watches. In regard to the American economy, this is more or less acceptable – in 1976 digital watches were about to become widespread – but in regard to the Soviet economy it distorts the comparison for the subgroup. Or, in other words, because of the fact that digital watches were not used by Soviet consumers in 1976, the price ratio for them should not be used as a price parity for the subgroup.

Thus, no serious conclusions about the reliability of the authors' estimates can be made without a special analysis of the question.

Second, although we do not have the sizes of all quality adjustments used, several questionable examples stand out. Thus, the authors essentially equated an American and Soviet boy's bicycle and were so confident of their price ratio that they presented it twice [59, 60]. But a Soviet newspaper says that 'only 5 per cent of the total output of children's bicycles fully meet modern demands'.[29] The same pertains to footwear, clothing, and many other goods, about which I have already said enough. I also spoke of the comparison of televisions the authors carried out, which formally looks correct but in essence is erroneous. In order to equate quality, they reduced the price of the American and Soviet TV sets, I by no means can agree that the difference is so small.

This is the main point, and I must with all certainty say that discussion of the authors' results should continue only after careful checking of their coefficients of comparative quality of sample goods and services.

Third, the authors' calculations unavoidably understand the comparative estimate of those goods that are in only the American and not the Soviet set. Indeed. The essence of the method is to evaluate these goods with the aid of price parities for other, similar goods included in the corresponding subgroup. But their absence from the Soviet set is not accidental; it is usually due to the fact that they are more difficult, i.e. more expensive, to produce. In Western economies, economies of surpluses, big difficulties in production do not prevent a good from being produced; they result in a correspondingly higher price. In the Soviet economy, an economy of shortages, such goods are simply not produced. Therefore, counting goods that are absent from the Soviet set at average price parities of the corresponding subgroups gives an undeserved advantage in the comparison to Soviet consumption. This is all the more significant because there are very many such goods.[30]

Related to this is my fourth remark. In establishing price ratios and corrections for quality for obsolete Soviet goods that are no longer produced in the US, the experts determined how much it would cost to produce the given Soviet good under current conditions in the US. But, as I already noted in Chapter 9, technical progress involves a more rapid growth of the consumer qualities of goods than of expenditures on their production. Thus, in determing how much it would cost *now* in the US to produce a contemporary Soviet sewing machine, the American experts again gave a definite advantage to indicators of Soviet consumption.

Fifth, a big part of foodstuffs – perishables – was not compared by the experts at all.

Finally, in establishing corrections for quality, they ignored such important elements as style, fashion, external appearance. And this, as hardly needs proof, gave Soviet goods a very large head start.

It is hard to be constructive in criticism here. It stands to reason that the authors should have paid more attention to this fundamental question. Also it is impossible not to lament once again that the authors did not resort to the life experience and professional knowledge of recent emigrants who know Soviet goods infinitely better. A study of prices in Moscow and Leningrad commission (second-hand) stores in their expeditionary forays would have provided much useful material; in these stores quality determines prices.

As I already said, general progress in consumption involves not so much an increase in quantity as an improvement in quality of goods and services. The USSR is more or less catching up, at least for some goods, to Western quantities, but it is hopelessly behind and lagging even further in quality. Precisely for this reason the problem of quality deserved and derserves the most special attention.

Other critical remarks I have made require discussion, and it is clear that not everyone will quickly agree with me. However, the need for a radical redefinition of the price ratios seems indisputable:

D)   We hardly need to hold it against the authors, but in many cases, encountering an absence of statistics, they were forced to make arbitrary estimates.[31] There are no data business trip expenditures, they could not break down roughly R12 billion in sales in retail trade [108], etc. We cannot assert with certainty that these arbitrary estimates necessarily overstate Soviet consumption,[32] but the potential for this is there.

What has been said is only a part of a much bigger problem – the reliability of Soviet statistics in general. I mentioned this briefly in Chapter 3 and repeat here that in itself the use of Soviet statistics is not something the authors should be blamed for. But one cannot but be distressed by the fact that the authors rarely inform us where they got their data, how they processed them, and what sort of doubts they themselves have. The absence of such information makes it impossible to critique the work in more detail. It might be that the largest part of the statistics the authors used is of good quality and supports their conclusions, but not having seen them, I cannot think so.

E)   My overview, in addition to its other shortcomings, is not perfect in a structural sense, and the next point I examine is perhaps the most important among the various aspects of consumption comparisons. But, self-criticism aside, I ask the reader to ponder the following. The idea of the unlimitedness of human demands is elementary and self-evident, but one point requires clarification. For starving Cambodians the Soviet ration would seem fantastically wonderful; for the Soviets themselves the American ration is in the literal sense of the word an impossible dream. But what about Americans themselves – do we have in America some dream, some still unreached dietary standard? Take a look at the table in the statistical handbook comparing the level of consumption of basic products in 1980 with the level in 1960.[37] In these 20 years the consumption of meat and fish increased and the comparison of eggs significantly declined, the consumption of milk fell, the consumption of butter and other fats fell sharply, somewhat fewer fruits and vegetables are eaten, but more juice is drunk, much less coffee and tea are consumed, but in general and overall the picture is about the same. What does this tell us? That already 20 years ago (actually earlier, but that is not important here) America had a dietary level which satisfied the population's requirements. And with a further increase in per capita income, say by two times, neither the volume of food nor its structure will change markedly. Or, in other words, the dietary level in America has reached a sort of plateau and in general further quantitative 'growth' is hardly likely.

Another example. In 1955 in America there was one car for every 3.5 people, while at the beginning of the 1970s there was 2.1 persons per car and since then the figure has fallen no further. Obviously demand has been satiated here, i.e. further growth is unlikely.

I could continue with such examples, but the idea is clear – after achieving a certain level, a satiation point is reached and growth decreases. Why then do we still speak of unlimited requirements – perhaps the Marxian slogan of consumption in the Communist society according to need' is correct? No. One reason is that new requirements and new means of satisfying them appear. A second, which is in principle inseparable from the first, and which is the subject of this entire discussion, is diversity.

Mankind as a whole, especially in connection with the slowing of birthrates, is coming closer and closer to the boundary where diversity becomes the main if not the only sign of further progress in consumption. America is in essence already crossing this boundary.

De Gaulle once remarked that it is hard to govern a country in which 200 different types of cheese exist, and he was absolutely right: the more we are all individuals, even in taste for cheese, the less manageable we are. But do we want to be 'well managed?' Let's turn de Gaulle's phrase around – precisely because it is easier for the Soviet leaders to manage there are so few types of cheese, and not only cheese, in the country.

The expansion of all sorts of diversity, the unfolding of various possibilities for satisfying the individual's requirements, also varied, and, to put it simply, increasing the freedom of choice is one of his most natural aspirations; greater diversity unquestionably means a higher standard of living, an improvement in the quantity of life. And precisely the constant striving for diversity makes human requirements unlimited.

Diversity, in addition to all else, makes life fuller and thus 'lengthens' it. I ask the reader to recall what he did three months ago on any ordinary day and his memory will not catch on anything in the everyday routine. But the day of an unusual trip ten years ago he easily remembers in full detail. Does the reader remember what was for dinner at home a week ago? But a meal that was unusual, different from the regular, although it was long ago digested, captured your attention and found its place in your memory. (Being married I will not continue with these examples.)

The problem is not always fully recognised. For economic reasons much is standardised in 'mass consumption' societies. The phrase that everybody wants to 'keep up with the Joneses' has become a cliche. However, the attentive observer could note that standardisation is more and more 'going into production'; the improvement of consumption, its real growth (difficult to measure using standard economic indices) is manifested much more in destandardisation, in the growth of diversity. And about the Joneses, the essential detail is that everyone wants to live '*no worse* than the Joneses', and given this indispensable condition, often pride themselves on being different, on the dissimilarity of what they have and consume.

Also not always taken account is an aspect of the problem that follows directly from the peculiarities of the Soviet economy of shortages. In 1972 my wife and I spent several days in Poland, and we tried, with all sorts of home-made calculations, to compare the standard of living with Soviet life. By direct comparisons of expendi tures and prices it was not higher, but we could see with our eyes that in fact the Poles lived better. Finally we understood the secret. The Poles had the opportunity to choose from many more varied goods what most suited them both in consumer qualities and in price. They could spend their income more rationally, with greater benefits and satisfaction. The same was true, incidentally, of Estonia in the 1960s. The level of income was not revolutionarily higher, Estonians hardly drank less than others, but the diversity and availability of goods (including cheap ones), provided a clearly better standard of living (in the 1970s this largely disappeared).

Is it, therefore, correct that since 1960, as the figures on per capita consumption of meat, butter and cucumbers tell us, as the careful calculation of economic indexes affirms, that the diet of Americans has not improved? The answer is obvious – during these years the diversity of products increased, new types and varieties appeared, the ranges of choice expanded, and all this *at the same quantities* improved the overall standard of consumption. It is unlikely that in America 20 years from now we will drink more juice and eat still more beef. But diversity will increase even more and precisely for this reason we will eat better.

Indeed, the overwhelming diversity of American goods is often excessive,[34] but lucky are the citizens of the country that can permit themselves such excesses.

We should, of course, not lose sight of the fact that diversity relates not only to goods but to the entire collection comprising consumption, i.e., not only to the packaging of vinegar and salt, the colour of wallpaper and cars, but to places to live, barbers, subjects in high schools and in universities, doctors,[35] television programme, etc.

Apparently, aesthetics and fashion can also (to some extent) be reduced to diversity. Objective measures of them simply do not exist; everything is decided by preferences (whims) of the mass consumer. We confidently say that Soviet men and women in provincial cities are dressed unfashionably, not because their appearance does not conform to our tastes, but because they do not have the possibility of buying what they like. Important here is only the 'existence of the absence' of the appropriate things in stores but the expensiveness of clothing and footwear. A fashionable young lady of Voronezh cannot look any different today than yesterday or the day before; the style of her dress is exactly the same as her girlfriend's; in a word, again there is no diversity.

By my taste, whites in America on the average dress worse than blacks. But since the choice of all consumers here is unlimited and expenditures on clothing and shoes are relatively low, any personal opinion on this makes no difference. No matter how foreign tourists like the appearance of Muscovites, and no matter how ironically Europeans speak of American checkered slacks, the elementary fact that, in addition to being priced affordably, American clothing and footwear are varied but Soviet are not, exhausts the question of comparison of aesthetics.

Although my assertions are understandably debatable, it is indisputable that diversity (or forced unification) and aesthetics and fashion are closely related to each other.

Thus, diversity in consumption is good, so good that I hardly need to further convince the reader.[36] And, very important, diversity costs money; standardisation is cheap. The diversity of all components of consumption in the US – from cucumbers to education – is incomparably greater than in the USSR. The authors mentioned the great American diversity several times, but did not consider this factor in their calculations. Why? Because this is not envisioned in the method they used, and how to do this is not very clear.

In the future it is necessary to try, first, to give a numerical estimate of comparative indicators of diversity – to determine by how many times various goods and services in the US are more diverse in types and models than in the USSR. This is not simple but at least a crude estimate is needed here. Second, with respect to introducing it into the calculations of levels of consumption themselves, a method of estimating through comparative indicators of production expenditures must be sought. Say 50 types of a certain product are produced and sold in the US, and only 5 in the USSR, and experts determine how much it would save to reduce the variety to only 5 types of this product in America and apply the derived coefficient to the comparative estimate. Of course, not everything is obviously simple here – for example, 'false diversity' spurred by competition must be discarded, identical goods produced by different firms must be excluded, etc. But seemingly, this is the only path.[37]

And while I confidently say that the comparative estimate of Soviet consumption must at a minimum be reduced by 25–30 per cent, the price of Soviet uniformity of consumption is no less. To pacify my opponents I will say that this estimate is included only partially in my attempt to determine the total size of the Soviet lag (Chapter 13).

F)   The authors themselves confess that they did not consider diversity, and my quantitative estimate is arbitrary and 'unscientific'

However, they did not even try to take into account another important element of consumption – trade as such, volume of its own services.

At first glance, expenditures on trade are considered 'automatically' through the prices of goods. Comparison, as the reader certainly remembers, is made with the aid of price ratios for more or less identical goods, and the compared prices include trade costs. However, the huge differences in the level of trade services (see the figures below), given the method the authors used, do not influence the results of comparison. Indeed! Assume for the moment that American trade is the same as Soviet and its costs are ten times smaller than they in fact are. Assume that their shares in the prices of all goods are identical. Assume that only things bought in the trade system are consumed and there are no services other than trade. Although the level of trade service changed by a factor of ten, this will not affect the result of the comparison of the overall level of consumption of the two countries. The retail prices of American goods under the conditions of this example would go down and the size of the price ratios will correspondingly diminish. However, the relation of American prices with each other would not change under our assumptions, and the overall result of comparing American and Soviet consumption should, by its very idea, be indifferent to the relation of the overall Soviet and American price levels. This is equivalent to a simultaneous increase (or decrease, it makes no difference) in all American prices by, say, 30 per cent; clearly, the result of the comparison of the levels of consumpton in the two countries should not change a bit. The sense of the method the authors used is that the comsumption of 1 kg of meat in the US should be equal (given equal 'quality') to the consumption of 1 kg of meat in the USSR. But the method is indifferent to how the consumer gets the meat, what sort of trade services he uses. Obviously, this is incorrect.[38]

Apparently, a special 'trade service' component should be introduced into the nomenclature of consumption. A technical difficulty is that trade markup should be singled out of all prices, price ratios and parities should be recalculated and expenditures for goods without the markup should be determined. A greater difficulty is the necessity of establishing a 'trade service sample' on a few samples, and it is not clear how to do it. Below I try to overcome both these dificulties, but my results are definitely not precise.[39]

Although the authors did not reflect differences in trade services in their calculations, they fully understand the actual backwardness of Soviet trade. They mention the endless queues and primitive organisation of trade, and report [11] that in the USSR there are only half as many stores (this, as we will soon see, is incorrect). These statements must be supplemented with statistics.

At the end of 1976 the USSR had 523 000 stores and 174 000 kiosks. Of the total number of stores, only 215 000, i.e., 41 per cent were state stores. The rest belonged to the trade cooperatives (*Tsentrosoyuz*). Since, on the other hand, only 30 per cent of all sales (excluding public dining) fall to cooperative trade we conclude from this alone that *Tsentrosoyuz* stores are primarily small. The yearbook gives information on the distribution by type only for the state trade network. More than half of the stores (including so-called 'mixed'), or 122 000, sell food products. Half of all food stores are specialised. How many stores had a full assortment of food products is unknown.

There were 91 000 non-food state stores, including 631 department stores, and 21 000 'non-specialised non-food' stores. Among specialised stores the most numerous types was drugstores – more than 25 000. (Soviet drugstores, unlike American, sell only medicines and sanitary articles). Among the rest were 45 stores for selling goods previously acquired from the population, and 1693 second-hand (commission) stores.

Employment in retail trade (in this case including cooperative trade but excluding public dining) totalled 4.4 m., and the total floor area of stores (excluding kiosks) was about 41 m. square metres.[40] Overall, per 10 000 population there were 20 stores and 7 kiosks with 1600 square metres of trade floor areas. The average floor space of a store (without counting kiosks) was less than 78 square metres, which should sooner be the size of an apartment (Soviet!), not a store.

Regarding American trade, as with other types of service, we have to work with imperfect statistics which count only those stores that are completely independent. In 1977 there were 1.487 m. different stores.[*] Food was sold in 252 000 stores, i.e. about 17 per cent of the total number. There were 48 900 department stores (77 times more than in the USSR), 12 700 book stores, 31 500 sporting goods and bicycle stores, 29 000 florists, 176 500 gasoline stations and auto repair stores etc. Overall per 10 000 population there were 145 stores, that is, 5 times more than in the USSR. Above I gave the number of state food stores in the USSR – 122 000. Taking into account cooperative stores as well the lag behind the US turns out to be relatively small. The explanation is that in America food is primarily sold in huge supermarkets, very rarely in specialised stores. But in non-food stores the USSR lags at minimum by about 15 times.

In 1976, 8.7 m. persons worked in retail trade in the US (excluding public dining)[42] i.e., 2.2 times more per capita than in the USSR.

Of course, statistics must be carefully read and supplemented with other data. The fact that the number of food stores in both countries is more or less identical in itself says that we should not rely on the indicator of number of stores. The number of people employed in trade must be viewed with an eye on the difference in labour productivity. I cannot compare data above on floor space in Soviet stores with corresponding figures for American stores, although it is clear that, having a much greater volume of trade, American stores are more filled with goods than with customers.

In general, that the American trade is incomparably more developed and better than Soviet is indisputable.[43] Advertising must also be included here. Its actual 'usefulness' may be debated; I cannot stand television commercials, but regardless of my personal tastes and predilections, advertising exists only because the mass consumer pays attention to it and pays for it.

The next conclusions would require a special study and hopefully someone will do it, but it should be quite clear that in trade services the USSR lags probably most of all.

I have already said that trade services should be taken into account. First, we need to have an estimate of their volume. For the USSR we have a direct figure – marketing cost in 1976 amounted to 9.6 per cent of the total volume of retail trade.[44] We will use this number, ignoring for simplicity consumption in kind.

Things are more complex with the American statistics – I did not discover such an indicator and had to calculate it. It turns out that the share of marketing cost in the total volume of American trade is almost 6 times larger – 40 per cent.[45]

Further calculations are presented in Table 12.1. I take the authors' figures on total consumption, and consumption of all goods as they are. Then, using the trade markup percentage determined above I establish their amounts (line 4) and the total for goods without the markup (line 5). For line 6 I take Soviet consumption of goods in rubles and American in dollars, as these figures are in the authors' calculations. But for determining the amounts of American goods in rubles and Soviet goods in dollars I use relations established by the authors for goods (line 2), including trade markup. The rest is arithmetic.[46]

As could be expected, introducing the trade markup into the calulations as a separate component of consumption reduces significantly total Soviet consumption compared with American (line 8).

Table 12.1 Per capita consumption figures recalculated considering differences in trade services

	Consumption in Rubles			Consumption in Dollars			Geometric mean
	USSR	US	USSR as % of US	USSR	US	USSR as % of US	USSR as % of US
1. Total consumption according to CIA[a]	1116	4039	27.6	2396	5599	42.8	34.4
2. Goods[a]	888	2863	31.0	1096	2532	43.3	36.6
3. Trade markup, per cent[b]	6.9	40.0	—	6.9	40.0	—	6.4
4. Trade markup, amount[c]	61	1145	5.4	76	1012	7.5	7.5
5. Goods excluding markup	827	2668[d]	31.0	658[e]	1520	43.3	36.6
6. Goods including recalculated markup[f]	888	3813	23.3	734	2532	29.0	26.0
7. Percent of change to CIA estimate	0	+33.2	−24.8	−33.0	0	33.0	29.9
8. Total consumption including recalculated markup[g]	1116	4989	22.4	2034	5599	36.3	28.5
9. Percentage of change to CIA estimate	0	+23.5	−17.8	−15.1	0	−15.2	−16.4

a[6]
bSee the text
cLines 2 and 3
d827 ÷ 0.31
e1520 ÷ 0.433
fLine 4 plus line 5
gLine 1 minus line 2 plus line 6

It should be said that my calculations are not accurate because the authors did take into account the difference in packaging. Another thing is that I took an average per cent of trade markup fot all goods.

The ratio that I obtained (line 4) – the USSR lags behind the US in trade services 16 times according to the geometric mean – can be disputed. But the figures that I presented above clearly say that the real lag is mammoth. Certainly, using for trade services the average price parity for goods can be considered arbitrary, but I see no other method. Still, in my final calculations (Table 13.1) in one variant I take the lag of the USSR in trade to be half as large as that calculated in Table 12.1.

G) Irrespective of the organisation of Soviet trade, of huge significance is its characteristic feature – the constant shortage of consumer goods as a direct consequence of the sharp imbalance between the population's money incomes and the possibilities of buying what they want.[47] The shortages are a great irritation to the population, further widening the scissors that were described back in Chapter 1.

Shortages are not simply a scarcity of goods due to low levels of production. This is a specific trait of the Soviet economic system which has no mechanism to bring the effective demand for and supply of goods into equilibrium. Theoretically, it is quite possible to imagine a situation in which, given the same quantity of goods, queues are not endless. I was told about the 'basic law of Soviet trade' formulated by a wise collective farm chairman: what is on the shelves today will be scarce tomorrow, and what is in short supply today might be back on the shelves tomorrow.[48]

Not so long ago Peter Wiles said at a sovietological conference in Cambridge that time lost standing in lines must be added to the working week. Another trait of scarcity already metioned above – the absence of goods for sale that exactly correspond to desires – forces the purchase of other less appropriate goods.

Scarcity in itself reduces the standard of living and worsens the quality of life. So a means of quantitatively estimating its impact on the overall level of consumption must be sought.

H) To finish with this group of questions, we will look at one point that completely escaped the authors' attention. As I tried to show under 'F' above, it is not only the quantity of goods that consumers buy that is important but how they are bought. The same relates to services.

I spoke above about the huge differences in the number of hotel rooms, but total 'consumption of hotels' should include such an unavoidable element as the amount of time and effort spent to get a hotel room. Or the difference in the 'consumption of transportation' should be determined not only by the quantity of cars and by the number of trips and flights but by service, including obtaining tickets.

To some extent all this should enter into the 'quality' of services that theoretically speaking is compared in establishing price ratios. However, such a comparison in no way includes the fact that employees of the Soviet service sphere will be extremely rude to you,[49] while in America (and the West in general) they will smile and thank you. The secrets of this difference are few – the significantly larger number of service enterprises, their magnificent equipment, a sufficient number of personnel, both owners and workers are interested in their work, but that is not the point. At issue is the fact that taking into account the 'quality of service in the service sphere' should also change the estimate of the comparative levels of consumption in the USSR and the US and to a noticeable extent.

I) Once again about a point that I mentioned several times. The standard of living (consumption) is determined not only by what is acquired in a certain year but also by what was a part of consumption earlier and is still there. Simply put, the issue is fixed assets. To a large extent the authors took into account the huge difference in the amounts of fixed capital in the two countries;[50] in particular their approach in determining expenditures on housing by rent payments rather than by expenditures on construction in the given year is methodologically correct.[51] However, as already noted, the authors understated the difference in consumption for durables and insufficiently considered the huge American fixed capital in health and education. They practically did not consider fixed capital in trade, which should be corrected by recalculating the trade markup that I propose.

The authors also absolutely overlooked the fixed capital in the dense network of first-class American roads (the amount collected in toll roads covers only a small fraction), but this is one of the main elements of the national wealth of the world's richest country. There are several methods of including these amounts in the calculation – for example, including their depreciation allowances in the amounts of consumption for public transportation. It is of no difference here what the real amounts of bookkeeping depreciation are, by what accounting method they are calculated, or to whose balance they are credited – not the actual flow of depreciation payments but a valid estimate of the true contributiuon of roads to the level of well-being is important here. Naturally, the calculation must also include the amount of depreciation for Soviet roads.

A stipulation is needed here. From the standpoint of GNP accounts and the general methodology of international comparisons, the authors' calculations are right. Using the example from Chapter 9, one but not four chairs must be included in the GNP of both countries. But this does not mean that the consumption component of GNP rightly reflects the real, actual standard of living, the population's welfare. I am not saying here that the authors' results must be corrected to take into account differences in capital stock, and in my final estimates in Chapter 13 I do not do it. However, in considering the estimates we should understand that because of this factor they substantially overstate the Soviet standard of living.

J)   The last remark. Although the CIA work I am examining is based almost entirely on official statistics, its final (summary) results do not coincide with the official indicators on national income. In 1976, R279.9 billion of national income was expended on consumption.[52] In the authors' basic calculation [20, 121], the total amount of Soviet consumption is R295.9 billion. I already mentioned that the authors also calculated a corrected indicator in a corresponding fashion [14], but it is accompanied by such brief explanations that we are at a loss to understand why they started with an amount of R286.2 billion, why the amount of turnover tax considered here is R58.3 billion[53] and why they finished the calculation with a total amount of Soviet consumption of R259.4 billion. I am not asserting that all three of these figures are incorrect, but as a reader I have a right to know how they were obtained and why the authors' total indicators differ from Soviet statistics. Moreover, in another publication (one of the authors of which is a co-author of this reviewed work), another figure is given for the total value of consumption – R285 billion[54] – and this completely muddles things.

Explanations might be proposed for certain divergences, but there should be no substantial divergences – their existence is evidence of errors in the interpretation of Soviet data. Of course, the data themselves might be contradictory, but then such cases should be indicated.

The specialist knows that attempts to determine the overall monetary income and expenditures of the Soviet population leads to the absurd result that expenditures exceed income. Possibly we are omitting some incomes, but it is more likely that we are overstating expenditures.[55] If the latter is correct, then the CIA calculations correspondingly overstate Soviet consumption.

I will not sum up this examination of methodological problems, but the method should in no way be considered perfect. And as I tried to show, in almost all cases its revision leads to a signficant reduction in the comparative indicators of Soviet consumption.

13 Conclusion

The major conclusions have already been stated, and here I will only repeat them briefly. The CIA study gives unique and priceless material for the analysis and further discussion of the problem. Without any exaggeration, its publication establishes a quantitatively new stage in the study of this problem – instead of general arguments and conjectures we can operate with concrete figures. Before a careful study of this work I could not justifiably quantify my own opinion about the extent of the Soviet lag. Having publicly stated a couple of years ago that Soviet consumption lags behind American by 4–5 times,[1] I more or less hit the mark, but this was intuition; now I can defend my estimate with facts and numbers.

At the same time I must decisively disagree with the CIA study's basic conclusions. The authors speak of the uncertainties and insurmountable difficulties in their work. They admit that their results 'surely overstate the Soviet position' and make statements such as 'on the less tangible aspects of quality, the bias is unmistakably in the USSR's favor'. However, they do not give even a hint of how big (small) these overstatements and biases are, so the reader might think that they are insignificant,[2] that the authors suppose their results to be close to the truth. Alas, the results are far from it.

How far? Regretfully, a 'precise' calculation is not possible. In considering the CIA work, I was forced to limit myself in many cases to expressing disagreement with the authors' results. But even when an alternative estimate was advanced it was often arbitrary. Besides, after my criticism in Chapter 13 of calculations in rubles, any pretence to a 'precise' estimate would look strange.

However, an attempt to determine the extent of my disagreement is quite appropriate. First, I remind the reader of my basic critical remarks:

a) Chapters 5-7 show that the Soviet lag for food must be adjusted downward by not less than 20 per cent;

b) Chapter 8 speaks of the need to reduce substantially the comparative estimate of Soviet consumption for all soft goods, in particular for footwear, by a factor of two;

c) in Chapter 9 the need to correct the estimate for durable goods is demonstrated. The reader saw that in the consumption of rugs the USSR lags 22 times; he saw that consumption of furniture, kitchen utensils, home appliances, cars, etc., is even lower than the minimal figures of authors;

d) Chapter 10 shows that the authors greatly overstated the comparative estimate of Soviet consumption for housing and for other subgroups like communications and recreation;

e) the material in Chapter 11 on education and health care is devoted primarily to difficulties with the problem and criticism of the authors' method. I do not venture any sort of quantitative estimates there, although, quite likely, the comparative estimate of Soviet consumption for this group is understated;

f) if the authors had considered the difference in trade services, this would have increased the comparative estimate of American consumption;

g) a detailed discussion of the cornerstone of the study – the experts' determination of 'quality coefficients' – show that they (both the experts and the coefficients) gave a significant edge to Soviet consumption;

h) a relatively minor point – the non-observance of standards in Soviet goods – should also reduce the estimate of Soviet consumption by a few per cent.

But even this is not all. As I tried to show in Chapter 12, a complete accounting of the differences in diversity in goods and services would further, and very substantially, reduce the overall estimate of Soviet consumption.

Thus, even without any calculations we see that the overstatement of Soviet consumption compared with America is very big. Let us try now to somehow quantify this conclusion. In Table 13.1, I present the results of some calculations.

First, I give geometric estimates by the CIA for all groups of consumption. Then I show four variants of corrections from minimal in variant I to maximal in variant IV.

In the text of the overview the only quantitative correction was on food (Table 7.1) and I use this figure, 20 per cent for all four variants. For other groups I make assumptions on the magnitude of the changes of the CIA estimates. In different variants I assume that the CIA estimates overstate Soviet consumption of soft goods and durables by 10–20 per cent and of household services by 15–25 per cent. On the contrary, because the CIA in my opinion understated Soviet consumption in education and medicine, I corrected them upwards: education by 10–20 per cent and medicine by 15–40 per cent.

Regarding trade services, as shown in Table 12.1, Soviet consump-

Table 13.1 Per capita Soviet consumption as a percentage of American

	According to CIA[a]	With corrections by variants							
		I		II		III		IV	
		% of correction	Consumption	% of correction	Consumption	% of correction	Consumption	% of correction	Consumption
Food	53.7	− 20.0	43.8	− 20.0	43.8	− 20.0	43.8	− 20.0	43.8
Soft goods	39.4	− 10.0	35.6	− 10.0	35.6	− 15.0	33.8	− 20.0	32.1
Durables	13.3	− 10.0	12.1	− 10.0	12.1	− 15.0	11.5	− 20.0	10.9
Total	36.6	− 14.8	31.5	− 14.8	31.5	− 17.4	31.8	− 20.0	20.9
Household services	17.8	− 15.0	15.3	− 15.0	15.3	− 20.0	14.5	− 25.0	13.8
Total goods and ser-vices	35.0	− 14.8	26.2	− 14.8	26.6	− 18.1	25.4	− 21.2	24.6
Education	76.7	+ 20.0	93.7	+ 15.0	93.2	+ 15.0	93.2	+ 10.0	84.7
Medicine	33.4	+ 40.0	51.3	+ 30.0	45.8	+ 30.0	45.8	+ 15.0	39.1
Total consumption[b]	34.4	− 2.2	32.9	− 4.6	32.4	− 7.3	31.6	− 12.9	30.1
With trade services[b]	—	− 14.5	30.4	− 29.0	27.8	− 29.0	27.2	− 29.0	26.0
With 'unquantifiable' factors[c]		− 10.0	30.6	− 15.0	29.0	− 20.0	27.3	− 20.0	26.1
Grand total	34.4	− 18.4	28.4	− 32.5	25.0	− 38.7	23.5	− 43.9	22.4

[a] [6]
[b] Corrections to goods only; consumption without taking into account the correction for trade services.
[c] Correction to goods and household services.

tion of all goods should be reduced by 29 per cent. In variant I, I guardedly correct the CIA figures by only half this amount, while the remaining three variants make the full correction. Of course, these corrections relate only to goods.

In Chapter 12 a lot of other critical remarks are made – on the non-observance of standards, the poor quality of even standard goods, the impact of shortages, the enormous difference in variety, etc. In Table 13.1, I call all these factors 'unquantifiable', and correct the CIA results for total goods and household services by 10–20 per cent.[3]

In Tables 13.2, 13.3 and 13.4 all these calculations are shown for variant I in detail, but I omit such detail for other variants.[4]

A few comments are needed here. Crucial, of course, is the issue of the reliability of my estimates. In fact, my entire overview is devoted to this very question. Hopefully, the mass of statistics I present themselves demonstrate convincingly that the scale of the Soviet lag is much larger than what follows from the CIA report.

I hope that my estimates will not be counterposed to the CIA results in degree of validity and 'scientificness'. The point is not only that I based a lot of them on the CIA work itself. By no means should the reader forget that at the foundations of the CIA work lie assumptions that have a decisive impact on their results (especially about the comparative quality of Soviet and American goods and services) and these assumptions are not more 'scientific' than mine. My corrections for soft goods and durables are as big as the corrections for food in only one variant, and the corrections for household services are bigger than food in only one variant. I analysed the figures for food most of all and corrected them minimally. We may think that in other groups the overstatement of Soviet consumption is not less.

In Chapters 8–10 I gave many examples of how the estimates of Soviet consumption of various goods and services (for example, of footwear and telephones) are overstated by a factor of two or more, and gave very few examples of the understatement of Soviet consumption. The reader should bear in mind that my correction of footwear alone reduces the estimate for the soft goods group by 10 per cent.

The modesty of my corrections is supported by the fact that for soft goods, durables and household services they are *less* than the corrections of education and medicine in the opposite direction.[5]

Regarding trade services, it is unquestionable that the corrections are needed and they should be large. One can argue that my corrections are too large but we cannot measure trade services in physical units, and any other approach here would be arbitrary.

Table 13.2 Total results of recalculations, variant I, Soviet per capita consumption as percentage of American[a]

	According to CIA			With corrections		
	In rubles	In dollars	Geom. mean	In rubles	In dollars	Geom. mean
Food	50.0	57.6	53.7	41.7	46.1	43.8
Soft goods	32.4	47.9	39.4	29.4	43.1	35.6
Durables	9.9	17.7	13.3	9.1	16.0	12.1
Total goods	31.0	43.3	36.6	27.3	36.4	31.5
Household services	14.1	22.4	17.8	12.3	19.0	15.3
Total goods and services	27.2	34.2	30.5	23.9	28.8	26.2
Education	63.2	93.0	76.7	78.8	116.6	93.7
Medicine	17.1	65.2	33.4	28.8	91.5	51.3
Total consumption	27.6	42.8	34.4	25.1	43.0	32.9
With trade services	—	—	—	23.0	40.3	30.4
With 'unquantifiable factors'	—	—	—	23.0	40.7	30.6
Grand total	27.6	42.8	33.4	21.2	38.0	28.4

[a]Tables 13.3 and 13.4.

Table 13.3 Recalculations, variant 1, in rubles

	According to CIA[a]			With corrections		
	USSR	US	USSR as % of US	% of corr.[b]	US New amount	USSR as % of US
Food	546	1092	50.0	+20.0	1310	41.7
Soft goods	239	740	32.4	+10.0	814	29.4
Durables	103	1031	9.9	+10.0	1134	9.1
Total goods	888	2863	31.0	+13.8	3258	27.3
Household services	116	822	14.1	+15.0	945	12.3
Total goods and services	1004	3685	27.2	+14.1	4203	23.9
Education	70	111	63.2	−20.0	89	78.7
Medicine	42	243	17.1	−40.0	146	28.8
Total consumption	1116	4039	27.6	9.9	4438	25.1
Correction for trade services[c]	—	—	—	+12.4	404	23.0
Correction for 'unquantifiable' factors[d]	—	—	—	+10.0	420	23.0
Grand total	1116	4039	27.6	+30.3	5262	21.2

[a][6]
[b]See the text.
[c]To goods (see Table 12.1).
[d]To total of goods and services.

Table 13.4 Recalculations, variant I, in dollars

	According to CIA[a]			With corrections		
	USSR	US	USSR as % of US	% of corr.[b]	New amount	USSR as % of US
Food	651	1131	57.6	−20.0	521	46.1
Soft goods	312	652	47.9	−10.0	281	43.1
Durables	133	749	17.7	−10.0	120	16.0
Total goods	1096	2532	43.3	−15.9	922	36.4
Household services	438	1956	22.4	−15.0	372	19.0
Total goods and household services	1534	4488	34.2	−15.6	1294	28.8
Education	457	491	93.0	+20.0	548	111.6
Medicine	405	620	65.2	+40.0	567	91.5
Total consumption	2396	5599	42.8	+0.5	2409	43.0
Correction for trade services[c]	—	—	—	−16.5	−152	40.3
Correction for 'unquantifiable' factors[d]	—	—	—	−10.0	−129	40.7
Grand total	2396	5599	42.8	−11.2	2128	38.0

[a][6]
[b]See the text.
[c]To goods (see Table 12.1).
[d]To total of goods and services.

The most debatable issue is that of 'unquantified' factors, but it is much better to have arbitrary estimates than to simply ignore them. And, taking into account the issue of variety, even the maximal estimate for 'unquantifiable' factors in Table 13.1 apparently underestimates rather than overestimates their actual impact. Considering the variety issue in Chapter 12, I gave a higher estimate for it than for all 'unquantifiable' factors in Table 13.1.

My corrections, as seen in Tables 13.3 and 13.4, increase the difference between the estimate in rubles and dollars. The CIA estimates for consumption as a whole are 27.6 per cent and 42.8 per cent respectively – that is, the second is larger than the first by 55 per cent; in my calculations the difference increased to 79 per cent. We may note that my estimates differ from the CIA estimates more in rubles than in dollars. The reason is obvious – the shares of education and especially of medicine increased in my calculations, and for them the difference between estimates in rubles and dollars is larger.

My calculations give results very different from the CIA report – Soviet consumption lags behind American not by 3, but by 4–5 times. Thinking again and again about all the material, about the many individual comparisons, and trying to see the full picture, I am inclined to the option that even variant IV – that Soviet per capita consumption in 1976 was 22.4 per cent of American – exaggerates the real picture; the Soviet living standard is even worse. But for further discussion I will stop here and consider that Soviet per capita consumption is four and a half times less than American. I hope that the attentive and open minded reader of my overview will agree with me.

One more thing. Quite recently the results of a big research project on comparisons of living standards and GNP in 34 countries were published. According to them, in 1975, per capita consumption as a percentage of American consumption was: in India – 6.2; Philippines – 12.7; Colombia – 21.8, Syria – 22.0; Brazil – 23.1; Iran – 24.4; Romania – 27.6; Yugoslavia – 35.3; Mexico – 38.5; Poland – 40.4; Hungary – 45.9; Spain – 58.1; Austria – 70.4; FRG – 74,1; France – 75.8.[6] As J. Gullula pointed out to me, if the CIA places the USSR near Yugoslavia and a little lower than Mexico, my estimates places the USSR near Syria, Colombia and Brazil.

Although these numbers are from a work done by the most authoritative specialists on international comparisons, not everything here looks convincing. I do not dare to say that these numbers are wrong but it is not easy to believe that the standard of living in Poland wa noticeably higher than in Yugoslavia, and Magyars live better tha

Yugoslavs by 30 per cent, that the living standard was so high in Spain, etc. Still, I have to admit these figures contradict my conclusions. For example, it turns out that Soviet consumption was twice as low as Polish and, on the other hand, that it was only three times as big as Indian, and neither of these comparisons looks right. Least of all do I wish to criticise the work by these specialists. But in expressing my doubts about their results, I would like to say that the question is not quite clear and should be discussed further.

Summarising, I will repeat my basic conclusion – the Soviet living standard, Soviet consumption, is less than American by at least a factor of 4.5. This conclusion can be used as a sort of rough estimate.[7]

In no way do I want to, and indeed I cannot, idealise our American standard of living. I am not closing my eyes to much that is, so to speak, not too wonderful. New York slums are horrible. I have seen beggars in New York and Washington and know that spending the night on a pile of old papers is not something Soviet journalists dreamed up. Though America has moved far ahead of the USSR, there are some houses that do not have telephones or even running water, air conditioners, or televisions. Far from every house that I have seen in visiting half of the states looks like a dream. In a remote valley of West Virginia, the television received only one channel. Not every good or service is necessarily of the highest quality. Trains run late. A snowfall paralyses life in the capital. Fresh fruits and vegetables in Europe (Western!) are tastier. Unemployment is certainly not a gift, just as finishing life on the meagre benefits for the poor is no present.

The list of 'not too wonderful' things in America could easily be continued; instead I will say that pointing out each of them will only enhance the significance of my conclusions – that although some things may not be so good about the American standard of living, in spite of our shortcomings, life in the Soviet Union, the Soviet standard of living, is 4.5 times worse.

Several words are appropriate about what the figures characterising the Soviet lag in consumption reflect. Does the CIA estimate of the three-fold Soviet lag mean that the American consumer is three times more satisfied with his consumption, or, following my estimate, that the Soviet consumer is 4.5 times less 'happy'?

There are no answers to such questions. Happiness is unmeasureable. And the degree of satisfaction, as I said in Chapter 1, is determined not by some absolute level but by the 'opening of the scissors' – by how far real consumption falls short of desires.

We must in no way forget the external juxtaposition of the material and the spiritual – appeals for simplicity, cursing luxury. Recall the joke at the beginning of the overview about the native completely satisfied with his serene idleness on the ocean beach. Still, mankind throughout history has strived and struggled for more material goods. Despite all reservations, limitations, and contradictory examples, the history of our civilisation is the history of the development of the economy. of the current and purposeful growth of production for consumption. And this is not only 'capitalist' ideology. At the basis of Marxism lies the promise of communism, under which consumption will not be limited and the blades of my scissors will come together. You can endlessly preach to people that luxury is harmful, that limitation to some 'rational minimum' is a virtue. Nevertheless, people want more, sooner, better. So, one cannot prove that the American consumer is 4.5 times more 'satisfied' than the Soviet; he is far from reaching the limits of consumption.[8]

It is not out of place to say that any characterisation of the total volume of consumption is necessarily conditional and abstract. In adding 'apples and oranges', butter and stools, we get only a rather abstract figure for which no satisfactory 'physical' equivalent exists. We must not forget that numerous conditions and simplifications underlie practically all economic measurements. Therefore, my estimate that Soviet consumption in 1976 was at best 22.4 per cent of the American level is conditional not only because I resorted to all sorts of simplifications and approximate estimates, but for the simple reason that all such estimates by their very nature cannot be accurate.[9]

What then does our estimate mean? No more and no less than the following. In order for the total volume of consumption of the average Soviet, in 1976, measured by the method used in the study, to be equal to the volume of consumption of the average American in the same year, production of 4.5 times as much as per capita of all consumer goods and services would be necessary. Hence, correspondingly larger inputs of various resources in the Soviet economy would be needed and they must be as efficiently used as in the US (or still more resources would be needed). In other words, in order to catch up to the US in consumption, the Soviet economy must correspondingly grow and improve. Assuming the share of the total national product expended on consumption remains unchanged, the volume of per capita GNP must be increased by a factor of 4.5.

Basic here is the lag in years. And if in Chapter 4 it was said that, in the CIA's opinion, decades would pass before the USSR could reach the 1976 level of American consumption, in fact, since the lag is so much greater, this will take *many* decades. In other words, many, many decades must pass for the average Soviet to reach the level of today's American diet, to be able to dress the same, to have such spacious and comfortable housing equipped with the same appliances, to spend as much on rest and recreation, to travel as much and as conveniently, to study in such buildings, be treated in such hospitals, etc. I remind the reader that according to simple esimates based entirely upon official Soviet data, the USSR will catch up to America of 1976 in meat in 57 years, fruit in 62 (or even in 172), cars in 138, housing in 155, telephones in 130 and roads in 260 years. They will reach this level if the rate of growth is at least maintained, for which there is little hope. We also saw the scale of the lag for durable goods and services. I will now present some other official data, taken from the last edition of the statistical yearbook.[10] First, let us examine the figures in Table 13.5. They show the movement of Soviet per capita consumption during the past 15 years both for basic food products and for those types of clothing and footwear for which data are published. Incidentally, the absence of data for other types of clothing gives cause for suspecting that the situation with them is still worse.

First of all note that the growth rate of per capita consumption declined sharply during these 15 years for all items shown in the yearbook with the exception of only vegetable oil, knitted underwear and hosiery. Moreover, regarding food, during the last five years there was no increase in the consumption of meat, and a slight decline in milk consumption. While we may consider the decline in consumption of potatoes and bread products as a positive phenomenon, we cannot assess positively the sharp reduction in per capita consumption of fruits and berries.

Without examining the indicators for food in Table 13.5 in detail (the reader can easily do this himself), we can confidently conclude that overall the quantity of food per capita did not increase during the past five years. From the official literature and the evidence of eyewitnesses we know that during these five years the quality of food did not improve; rather it grew worse. Consequently, the *volume of comparison* for this group could not have increased. True, there are a number of signs of an increase in the consumption of alcohol (possibly this is precisely the reason for a certain growth of the consumption of sugar), but this is not a positive factor.[11]

Now let us examine non-food goods. Here also things are bad. Although in the last five-year period the overall consumption of fabrics grew somewhat (less than in the previous period) consumption of silk

Table 13.5 Per capita consumption in the USSR[a]

Food	1965 Absolute	1970 Absolute	1970 5-year growth, %	1975 Absolute	1975 5-year growth, %	1980 Absolute	1980 5-year growth, %
Meat and meat products, kg	41	48	17	57	19	57	0
Milk and milk products, kg	251	307	22	316	3	314	− 1
Eggs, number	124	159	28	216	36	238	10
Fish and fish products, kg	12.6	15.4	22	16.8	9	17.0	1[c]
Sugar, kg	34.2	38.8	13	40.9	5	42.2	3
Vegetable oil, kg	7.1	6.8	− 4	7.6	12	8.6	13
Potatoes, kg	142	130	− 8	120	− 8	112	− 7
Vegetables and melons, kg	72	82	14	89	9	93	4
Fruits and berries (excl. use in wine), kg	28	35	25	39	11	34	− 13
Bread products, kg	156	149	− 5	141	− 5	139	− 1
Non-food products							
Fabrics, total, m²	26.5	30.4	15	32.5	7	34.6	6
including:							
Cotton	19.1	21.2	11	22.0	4	23.8	8
Wool	2.5	2.7	8	2.8	4	2.7	− 4
Silk	3.6	4.7	30	5.9	25	6.6	12
Linen	1.3	1.8	38	1.8	0	1.5	− 17
Knitted outerwear, units	0.9	1.8	100	2.0	11	2.1	5
Knitted underwear, units	3.3	3.5	6	3.9	11	4.4	13
Hosiery, pair	5.8	6.0	3	6.1	2	6.8	11
Leather[b] footwear, pair	2.4	3.0	25	3.2	7	3.2	0

[a] *Narkhoz-80*, pp. 405–6.
[b] As we saw in Chapter 8, only a part of this is really 'leather'.
[c] Fell by 5 per cent in comparison with 1976.

fabrics has slowed sharply. For fabric consumption the reader should also attentively examine the per capita figures themselves – clearer than anything else, they say that the Soviet population cannot dress decently.

During the last five years there was absolutely no growth in footwear, an insignificant increase in the consumption of knitted outwear, and this from an extremely low absolute level of consumption.

While in 1960, 121 apartments were built per 10 000 population, 93 were built in 1970, 88 in 1975, and only 77 in 1980.[12]

Let us turn now to Table 13.6, which shows how well supplied the population is with various durable goods. Here the picture is more complicated, although it also unquestionably shows a general trend of a sharp slowing of growth. During the last five years the growth in the consumption of all durables except cameras was slower than in 1971–5, and much slower than in 1965–70.

The table shows that the growth of the consumption of durables is continuing. However, this is primarily quantitiative growth. The consumption of almost all items is still far below norms.[13] We have reason to believe that the transition to the production of better quality, more modern durables will sharply slow this quantitative growth. A lot of time will be required to achieve 'normative' consumption, but the norms are much lower than consumption already actually achieved in the US. Note that there are no norms for many machines widespread in America – dishwashers, garbage disposals, etc.

According to A. Tretyakova's estimates, in 1976 in the US, per capita expenditures of electric power directly in homes was 2840 kwh and in the USSR 246 kwh (298 in cities and 164 in the countryside). The difference is more than 10 times.

Chapter 11 shows that the question of comparing education in the two countries is not very easy. Note an obvious sharp slowdown in the rate of growth of higher and secondary education in the USSR. Between 1950 and 1960 the number of students admitted to higher educational institutions grew by 70 per cent, and to *tekhnikums* by 80 per cent. Between 1960 and 1970, admissions to higher educational institutions increased by 54 per cent and to *teknikums* by 74 per cent. But during the decade 1970–80 admissions to higher educational institutions increased only by 15 per cent and *tekhnikums* by 9 per cent. During the same decade the total population grew by 10 per cent.[14]

In order to overcome the lag, the Soviet economy will have to develop, the production of agricultural products and industrial con-

166

Table 13.6 Quantity of durables, units[a]

	Rational norm	1965 Absolute	1970 Absolute	1970 Growth %	1975 Absolute	1975 Growth %	1980 Absolute	1980 Growth %	1980, per 100 families, absolute
Watches	600	885	1193	34	1319	11	1523	15	518
Radios	250	165	199	21	230	12	250	9	85
Televisions	135	68	143	110	215	50	249	16	85
Cameras	?	67	77	15	77	0	91	18	31
Refrigerators	110	29	89	207	178	100	252	42	86
Washing machines	72	59	141	139	189	34	205	8	70
Vacuum cleaners	?	18	31	72	52	68	84	62	29
Motorcycles and motor-scooters	15	17	21	24	25	19	29	16	10
Bicycles and mopeds	70	134	145	8	156	8	144	– 8	49
Sewing machines	98	144	161	12	178	11	190	7	65

[a]At the end of the corresponding year, Narkhoz-80, p. 406; norms from Mayer, Uroven' zhizni naseleniya SSSR, M., 1977, p. 105.

sumer goods will have to grow, and housing and agricultural construction will have to move at a faster pace. However, without serious structural changes, i.e. without a radical rebuilding of the entire economic system, the Soviet economy will not move ahead at all. Overall growth of production per capita has already almost ceased, and before long the volume of production will begin to fall – the country will enter a period of negative growth.[15]

Even if some change is made and the economy begins to move ahead, it is unlikely that the American economy will stand in place; in spite of inflation and various crises the standard of living will grow.

From this the conclusion is clear that under the economic system existing in the country the Soviet people will continue to live much worse than Americans or than the people of Western Europe and Japan. Even with radical economic changes in the USSR there is a little chance of overcoming the gap in the coming decades.

A caveat is necessary. All my calculations should not be taken very literally. When I say that the lag behind America in roads is 260 years, I am not saying that their length per capita in the USSR in the year 2240 will be equal to the American. Not to mention that in general to guess at such times, the future of road construction, and the fates of states and peoples is ridiculous, this calculation presupposes numerous conditions – a complete halt of road construction in the US, the continuation of this type of demand, the uniformity of the volume of road construction in the USSR throughout these 260 years, etc. V. Chalidze pointed out to me that the analogous calculation for telephones is in principle incorrect since, surely, there will be several technological revolutions in this area. Certainly, revolutions, bloodless I hope, will also take place in the production of fruits and meat.

In spite of all this, the calculations demonstrate the overall scale of the Soviet lag. They unquestionably say that, even working with Soviet statistics, one should in no way think this lag will be overcome in, say, 20–30 years. At the very beginning I promised to present facts and figures and avoid epithets and exclamation marks. And here in this indeed emotional place I will try to give my final conclusion as quietly as possible. The Soviet citizens joked about Khruschev's promise to overtake and surpass America by 1980 and about the 'building of the foundation of communist society'. Some people were very serious about Andrei Amal'rik's prediction that the USSR will cease to exist by 1984. Not at all joking, if the USSR not only does not fall apart within the years to come and continues to exist in more or less the same form, even the youngest Soviets and even their children and grandchildren will not live to see the level of consumption achieved in America in 1976. Such is the sad but unavoidable conclusion of our entire analysis.

Appendix I: Estimating Soviet National Product and Military Expenditures

Of no less significance are other conclusions from our analysis. I turn to them now but first will reiterate what was said at the very beginning – the purpose of the entire CIA study was not so much to investigate the levels of consumption themselves as to make calculations necessary for the comparison of the total national product of the USSR and the US. The study itself cites this larger task, on which CIA economists constantly work. And, just the opposite, the publications on comparison of national product cite the calculations for consumption.

We will note two circumstances here. On one hand, it is hard to exaggerate the significance of the very problem of comparing the sizes of national product. Only they enable comparing the scales of the economies, demonstrating the economic (and, hence, all other), might of a country. It is no accident, therefore, that in standard Western textbooks, in speaking of the Soviet economy, the authors indicate first of all that it produces about 60 per cent of the American national product (per capita, of course, less), and the same is repeated in countless newspapers and magazine articles. However, on the other hand, as far as I know, this figure, established by the CIA, has never been checked by anyone. The corresponding methodology is known only approximately, the progression of calculations is not published, and no other organisation carries out alternative calculations.

The publication of the work we are examining in essence for the first time gives the possibility of peering into the CIA's calculating kitchen, looking over the methodology and results of calculations for the most significant component of the national product.

We must turn attention to a fact that I have difficulty satisfactorily explaining. Having made such significant efforts at determining consumption, for the first time making concrete comparisons of goods, and carrying out special complex and voluminous calculations, the CIA economists arrived at conclusions that do not make even trifling changes in their previous overall estimate of Soviet national product: in carrying out a special study of consumption the CIA got exactly the same numerical result that they had earlier. Indeed, already in 1975 the CIA testified before Congress that Soviet per capita consumption in 1973 was 34 per cent of American.[1] True, the results of comparisons for individual groups shown then differ from the figures obtained in this study, and they were comparing 1973 and not 1976. None the less, the exact coincidence of the overall indicators attracts special attention. To anyone who has studied statistics such a coincidence looks strange.

Soviet definitions of national product differ significantly from Western. In

168

both the USSR and the West, indicators of *national income* are calculated, but they are not comparable with each other primarily because Soviet-style national income encompasses only so-called material production. We will designate national income according to Soviet methodology as SNI. Western economists usually work with the indicator *gross national product* (GNP), which is not determined at all in the USSR.[2]

Back in the 1940s A. Bergson proposed a special methodology for calculating Soviet GNP in rubles in 'prevailing' prices. The method was a first-rate scientific achievement; without it, comparison of the Soviet economy with Western countries in categories that Western economists and the public understand (are used to) is impossible. Subsequently the method was developed and used for concrete calculations by A. Becker of Rand and also by CIA economists. I have made several comments on this method,[3] the main one being that it is insufficient for separating out the military component from total GNP. Indeed, although the method itself envisions determining not only total GNP but also the military expenditures as a component, and the corresponding determinations are made, for a long time the CIA supposed that Soviet military expenditures take practically the same percentage of GNP as in America. In particular, for 1970 the share of military expenditures in Soviet GNP was determined to be 5.5 per cent, and this percentage was given in a study describing the results of GNP calculations.[4] Then, the estimate of the size of military expenditures was re-examined and doubled. That the estimate was revised is well known, but little attention is paid to the fact that this was done without re-examining the methodology of GNP calculations.

Irrespective of the quality of the methodology, it is in itself insufficient for comparing the size of GNP with other countries since its size is established in rubles.[5] In order to compare Soviet GNP in rubles with American GNP in dollars, the same methodology used in comparing consumption must be employed, which is why I discuss this question here. And the results of the comparison of GNP in the USSR and the US raise very serious questions.

According to the CIA publication, in 1976 Soviet GNP in comparison with American was: 49.5 per cent calculated in rubles, 73.7 per cent calculated in dollars, and 60.4 per cent by the geometric mean.[6] The estimate is in effect *greater* than the corresponding estimate of ... the USSR Central Statistical Adminstration (TsSU) which asserts that Soviet national income in the same year was 67 per cent of American.[7] At first glance this is not apparent, but only at first glance. On the same page of the yearbook where the 67 per cent indicator is published, nothing is said about how it is calculated. But three pages later we learn that the comparison is made in dollars and that Soviet SNI amounts to 54.2 per cent of American 'at the official exchange rate' and 66.5 per cent 'based on the correlation of prices'.[8] We may conjecture (it is not explained) precisely what calculation 'at exchange rates' means, but this is not of importance here. Still, we will note that this estimate is lower than that 'based on the correlation of prices'. We will note also that there are no grounds for thinking that such a calculation is equivalent to a calculation in rubles. In other words, we cannot calculate a geometric mean based upon TsSU data. More important is the fact that the highest of the two TsSu estimates – 66.5 (67) per cent – is in dollars, and it is much less than the CIA estimate also in dollars – 73.7 per cent![9] One might object that I am comparing a TsSU estimate of SNI with a CIA estimate of GNP.[10] However, to a specialist it should be clear that comparisons based upon SNI should give better results for the Soviet economy than comparisons based upon GNP. Indeed, without drowning the reader in excess details and calculations, I will simply say that the GNP indicators differ from the SNI indicators primarily in depreciation and services to the population (the latter according to Soviet theory do not relate to the sphere of material production). And precisely in these respects – in total depreciation and total services – the US is significantly further ahead of the USSR for other indicators.[11] The conclusion is unavoidable: the CIA estimates the USSR lag behind the US in national product to be significantly, at least 15 per cent, smaller than the deliberately propagandistic indicators of the USSR Central Statistical Administration.

This fact alone should suffice to make it clear – the CIA is mistaken here. The most important task of the TsSU in such comparisons is to proclaim the grandiosity of Soviet successes. I already said that Soviet statistics are not always necessarily incorrect; many TsSU indicators can essentially be trusted. In general, things are not simply blatantly falsified; 4 is not 'simply' changed into 2 and 10 into 100: each published figure is somehow calculated, somehow substantiated and not 'taken out of thin air'. Usually you must only know the methodology of calculation and, knowing it, the statistics, however poor, can be used.[12] And I myself based most of the conclusions in this overview upon official statistics. But in this case the yearbook does not even give a hint of how this indicator was calculated, how the 67 per cent was obtained. True, articles in special journals speak of the corresponding method, but vaguely without details.[13] Why such modesty? Is this some sort of military secret which if revealed will damage defence capability? Or perhaps the scholars who authored the method are avoiding their desired fame? To be sure, the method of determining the size of national income itself is described in rather great detail in standard college textbooks. Why do they carefully guard this secret method of comparing a non-secret value of Soviet national income with the even less secret value of American national income, which is published in the same yearbooks? The only explanation is that the authors of the method know that there are flaws in it, and detailed publication would reveal them. What sort of flaws? The answer to that question is also clear – the method does not understate Soviet successes, which would be diametrically opposed to the entire direction of propaganda. The indicator is overstated, i.e. the Soviet economy in fact produces much less in comparison with the American and the authors of the method know this well.[14]

My arguments are by no means limited to this reasoning. We have far from enough material to comprehensively examine the CIA calculations and determine the direct source of such an error (see also below), but what is published is certainly enough for a concrete discussion of the essence of this estimate. Let us discuss the problem first on the assumption that we are fully satisfied with the CIA calculations for consumption, that they are completely accurate.

As I already said, GNP must be compared by the same method, i.e. sample goods are selected, weights are established, price ratios are determined, price parities are calculated, etc. In addition to consumption, the total value of GNP includes investment (usually subdivided into equipment and construction work), defence (including space), and administration.[15] But the use of the method for components of GNP other than consumption encounters obvious obstacles. The selection and comparison of sample goods here is much more difficult, and in general much less information is available about both prices and the shares of sample goods in their groups. Prices could be obtained only accidentally. The CIA could not carry out a 'spy' operation for these components analogous to that for consumption. Buying models of Soviet equipment and giving them to experts for comparative evaluation is cumbersome, expensive, and not very efficienct. Soviet equipment for export differs sharply in quality from 'normal', and many types of Soviet equipment are not sold or are not transportable. This is even more true of the output of construction. Regarding military equipment, some models are available,[16] but the technical characteristics of the mightiest, and hence most expensive, types of arms are known only approximately.

Under these conditions the CIA did the best possible. As is apparent from two publications,[17] some sample goods were compared and price ratios were determined, based upon data in the literature. They carefully analysed special price handbooks for the revaluation of fixed capital in 1972–3, and also some other material on the estimated cost of construction-assembly work. These documents include prices (estimated cost – *smetnaya stoimost'*) and various technical specifications, which were used as the basis of price ratios.

How they compared administration we are not told, but presumably it was done by the same method as in comparing health care and education, although for administration the CIA economists must have had far fewer data.

We are also not told how they concretely compared military expenditures. But we know that the prices at which Soviet industry delivers arms and other equipment to the Minister of Defence are not known in the West. Also unknown is the amount in rubles that is actually spent on defence (since 1976 the CIA also does not believe the official indicator), to say nothing of the breakdown of this amount into components. Only the money payments to military personnel and expenditures on 'other allowances' for them can be determined more or less accurately.[18]

Thus, the data were best for investment, but even they were far from desirable. Initial calculations were made in 1967 prices, which then somehow, i.e. not very accurately,[19] had to be converted to 1976 prices. It was necessary to work with price-estimate handbooks which present a greatly idealised picture. In actuality the quality of both equipment and construction is always poorer than listed in these handbooks, and this must greatly overstate Soviet 'quality' in establishing price ratios. The CIA economists must also have known that actual expenditures are always (!) higher than estimated cost; the literature is full of complaints about exceeding it by one and a half to two times and more. This should have led to a perceptible exaggeration of the physical volume of investment. Thus, even for investment, where relatively more material than for military expenditures was available, it was still clearly insufficient for reliable conclusions. By no accident, not one substantial work on Soviet investment has been published in the West in the last 20 years, and it is no accident that the CIA made a major error here (see below).

Therefore, in general for the examined components of GNP the difficulties in

selecting sample goods, comparing them, and calculating price ratios and
parities were incomparably greater than for consumption. Therefore, there are
no grounds for thinking that better results could be achieved here.

Keeping all this in mind, let us examine (Table A1.1) the price parities the
CIA calculated in comparing GNP in the USSR and the US. We will not
concern ourselves with administration, which amounts to only 2 per cent of

Table A1.1   Ruble–dollar price parities for 1976[a]

	Soviet weights	American weights	Geometric mean
Consumption[b]	0.443	0.682	0.55
Investment, total	0.364	0.474	0.42
including			
Machinery and equipment	0.266	0.434	0.34
Construction and other	0.459	0.502	0.48
Administration	0.151	0.163	0.16
Defence and Space	0.473	0.523	0.50
Total GNP	0.403	0.600	0.49

[a]Figures in the first two columns are from *Soviet Economy* . . ., p. 379.
[b]The parities given here differ from those presented in Chapter 4, presumably
because the amounts of turnover tax, subsidies, etc., are taken into account in
the GNP calculations.

GNP.[20] Let us turn to the other two components. The parities for investment
look strange. Soviet economists know well that prices of products of so-called
Department I of social production (production of the means of production) are
understated in comparison with the prices of Department II products (production of means of consumption).[21] Therefore, the lower price parities for
investment in comparison with the parities for consumption in themselves raise
no objections; this is how it should be. However, the size of the difference,
especially the closeness of the parities for construction work to parities for
consumption does not look correct. Using precisely these parities, the CIA
came to the conclusion that in 1976 Soviet investment was, by the geometric
mean, 123 per cent of American. A very interesting conclusion, all the more so
since according to the TsSU estimate Soviet capital investment in this same
year was 'over 100 per cent' of American, where 'over' must mean something in
the order of 1 per cent.[22] Once again I repeat that the TsSU has absolutely no
need to understate Soviet successes, and CIA economists should have paid
careful attention to this.[23]

The greatest objections are raised by the parities for defence and space.
Determining the actual size of Soviet military expenditures is the most difficult
problem facing Western specialists on the Soviet economy. In efforts to solve it
a very fundamental fact is hardly considered – military industry works under

exceptionally favourable conditions. It is supplied on a top-priority basis and without interruptions, it is given the best of everything, the best personnel work in it, etc. Apparently the budget does not cover losses of the defence industry, i.e. the prices of its products formally cover expenditures. But only formally; if these exceptional conditions were taken into account, the real amount of expenditures on the production of arms (including scientific research and experimental design work) must be much higher than appears in the accounting books. And precisely this 'secret' is ignored by the CIA calculations. Ignored in spite of some Western works about this phenomenon. In taking a price parity for defence that is practically equal to the parity for total GNP (the entire economy), the CIA economists are telling us that in their calculations the conditions of work in all branches of the economy are identical.

Just above I said that, before 1976, the CIA estimates agreed with the offical Soviet indicator of military expenditures. Then the CIA changed its estimates, doubling it for 1970 and raising it even more for subsequent years. However, seeing such an equality of parities, I am puzzled by how they raised their estimates; what did they change? A careful examination of the expenditure side of the Soviet state budget shows that there is no place there to 'hide' very large amounts of expenditures for defence. What then is the source of these expenditures; what does the CIA think about this?

Let's move on. We are assuming for now that the CIA calculations for consumption are correct, which, alas, they are not. How does the overstatement of Soviet consumption affect the estimate of GNP? According to the CIA's calculations, the picture in 1976 was as shown in Table A1.2. Let us assume now that in fact Soviet consumption lagged behind American in dollars not by two (1186:644), but by three times. Then its value would be $1186 \div 3 = \$395$ billion, and, correspondingly, GNP would be $1253 - 644 + 395 = \$1004$ billion, i.e. only 59 per cent of American, 15 per cent less than the TsSU estimate (in rubles almost 10 per cent).

Table A1.2   Consumption and GNP

	1976 values ($bil.)[a]		USSR as a percentage of US
	USSR	US	
Total consumption	644	1186	54
GNP	1253	1700	74

Soviet Economy . . ., p. 378.

This calculation serves to illustrate the significance of such a revision, but in addition to all else we would need a precise estimate of the actual lag of Soviet consumption behind American. The estimate of Soviet investment in comparison with the US must also be substantially corrected.

The following objection must be expected. Among my basic disagreements with the CIA work, one of the main ones is that it took insufficient account of the abominable quality of Soviet goods. However, it is thought that the difference in quality from the West is much less for non-consumer goods, in particular for arms. A detailed examination of this problem would take us far afield, and I am not an expert on it. None the less, the quality of *any* Soviet good should in no way be overrated. It is enough to mention computers, where the lag is not shrinking but growing. And the simple fact that the USSR tries in every way to get Western equipment and technology and sells raw materials undermines this argument.

Speaking of arms, it must be said that they are also not of the best quality. In particular, high officials in military intelligence have testified before Congress that Americans arms are more refined, which, in their opinion, somewhat reduces the effect of the larger quantity of Soviet arms. One might also object that while a correction of the value of Soviet consumption should reduce the comparative estimate of GNP, an increase in the share of military expenditures should have the opposite effect. Indeed, assuming that they compose at a minimum 20 per cent of GNP, we thus increase its total comparative size. This is not the place to examine the complicated problem of international comparisons of military expenditures, but it has at least two aspects. On the one hand, there is an effort to compare military might, and on the other to determine the share of the military burden for each economy.[25] It is difficult to say what are the relative military strengths of the two countries are; published estimates are contradictory. My criticism of the CIA estimates relates precisely to the share of military expenditures. Soviet arms are extremely expensive; all of the best in the country goes for rockets, bombs, and other such dreadful toys. However, I can say nothing about their total volume, the, so to speak, results of these expenditures. In other words, in itself a revision of the share of military expenditures does not necessarily lead to a revision of their amount.

I know that my remarks are too brief and I will return to them in another work.[26] But overall I believe that the *CIA substantially overstates the Soviet GNP in comparison with American.*[27] In its most recent publication, the CIA stated that Soviet GNP is 55 per cent of American.[28] I think that it is no more than 30 per cent. The importance of this conclusion of our short analysis needs no special explanation. It is worth repeating what I already wrote elsewhere: in the study of the economy of any country, knowing the size of its national product is no less important than chronology is in the study of history.

Why are such mistakes made? I have not the slightest doubt about the honesty of those who make these calculations, about their good intentions and devotion to this difficult job. And their qualifications are high; participants in this work include not only CIA economists who have graduated from the best American universities but also professors from those same best universities.

The reader should not be fooled by the simplicity of many of my argument and passages; for clarity I often intentionally simplified. The study of the Soviet economy in general and especially in the West is difficult business and, strictly speaking, this difficulty is the first reason for mistaken estimates. Indeed methods that are not at all obvious must be employed, uncharted areas of statistics must be corrected; the answer sought is far from always seen immediately, and success – a correct research result – even with great efforts is not always guaranteed.

Speaking more concretely about our case, in itself the method of determining Soviet GNP in rubles is more or less acceptable; in spite of all the obvious shortcomings of both the method itself and the Soviet statistics upon which it is based, in spite of the fact that the definitions of GNP cannot be made fully compatible with the definitions of SNI, no better approach is known. However, efforts to create a satisfactory method (considering all the significant concrete details of the given case) of translating Soviet GNP in rubles into a dollar figure with American indicators have clearly not been sucessful. In the basic text of this overview the reader saw examples of various mistakes in initial information, determination of price ratios and parities. Many more serious mistakes were unavoidable in comparing the other two elements of national product where there was so much less information – investment and military expenditures. And moreover, as I tried to show in Chapter 12, there are a lot of methodological problems. Even more, although the problems indicated in Chapter 12 relate to consumption, there must be no less difficult analogous problems with calculations for investment and military expenditures.[29]

In sum, long and persistent work lies ahead in order to work out some sort of acceptable method.

The second reason is the absence of an appropriate theoretical foundation. Modern Western economic theories do not describe the realities of the Western economies themselves very well, and they are notoriously unsuitable for the analysis of Soviet-type economies. Using them leads to the confusion about which I wrote in Chapter 12.[30] But, alas, there is no other. And regrettably, sovietology pays too little attention to Soviet economic theory. I am not saying that the theory is good; the 'successes' of the Soviet economy being guided by it express enough, and the statistics follow this theory, but we will not understand the Soviet economy without a precise knowledge of it.

A significant third reason is, as I already wrote at the beginning of this overview, that CIA economists work without competition and, hence, without serious scientific criticism. It is hardly possible for a lone outsider to check the CIA's calculations, even if he were given all the material, much less carry out alternative calculations. In other words, CIA indicators can only be criticised speculatively, and there is no one to appeal to – for the 'general public', all these things are too specialised.[31]

In closing my overview, I must also speak of still one more reason – the obvious psychological trap into which CIA economists have fallen. I speak with certainty about this because in the past I also was involved in large-scale calculations with huge masses of information (so-called optimal branch planning) and fell into a similar trap: the 'magic of calculation'. It often happens that an economist must measure something that defies measurement. Then a lot of assumptions and approximate estimates must be made. In making them, the researcher hesitates, questions, endlessly corrects and adjusts. But having finished some sort of final calculation, and then publishing it, having defended it in superficial debates with opponents who note only the most obvious errors the author himself begins to believe in the results and forgets about the assumptions and his own doubts.

Only in this way can I explain to myself that the CIA economists persistently cling to their twenty-year-old estimates, that in spite of an avalanche of new information, in spite of their own cardinal revision of Soviet military expenditures, and a special study of the comparative levels of consumption, they continue to stick to their old views on the size of the Soviet economy.

Given all this, of no less importance is the development of a certain impression of the Soviet economy in the West over decades, and it is still worth lingering on this point. From the beginning, many recognized that the initial level – the economy of tsarist Russia – was terribly low. Some, though far from all, understood that the socialist economic system by its very essence could not but be much worse than Western systems. This understanding was, of course, shaken by the crisis of the 1930s.

Before the war almost no one in the West was involved in the scientific study of the Soviet economy. It began only during the war, primarily in the Office of Strategic Services, a forerunner of the CIA. And then a big role was played not only by economic but psychological factors. The USSR was an ally. The victory over Hitler made deep impressions; it was clear that victory was made possible not only by the Soviet army and the second front, but by the Soviet economy.

After the war, the appearance of the atom bomb then the hydrogen bomb and especially Gagarin's flight had still greater psychological effects; one does not have to be an economist to understand the need for powerful industry to accomplish these things. Specialists did not readily criticise Soviet statistics; they themselves after all were drinking at the trough of Soviet statistics. Predictions of a crash (political, national, and most of all economic) were never vindicated. And no one wanted to be known as a 'fervent anti-Soviet'; although the term was invented in Moscow, it is in most use in the West. Not being that meant demonstrating objectivity on every occassion, and even without occasion. If one were to criticise the USSR, then it would not be too strongly, and such light criticism would be balanced by emphasis on some positive things. Gradually in the 1960s the point of view prevailed that the Soviet economy in spite of all its shortcomings was really not so weak.

True, emigrants of the first and second waves repeated over and over that the real state of the Soviet economy was much worse than portrayed by propaganda and statistics, but they were not believed much. The most scandalous case was, if you will, with Naum Jasny, who tried for a long time to explain that the grain harvest statistics were shameless lies. It is not that anyone publicly argued with him – it was more effective to just keep quiet. Only when Khruschev published 'the secret' – the harvest was determined not 'in granaries' but by the 'standing crop' – dit it become necessary to admit unwillingly that Jasny was right.

In examining the history of the development of the impression of the Soviet economy, the significance of several studies in the early 1960s cannot be exaggerated. Among them three works that established the level of Soviet consumption in 1955 in comparison with American. All of them gave the same result [15] – Soviet consumption was 24–6 per cent of American by the geometric mean.[32] These works themselves were not published and therefore we cannot examine them in detail. For concrete examination, Soviet statistics are also lacking – the yearbooks give them only for 1950 and 1960 (there are some figures also for 1958) – and, incidentally, it is not very clear why these important comparisons were done precisely for 1955. None the less, elementar reasoning shows that the result of these studies cannot be right. Indeed the country had just recovered from the most destructive war in its history and had still not left the Stalinist camp. Housing construction had not yet begun. More than half of the population lived in the countryside and literally begged; the urban population was on the edge of starvation. Consumption of durable goods was less than minimal. Watches were considered almost a luxury. And at that time the standard of living in the US was not fundamentally different than now; it had continuously grown in the postwar period.[33]

It is quite obvious how these results were obtained. From A. Bergson's description of his calculations we can see that he used the 'indirect method' which gives significantly less accurate results when information is lacking. Besides, his calculations (like, presumably, the two others) ignored the comparative quality of Soviet and American goods. As one former CIA analyst put it: one horsepower was equated with one horsepower. In trying to be just, I should say that Bergson's description included a lot of caveats. But such caveats are usually of interest only to specialists and even they rather soon forget them. I understand how these results were obtained in the 1960s when the iron curtain was only beginning to rust. But now it is time to re-evaluate those estimates.[34]

Why do I say that the significance of these works is exaggerated? Because it was precisely on the basis of these studies and certain other calculations that the opinion of Western economists about the comparative size of the Soviet economy was formed. Numerous other measurements were built primarily by applying time series to this base.

Precisely these works are at the bottom of both the mistaken impression of the total size of the Soviet economy and the no less mistaken impression of the share of military expenditures in it.

Also of great significance is the following. It would seem from a statement about the weakness of the Soviet economy that it is not capable of continuing the arms race, of further extending its enormous military expenditures.[35] We must presume that when venerable Mr Nixinger undertook the celebrated detente, the hope was in part that the Kremlin would jump at the chance of avoiding at least a part of the ruinous military expenditures.[36]

As we know, reality turned out to be different. Having attained detente, the USSR did not reduce the military spending, but expanded it. As far as I know, this was never explained,[37] which gave still more weight to the arguments of those who persisted in speaking of the might of the Soviet economy.

As a result of a complex interlacing of circumstances, it turned out that 'hawks', pressing for a sharp increase in American military spending, tended toward the opinion of the strength, while 'doves', liberals, held to the weakness of the Soviet economy.[38]

Obviously, at the base of these incorrect, mortally dangerous impressions lies lack of understanding of a simple fact – the share of Soviet GNP allocated for military purposes is extraordinarily high. For the Western observer, the Sovietologist, it is almost impossible to imagine what part of national product, national efforts, the Soviet rulers set aside for war preparations. Precisely this enables them to have *tremendous military strength with a weak economy*. This misunderstanding, the root of which is transferring Western impressions to Soviet reality, is the basis of many of the CIA estimates. It is clear both what caused it and why it led to mistakes.

Regarding the reasons for this misunderstanding, the CIA economists, like other sovietologists, were guided primarily by Soviet statistics and Soviet prices. Neither prices nor statistics show the main thing here – Soviet defence industry employs the best brains and the best hands, it works under exceptional conditions being, in fact, excluded from the economy of shortages. This fact was ignored by Bergson's model, which the CIA used. I would not say that the model is grossly incorrect, but its role was limited by assumptions about the 'correctness' of Soviet prices.

Regarding the significance of this misunderstanding, the CIA economists, believing in a modest share of military expenditures, unavoidably had to believe also in the very big overall size of the Soviet economy.

The meticulous reader will pose a reasonable question. Suppose I am right in my arguments about such impressions of sovietologists; however, CIA economists, inasmuch as they are economists, work not with impressions but with figures, they not so much 'reason' as calculate; what then is the significance of such impressions? The problem is that large-scale economic calculations, especially international comparisons, and still more so comparisons with the USSR, inevitably involve conditionalities, assumptions and arbitrary estimates. Upon finishing a calculation of this kind an economist often does not have the possibility of comparing the result with other and reliable information and thus assure himself that the result is correct. The results can be checked only by common sense, by indirect comparisons, by all sorts of reasoning. And this is just where impressions of the remarkable successes of the Soviet economy played a fatal role.

I already spoke of three calculations which showed Soviet consumption in 1955 as a quarter of American. If Soviet economists of past or current times got such a result, it would shock us in the extreme; we would immediately search for an error, understanding that it was mistaken in the initial premises, assumptions, or in the calculations themselves. But given the impression that the Soviet economy works better even than the USSR Central Statistical Administration asserts, such a result seemed, and still seems, natural, correct, that is, needing only minor revision.[39]

With these impressions, CIA economists quietly went to sleep, having reported that Soviet military expenditures account for only 5 per cent of GNP and they are sleeping serenely now reporting that this share is on the order of 12–14 per cent, and that the size of the Soviet economy is approaching two thirds of the American.

We have departed from our basic theme of comparing consumption in the two countries and it is high time to conclude before the reader falls asleep. Sharply disagreeing with many of the CIA economists' conclusions, and having noted and criticised various imperfections, I want to emphasise for the last time – they arise primarily from the exceptional difficulty of the task. By no means accidentally, I myself was forced to avoid alternative estimates for both consumption and the national product. The authors of the study did what they could and in general they moved ahead toward the solution of an extremely difficult problem, although for better results greater efforts will be needed. These efforts, of course, must be made.

Appendix 2: The Soviet Economy: Alternative Views*

I know that most men – not only those considered clever, but those who are clever and capable of understanding the most difficult scientific, mathematical, or philosophical problems – can seldom discern even the simplest and most obvious truth if it be such as obliges them to admit the falsity of conclusions they have formed, perhaps with much difficulty – conclusions of which they are proud, which they have taught to others, and on which they have built their lives.

Leo Tolstoy

Exactly a dozen years ago, Professor Zvi Griliches of Harvard told us in Moscow that American interest in Soviet economics was minimal. In a few months I discovered that, indeed, it was not too great.

Some interest existed in the sovietological community. I was invited to speak here, at MIT, and at some other oases of curiosity. At those appearances, I was not particularly good. My English then was not a real means of communication. I did not know what could be of significance to sovietologists, to the US government, or to the public. Cultural differences played a role. I did not understand the political, partisan differences within this society, particularly how my hawkish stance immediately made me next to a pariah within the community. On many occasions, I insulted people by voicing their obvious (to me) mistakes (an unforgivable sin), and, even more importantly, by paying too little attention to their own work. A typical example: a sovietologist told me that the director of a Soviet institute took from his table a book, and said: 'When we have a serious question about our economy, we look here, in your book, Professor Such-and-such.' I could not resist a laugh.

Back in Moscow, I was convinced outsiders could not know what was going on in the USSR in general, and in its economy in particular. Only gradually did I recognise that this notion was wrong, and I am of a high opinion about some of the achievements in economic sovietology. Indeed, a lot was done under extremely different circumstances. However, step by step, I arrived at the conclusion that the picture of the Soviet economy drawn by sovietology is not exactly 20/20.

I will follow the main line, avoiding technicalities, minor points, and jargon. My presentation could look too simple. I do so on purpose, and please make no mistake: I am perfectly willing to discuss all technicalities.

The text of a presentation at the Harvard Russian Research Center, 13 March, 1985. My thanks go to participants in the seminar, as well as to Roger Clarke, David Epstein, James Gillula, Alexander Korsunsky, and Peter Wiles for criticism. The unabridged text was published in *Russia*, 1986, No. 12.

A) I begin with a summary of the general picture of the Soviet economy painted by sovietology:
 – it produces something like 60 per cent of the American level, or 50 per cent per capita;
 – the standard of living is three times lower than in America;
 – the military share of GNP is 12–14 per cent;
 – there are no financial problems: marginal propensity to save is quite normal, the state budget has a permanent surplus, inflation is controlled, etc.;
 – aside from grain and advanced technology, the USSR benefits little from foreign trade; the country does not depend on others, and what is bought abroad is only a fraction of the national product;
 – the productivity of the economy is declining – its growth became negative around 1970. But in spite of difficulties, it will somehow 'muddle through', and with some reforms, the economy will continue to grow in the decades to come. The book *The Soviet Economy Toward the Year 2000* concludes with Professor Evsey Domar's words that the American economy has its problems, as well.

Such is the picture, and, interestingly enough, this vision is shared by practically all the community. Only on military expenditures are there some disagreements, but they involve merely three: William Lee, Steven Rosefielde and Franklyn Holzman.

This is remarkable. The issues are very difficult, indeed. Still, all the community agrees on them, nobody dissents. In this country, built on competition, there is no alternative to the views which I have just listed. Such uniformity, which is to say such a monopoly of opinions, in itself should look suspicious.

My list seems to include the most fundamental issues. There is hardly a question of significance which does not relate directly to this.

B) My claim is that this picture is not correct,[1] and below I present my alternative views. But first, my methodological disagreements – that is, the reasons why those incorrect conclusions were arrived at.

1. *Statistics*   Like it or not, we have no alternative to Soviet statistics, so we cannot just deny them. However, the reliance on those statistics has been excessive. The examples are endless. The most striking: prior to the mid-1970s the official data on military expenditures were believed. Other examples: the foreign-trade ingredient is not excluded from the National Income Produced figures; the reported figures on construction are not refined by deleting unfinished construction; the harvest figures are not corrected for losses, etc.[2]

The figures for investment and fixed capital are very strange. No data for investment in current prices are published. The Soviet literature is overfilled with direct statements about the falsity of the figures. However, in no Western studies are those numbers adjusted.

When, seven years ago, I said here that the assertion about the state budget having no deficit was ridiculous, you did not believe me, you believed Soviet statistics.

True, there are some works in which questions are raised, there are cases of adjustments and corrections; still, an alternative to, so-to-speak, the figures from *Narkhoz* (i.e. Soviet statistical annual) does not exist. The only exception is the CIA series of GNP, which I will address later.

When in 1983 I began a project on productivity,[3] I had to create an alternative statistical base. This is the only way to improve our estimates radically.

An interesting attempt is now being undertaken by Dimitri Steinberg, but his work has not yet been completed.

2. *Rubles and Dollars*   I am ashamed to talk about such obvious things; still, sometimes people forget that the Soviet economy works in rubles and kopecks, but not in dollars and cents. The price structure of the Soviet economy is so unique that it simply must not be measured in foreign currencies.

For example, experts follow Soviet statistics on foreign trade, which are in dollars (or in so-called foreign rubles), and reach erroneous conclusions.

The most recent example: the discovery that in the last few years, the Soviet military buildup has stopped (see below). The scientific basis is the measurement in dollars.

3. *Theory and Models*   No doubt, Marxian theory is not the only summit of economic thought, but I humbly question the decision to base all studies of the Soviet economy on modern Western theories. Here are the reasons.

The Western theories are not universal: they somehow describe the Western economies, but the Soviet one is of a different kind. An example: such concepts as marginal propensity to save (or to consume) have very different meanings, if they have any meaning at all: in the Soviet economy, the consumer of productivity, a lot was done on capital–labour substitution, but Soviet managers do not operate in the Western environment.

It is very unfortunate that, to my best knowledge, no attempt has been made to create a special theory of Soviet-type economies. I do not, as we say in Russian, hold God by his beard; the creation of such a theory is a monumental task. Years ago, I suggested as one of its basic ingredients that an economy of the Soviet type is governed by shortage. Later, I discovered that, as early as 1924, L. N. Kritsman demonstrated the theoretical inevitability of demand exceeding supply under socialism.[5] Professor Janos Kornai's *Economics of Shortage* was also published, so I do not pretend to be original. But this very consideration – that the Soviet economy is one of shortage – is quite instrumental in theoretical explanations of various phenomena.[6]

4. *Models and Realities*   Let me turn now to perhaps the most serious point. Many times I asked myself why we disagree so sharply on so many issues. My personality aside, what so divides my views from those of all the community?[7] To repeat, I was wrong about the impossibility of understanding the economy from the outside. But possible does not mean easy. An outsider has to deal with artifacts: he is never certain. From this uncertainty, two things follow. First, the outsider is very defensive about his work, and takes any critique as anathema. Second, lacking data and understanding of real facts, outsiders have had to rely heavily on models, on what they call the quantitative approach.

Let me explain. I have nothing against modelling, modellers, and quantitative studies. In my old country, I published a few books, and perhaps too many articles, on linear programming and its practical applications. But excessive reliance on models is, frankly, too often an instrument for dismissing criticism and avoiding discussion of realities. The most vivid example is Bill Lee. For years he insisted that the CIA figures on military expenditures were wrong, but even when his figures were accepted, it was said (but not proven!) that he was right for the wrong reasons. I could give other examples, but rather, will say the following. On the one hand, before taking seriously the results of calculations with models, we should first look at the data used. Unfortunately, models are often much better than data. On the other hand, ideas and assertions should not be dismissed because they are not supported by models. Having lived in that country for forty-five years, and having studied its economy from outside for another eleven, I trust my intuition not less than models. I am not saying that all models are bad, or should not be used, but I suggest that reasoning, simple logic, and the like, which are called anecdotal economics, must not be dismissed. And, of course, I prefer to be right for the wrong reasons than to be wrong for the right reasons.[8]

The scientific basis for studies of the economy was created 20–40 years ago, particularly by Professor Bergson. For that time, the basis was very good, especially considering the scarcity of information. But since then, the latter has mushroomed radically. And, surprisingly, over the last couple of decades, that basis has hardly been improved.

Most surprisingly, not only the analysis, but even the conclusions published now are similar to those published decades ago.[9]

Finally, there is no doubt that people working in economic sovietology, including those at the CIA, are honest, devoted and highly qualified. Why, then, are their results, in my opinion, not so good? Certainly because of the unspeakable difficulty of the subject. Certainly because there is no real competition in the field. But no less certainly, a good theory is lacking. Without it, we could not expect radical improvement in the results.

C) A separate comment about Professor Bergson's model of GNP accounts, developed some 40 years ago. I will not waste your time extolling the virtues of the model and its creator; clearly it was a first-rate achievement. Let me instead focus on some of its shortcomings.

The very idea of presenting the national product of the USSR in accordance with Western concepts is marvellous. However, some problems happen to be insuperable. The first is the so-called non-material sector, services. Indeed, to determine the size of that sector, we should know wages, profits and depreciation. Wages are more or less determinable. Profits and depreciation are not. The most difficult is of course the military sector, but health care, education, housing, etc., are not a piece of cake, either. In the CIA calculations, the share of services in GNP falls from 29 per cent in 1950 to 20 per cent in 1980.[10] Is this true? I doubt it. The significance of the impossibility of measuring properly the profits and depreciation in the non-productive sphere means, to say it straightforwardly, that the attempts to determine Soviet GNP cannot be fully successful.[11]

Further, the calculations with the model have two gaps. One is that, in them, incomes of the population are always considerably less than expenditures, which is impossible, but no explanation of hypothesis was suggested. Another gap is in the public sector – there, incomes (revenues) are not large enough to explain the enormous military expenditures. Since equalizing incomes and expenditures in both sectors is one of the fundamentals of the model, the significance of the gaps cannot be underestimated.

This leads me to the next point – the model cannot determine Soviet military expenditures. Suffice it to say that in the first version of the CIA's GNP accounts of 1970, military expenditures were equal to offical data with adjustments for science.[12] A year later, the Agency published a new version of the accounts, in which the military expenditures were twice as large. This is remarkable: the model is so universal that you obtain military shares both of 5–6 per cent and 12–14 per cent of the total.

I have other problems with the model. In particular, it ignores the huge deficit of the state budget, and underestimates the even greater gains of foreign trade.

One more point. Let us agree with the idea that instead of using Soviet figures of National Income or GVO (Gross Value Output), figures for GNP should be used as more correct. But in every kind of analysis, you have to use other Soviet statistics which do not correspond to GNP figures.

I do not say that the model should be abandoned. On the contrary, serious work must be done to improve it. In particular, the CIA's attemnpt to use the model to determine the real rate of growth (deflated series) is to answer one of the most urgent questions.[13] However, *in addition*, a special model must be developed which follows Soviet concepts and definitions presenting the Soviet economy in its own figures. Input–output analysis is only part of this task.

Above, I said that we have no alternative to Soviet statistics. Unfortunately, the GNP model does not provide a reliable option.

D) Let me now turn to Soviet–American comparisons, and begin with the standard of living. By itself, the question is of major importance, particularly because the methodology employed in comparisons of living standards, which is practically the same as that for GNP and military expenditures. (I shortened this part of the paper for this book.)

The authors of the study worked honestly and with devotion. I am thankful to them for providing me with a good object for criticism. Still, I have major disagreements with the results.

The authors made a large number of varied mistakes. Their samples are not always typical. They overstated some prices. In many instances they did not adjust for obvious Soviet statistical distortions, such as the fat content of milk.

Though efforts were made to take quality differences into account, they were not sufficient. From the study we might conclude that Soviet meat is of the same quality as American, that Soviet bicycles are also of the same quality, etc.

I have a number of serious methodological disagreements, particularly that the enormous differences in trade services were ignored.[14] The study claims that Soviet per capita consumption is something like a third of America; in my estimation, because of this very factor (trade services) alone, it is, rather, a quarter. The mammoth variety of American goods and services was ignored, and so on.

In sum, on the basis of a very detailed examination of the study, I concluded that Soviet per capita consumption was at best something like a fifth of American. I agree with Professor Pipes, who, in his *Survival is Not Enough*, calls the CIA estimate fantastic.

I submitted my report to the Pentagon in 1983. Copies were circulated, including to the CIA; no response followed. The only one was from Dr John Hardt of the Library of Congress, who judged my work qualitative but not quantitative, and without further comment, dismissed my conclusions.

E) Turning now to GNP comparison, I remind you that according to the CIA's calculations, Soviet GNP was 60 per cent of American in 1976,[15] and 55 per cent in 1982. I disagree. Having examined the CIA comparison of consumption, I just cannot believe other figures without similar checking, but unfortunately, we do not have a publication on GNP comparisons with all the necessary details. Here are my arguments.

The figure of 60 per cent is based on comparison of the three elements – personal consumption, investment, and military expenditures. Even if we believe the two other elements, because of my correction of consumption, Soviet GNP was not 60 per cent of American, but much less. Let me emphasise that my correction of consumption comparison is minimal.

In regard to investment, the CIA claim that, in 1976, Soviet investment was about 20 per cent higher than American is ridiculous. Housing construction in the US is much larger. The American economy is also much larger, and renewal of its equipment occurs much faster. Only in so-called capital repair is Soviet investment larger, but its real value is at best questionable.

Let me add that the official Soviet figures, produced with the sole purpose of propaganda, show that Soviet investment is not larger than American.

In regard to military expenditures, the CIA reports that in 1976 the Soviets spent 136 per cent of American expenditures, which is also unbelievable. If we take out expenditures for personnel, the figure means that the Soviets invested in weapons procurement at least twice as much as we did. Later we will talk about military expenditures, but I will tell you now that the CIA underestimates their share in the Soviet national product. I shall also add that, being a hawk, I am not inclined to underestimate the Soviet military buildup. Still, the assertion that Soviet military procurement was twice as large as ours does not hold. And it contradicts the Agency's assertions about comparative numbers of weapons *in natura*.[16]

In other words, those simple considerations of the GNP elements indicate clearly that it is much smaller than commonly believed.

Earlier in the 1960s, Professor Bergson compared the sizes of the two economies. In his calculations, he did not take into account the differences in the qualities of Soviet and American goods.[17] The comparison was really quantitative, so Dr John Hardt evidently liked it. Professor Bergson wrote[18] that in those comparisons for 1965, the USSR produced 35 per cent of American GNP in 'ruble valuation' and 57.5 per cent in 'dollar valuation' – that is, something like an average of 45 per cent. Let us believe those figures. But if, additionally, quality differences were taken into account, the size of the Soviet economy would be not 45%, but much less. Those differences are so enormous that in the same calculations, the comparative size of the Soviet economy, if the quality differences are counted, would be, I estimate, at best 30 per cent of the American. If so, how can we believe that for 1965–76, the gap was bridged so significantly – to 60 per cent.

Next, I am also troubled that those estimates portray the Soviet economy larger than do propagandistic exercises by Moscow statisticians.

Finally, let me submit another very simple consideration. American agriculture produces more than does the Soviet. Though our population is smaller, we eat much better, and export food, whereas the USSR imports it.[19] Nevertheless, let's assume that the two agricultures' sizes are equal. American agriculture is something like 3 per cent of GNP.[20] In regard to Soviet agriculture, it is not so clear; estimates vary. According to the CIA, in 1976, Soviet agriculture produced 16.7 per cent of GNP.[21] From this you may easily conclude that the total Soviet GNP was at most five-and-a-half times less than the American.

You may say that one percentage is in rubles and the other in dollars, so the geometric mean will look different. Granted, though in the CIA comparisons, ruble–dollar and dollar–ruble price ratios for food with American and Soviet weights are rather close to each other. I would add that parities for agriculture are not too far from the parities for the economy as a whole. Certainly we have to compare carefully the American and Soviet definitions of agriculture. And, of course, I am not saying that the Soviet GNP is precisely five-and-a-half times smaller than the American. Still, I cannot imagine how those who claim that the Soviet GNP is 60 per cent of ours would explain the results of this comparison of agricultures.

The question is not easy. I cannot myself assuredly state the precise comparative size of the Soviet national product. But I do say that the economy is much smaller than is believed, and in any case, it is not the second in the world; in particular, it is less than that of Japan.

To repeat what I have already written elsewhere – for economic sovietology, this question is as fundamental as chronology is for historians.

Thus, my reading of the economy is very different from that commonly held, and the question is, why? Varied reasons are listed in my publications – among them, obvious mistakes in price parities, which do not properly take into account differences in quality. I shall add one more.

The Soviet economy has an enormous number of employees, tremendous fixed capital, vast areas of arable land, and maybe the largest deposits of natural resources in the world, but this huge economic potential is used extremely inefficiently. A lot of what is produced goes to intermediate goods, and is then lost. Think, for example, that only a quarter of all potatoes grown leave their producers;[22] that the country produces more steel, more oil, more cement, and more milk than we do; that only a quarter of total industrial production goes to personal consumption; etc. All this is very well known, and you would say that it is one of the reasons why, in the West, the Soviet national product is measured not in GVO, but using the GNP concept; allegedly the latter takes into account only so-called final products. Alas, it is not quite so. This question – how our measurements reflect that the Soviet economy produces more intermediate than final products – should be looked at.

F) Now on military expenditures. The question is too broad and complex, and I will limit myself to very brief considerations.

First, the basic model of GDP, as I already said, does not provide a way to determine the amount of military expenditures in rubles.

Even intuitively, it is quite obvious that the military share of Soviet GNP cannot be as low as 12–14 per cent.[23] We are told that such is the result of special calculations. This does not convince me. Professor Henry Rowen, in an excellent recent paper, said that the very preciseness of such an estimate makes one suspicious. And of course, what we know about the calculating procedure is not very encouraging. Indeed, Soviet weapons costs are estimated as if they were produced in the US, and then the dollars are converted into rubles. The procedure is very far from perfect, but that is not my main point. As we know, the basic secret of Soviet military expenditures is the exceptionally good conditions of military industries, which are not reflected in cost. And I could not believe my eyes when I saw that ruble–dollar ratios for defence and space are practically the same as for all GNP.[24] When I talked in 1983 to a special CIA commission, Dr Abraham Becker told me that the secret is known and taken into consideration; however, his statement contradicts the official publication just quoted.

Why do I disagree with the notion that the military share of GNP is as low as 12–14 per cent. First, it follows from my comparisons of total size of Soviet and American GNP.[25]

Further, it follows from what I just said – that the CIA calculation ignores the exceptionally good conditions of military industries. I see no way to quantify the factor *precisely*, but would dare to say that conditions in military industries are at least twice as good as in others. So, if the CIA estimates the military share as 12–14 per cent, I would assert that it is at least 20 per cent of GNP.

For the last several months, over and over again, statements have been made that the Soviet expenditures for military procurement have hardly grown since 1977. Why? Because such is the estimate of both the CIA and DIA. Bob Kaiser of *The Washington Post* referred to this as the unmasking of one of the myths of the Reagan administration. At least two comments are in order. First, maybe an even more important element of military expenditures is science and production of weapons prototypes, but the estimate pertains only to procurement. (Reported expenditures on science have grown rapidly.) Second, the estimate confuses the issue because the calculation is in dollars. Indeed, in rubles, the dynamics can be, and, I am sure, are, quite different. We can hardly believe that, starting in 1977, the USSR has frozen its expenditures for procurement. It is very unfortunate that practically all the community's efforts have been concentrated on an artificial procedure of comparing military expenditures in dollars.

I agree with Bill Lee, who years ago insisted on more thorough studies of the military share of national product in rubles. The task is exceptionally difficult, but not insoluble.

On 22 Februrary 1985, *The Wall Street Journal*, p. 35, reported that, according to Professor Bergson, 'the U.S. intelligence community, in estimating Soviet military expenditures, does as well as can be expected', that 'It's the only game in town, and if you don't take it too literally, you won't be too misled.'

Having made a lot of mistakes in my life, I recognise that humans are not gods: mistakes happen. What I do not understand and do not accept is self-satisfaction in science. I do not know what is expected from the community, and perhaps, indeed, the estimates are close to Professor Bergson's expectations. But with all my respect, even if you don't take the estimates too literally, you will be misled, and you have been. Of course, the situation results from the fact that 'it is only game in town'.

G) I will skip the financial matters, since my views have been published.[26] So far, I've heard no objections to my conclusions that the state budget is permanently in the red, that the population's savings are the headache of the regime, that the financial crisis is terrible. So I will go directly to foreign trade.

The price structure of the Soviet economy is vastly different from that of world markets, due to the financial iron curtain. Therefore, though the foreign trade balance in dollars is slightly negative,[27] in rubles it is very positive. This fact has been ignored. In my works on Soviet finance, I demonstrated that earnings, from foreign trade, namely imports minus exports, both in rubles, covered much, but not all (!), of the budget deficit. In other words, by selling grain to the USSR, we, in addition to feeding Soviet cattle, plug a huge hole in the state budget.

But this is only part of the picture. Soviet statisticians include the foreign trade balance in reported figures of national product. According to my calculations, now the balance gives not less than 11 per cent of reported national income produced.[28] The significance is manifold.

First, the reported figures overstate both output and its rates of growth – when you exclude the foreign trade earnings, they become much smaller.

Second, foreign trade earnings must be excluded from calculations of productivity – this was never done.

Third, in the CIA accounts of GNP, this phenomenom was not understood. The accounts, the model, follow Soviet statistics, which include earnings not in national income utilised where they belong, but in national income produced, where they do not. In the published GNP accounts for 1970, the import–export balance was included as R7.6 billion, which is about right. But it is included in National Product by Sector of Origin (national product produced), which is not correct; no sector of the economy originated this 7.6 billion.[29]

On the other hand, I am not sure that the CIA accounts of GNP for consecutive years to 1970 include the import–export balance on a full scale. Now it is not less than 60 billion rubles, and perhaps right here we should seek part of the funding of military expenditures.

H) My last issue is the current and prospective economic situation. Here too a lot of disagreement exists.

First, all measurements of productivity were strongly biased by an unfortunate mistake. They took the CIA figures for output (GNP) and Soviet official data on capital stock. Aside from other problems with the figures (I address them in the report to the Office of Net Assessment), the GNP series is allegedly corrected for inflation, but the official series on capital is not. Therefore, inadvertently, the calculations show longer-than-actual productivity. Thus, in them, productivity growth became negative ten years ago. If so, how could we explain that the Soviet economy survived, and even managed a military buildup in the 1970s?[30] Amusingly, the authors of those calculations apparently did not believe their own figures. Indeed, in my first major disagreement with the community, I asserted that the Soviet economy was in trouble, and even those who established the negative growth of productivity rejected the assertion. Only sometimes in 1981, or maybe in 1982, did people begin talking about problems with the Soviet economy.

When I arrived here in 1974, I was very much surprised, among other things, by the too-rosy image of the USSR's economy. Obvious problems were explained away in an optimistic tone. Some talked about maturation. Professor Berliner, commenting several years ago on my presentation, said that certain economies – for example, the Swiss – function successfully with a very slow growth rate. A lot was said and written about bad weather, the soil situation, demographic difficulties, etc., which, while true in itself, distracts from the economy's real main characteristics.

I am saying something different. If you trust the CIA measurements of productivity, if you believe in the maturation and in the decisive significance of the oil situation, you will think that the economy, as experts claim, will somehow muddle through further: it did muddle through for more than a decade with negative productivity. In my opinion, the negative growth of productivity starting only at the end of the 1970s marks the beginning of the end of the Soviet economic system.

A few things must be explained here. First of all, I reached my conclusion about the crisis before doing calculations of productivity; the latter only confirmed it. To put it briefly, the system does not work. For a long while this was not so clear because of the huge reserves of unused labour, because everything was given to investment, because, I repeat, the statistics were excessively believed. After the 1973 oil crisis, when Western systems began their adjustment, the critics of capitalism, inspired by detente, once again pointed to the USSR as a pattern. I remember how, in 1975, Professor Galbraith wrote in *The New York Times* that there were no unemployment and no inflation in the Soviet Union. I remember how a special bill about planning the American economy was introduced.

One may say, and some (for example, Professor Schroeder in her recent piece in *Soviet Union*) do, that the USSR has achieved significant successes. The assertion can be argued, but a few things are indisputable, namely:

– regardless of what statistics you use and how you interpret them, all show the same general trend: the pace of the economy is slowing;

– the sources of extensive growth are approaching their limits, and the Soviets may rely only on intensive development;

– the economy does not operate in cycles: a downturn is not followed by an upturn (by the way, this is one more example of the non-applicability of Western economic theories to the Soviet economy);

– there is no known way to improve economic performance radically. Ten years ago at a seminar here, somebody asked me, 'What would you do if you were in Kosygin's place?' My answer – quit immediately – was not a joke. The Soviet economic situation is so tragic that only a real miracle, such as, for example, the discovery of a very cheap and safe method of harnessing nuclear energy, can, if not save, at least prolong, it.

For years I have kept repeating the same very simple syllogism, and wonder why it is ignored. Maybe, once again, my crime is that I did not convert it into a model? The syllogism goes like this. The general tendency of practically all basic indicators is down: official statistics and CIA figures, rates of production output and of capital investment, labour productivity and the budget deficit (this is up, but the meaning is the same). I understand that the details of each particular measurement are disputable; that some would even disagree with me about the budget deficit; but you cannot deny that the economy is performing worse and worse. What can we expect?

In spite of this long-term tendency, experts say that the economy will 'muddle through'. Why? Because such are the calculations with SOVMOD (a special model developed for measurement). Well, the model is based on extrapolation with additional fancy tricks, How the model could extrapolate falling rates of growth in stable growth is a mystery. But those who insist that the economy will continue to grow at a rate of 2–3 per cent a year should give at least one reason how and why the regime will, if not reverse, then at least arrest the continuation of the same tendency.

Some say that the economy has huge reserves. For example, the labour shortage is a result of low productivity, so as soon as the problem is resolved, the economy will rush ahead. It is very true that the economy is extremely inefficient, and in this sense it has colossal reserves. But to use the reserves you need another economic system.

You may argue that there were two upturns in the economy – in the second half of the 1960s, and during the last two years. Well, the first must be looked at more attentively, but the second did not happen. The Soviet statistics are incorrect, which can be easily demonstrated. In other words, the economy is not growing: at best, it is already stagnating.

Aside from statistics, the basic fact is that nothing has happened during the last few years which could turn the economy up. Once again, I ask the same question: what of real significance occured in the Soviet economy that turned it around? And because I see no answer in either Soviet or sovietological literature, I cannot believe that the economy is performing better.

Something should be explained here. Why do capitalist economies have cycles, go up and down? Among other reasons, three are fundamental: investment cycles, psychological 'waves', and huge reserves of everything (economies of abundance). But in the Soviet economy, there are no possibilities of increasing investment; the economy is not governed by the consumer psychology; and the economy of shortage does not have reserves.

The following question should have intrigued curious minds: the Soviet economy is very unbalanced – how were the imbalances overcome, how could the economy operate without sufficient reserves? My answer is that during fast growth, the impact of imbalances was lessened by increments in production – in fact, the increments were planned for this very purpose. And of course, the slower the growth is, the smaller the possibilities are to struggle with imbalances.

Some observers suggest: that slow growth of the Soviet economy prepares it for a renaissance. Professor Schroeder explains the slowdown of the late 1970s as a planners' decision.[31] Just the contrary. Low plan targets are not the reason, but the result. And low rates of growth do not prepare for an upturn, they increase the impact of imbalances. In other words, here we see the notorious vicious circle – the slowdown will increase imbalances, and imbalances will slow the economy down even more.

The crucial question is, what can happen in the future? Or, to put it differently, can we expect that the Kremlin chieftain will reform the economy? Even if he does, the reforms will not save it.

I have seen an endless number of brilliantly written articles about reform, comparisons with Hungary (comparisons with Yugoslavia are not fashionable now, and after Professor Kornai's article in *The Journal of Comparative Economics*, comparisons with Hungary are not going to be fashionable, either), scenarios and political exercises. Surprisingly, all the articles miss the main points – ownership and transition.

In regard to ownership, decentralisation can be effective only if those who make decisions and those who implement them are ruled by their selfish interest – it's axiomatic. But please explain to me how this can be done without private ownership. The market system is a capitalist system, which cannot work without capitalists; it is as simple as that. Market socialism makes no more sense than socialism (of the Soviet type) with a human face.

In regard to transition, even if somebody somehow invented some economic system workable under the Soviet regime, and this invention were accepted by the rulers, the transition would not be easy and would take decades to be implemented.

A few words about China. Many people speak and write about reforms there, and it looks as though Comrade Deng has given them new hope. But remember the hopes inspired by Comrades Tito, Gomulka and Kadar. There are at least a few problems with application of what we observe in China to the USSR. The Chinese economy is on a very primitive level. There are living capitalists and huge reserves of labour. Still, if we live long enough, we will see that the Chinese economy will not be more successful than other socialist economies.

Summarising, the Soviet economy will not muddle through; it will deteriorate further.

In Moscow we used to say that each new scientific idea goes through three stages: first, everybody says that it is nonsense; second, some say, well, there is something there, but still . . . ; third, they ask, what is he talking about? We have always thought the same way. I wonder at what stage we are now.

Notes and References

Preface

1. For example, a 1987 novel, *The Trap on the Potomac*, claims that the Agency set up Watergate in order to get rid of Nixon's detente.
2. *Ekonomika nedostach*, Chalidze Publications (New York, 1983).
3. *Russia*, 1983, # 7–8.
4. *Russia*, 1986, # 12; *Survey*, 1985, vol. 29, # 2 (125); *The Atlantic Community Quarterly*, 1986–7, vol. 24, # 4. See the text in Appendix 2.
5. *Izvestia*, 18 Sept. 1987, p. 1.

Introductory Remarks

1. *Consumption in the USSR: An International Comparison*, A Study Prepared for the Use of the Joint Economic Committee, Congress of the United States, Washington, D.C., 17 August 1981.
2. The authors refer several times to a similar work completed by the CIA in 1964 in which Soviet consumption in 1955 was studied (on its basic conclusions, see Chapter 14), but as far as I could determine, it is still (why?) stamped secret.
3. Although relatively few sources are cited in the text of the study itself (which is not one of the publication's merits), it is clear that, in fact, the authors examined a huge number of Soviet books, journals, and newspaper articles.
   Sovietological literature has given rather little attention to the population's consumption. I have not seen a more or less comprehensive study. A work familiar to specialists is Alastair McAuley, *Economic Welfare in the Soviet Union* (University of Wisconsin Press, 1979), devoted to a related, but separate question – the distribution of income among various population groups. There were also several publications – by Aron Vinokur and Gur Ofer of Israel – on surveys of recent immigrants that they conducted. Others who have written on the topic include Janet Chapman, Alec Nove, Barbara Severin, Gertrude Schroeder and Peter Wiles. In most cases, sovietologists have based their studies upon the Soviet literature, and I preferred to use primary sources.
4. One cannot but be amazed that, judging from the text, the works made absolutely no use of the experience of recent emigrants from the USSR. There is mention of a survey conducted in Israel, but the professional knowledge of former Soviet sociologists, economists, lawyers, and other specialists apparently – at least for this work – rests once again in vain.
5. The manuscript was read and quite usefully commented on by Jack Alterman, Alexander Babyonyshev, Valery Chalidze, David Epstein, James Gillula, Dina Kaminskaya, Alexander Korsunsky, Yuri Markish, Henry Morton, Marianne Sheinman, Konstantin Simis and Albina

191

Tretyakova. I also had useful conversations with Godfrey Baldwin, Eva Jacobs, Barry Kostinsky and Donny Rothwell. I am especially indebted to James Gillula for excellent translation and many comments, to Albina Tretyakova for her suggestions, for supplying me with a mass of material and correcting many mistakes, and to Jack Alterman for extensive and extremely helpful criticism.

6. I wrote about this phenomenon, which actually pertains to phenomenology, in *Vremya i my*, 1978, no. 29.
7. In particular, I did not discover data on 'home' production of fruits and vegetables, imports of bananas in physical units, the production of Pepsi and Coca-Cola in physical units, etc. American statistics ignore the effect of consumption by foreign tourists and 'illegal' immigrants. The authors complain [96] about the lack of data on private schools. The figures on the production of clothing look strange, and there is a difference between the handbooks of the Census Bureau (*StAb*) and the Department of Agriculture (*AgSt*). The production (harvest) of fruits is often given in 'boxes', and the weight of a box is different for different states, so the total weight can be found only approximately.

    Many indicators are calculated in the way that is most convenient for the statisicians. For example, the number of 'eating and drinking places', (restaurants, cafes, cafeterias, etc.) is determined by a special census excluding those 'places' that are in hotels if the places belong to them, and excluding school, university and other cafeterias. The significance of this is apparent from the fact that in 1977 in bowling alleys alone $500 m. was spent on food and drink.

    Many figures are revised after a period of time. In particular, the population for a given year is quite different in the stastitical yearbooks for different years; see, for example, *StAb-78*, p. 6, and *StAb-81*, p. 5 (due to a post-census revision).

1 What For?

1. *Narkhoz-80*, pp. 38, 48, 59, 85–9, 92.
2. Soviet statistics also carefully avoid publishing data on the structure of consumption. An exception is the 'budgets of the families of workers and employees and collective farmers' (e.g., *Narkhoz-80*, pp. 383–5), but these data are very suspicious. It is sufficient to say that the parts do not add up to the total even though one of the items is labelled 'other expenditures'.
3. I may include myself in this survey. Without detailed calculations, several years ago I estimated that the level of Soviet consumption must be one-fourth to one-fifth of American consumption, and I published this estimate (see Chapter 14).
4. I wrote about the 'scissors' in 'Protivorechivyye protivorechiya', in *SSSR. Vnutrenniye protivorechiya*, New York, 1981, no. 1.
5. In particular, if the blade 'consumption' is moving very slowly, it means that the spread is growing. It is also understandable that the greater the Soviet lag in consumption behind that of other countries, the wider the spread.

2 Methodological Basis

1. This and the following chapter play a service role. They are primarily for readers who are little acquainted with the problem being discussed. I do not pretend to offer any original opinions here. Moreover, I simplify a number of things and do not speak of the debates and disagreements that are abundant in the special literature. Incidentally, quite a lot has been published in Russian on the methodology of international comparisons, especially on comparisons within 'the socialist camp'. One such work is O. K. Rybakov, *Metodologiya sravneniya ekonomischeskikh pokazateley stran sotsializma*, M., 1968.

2. Here is a joke with a deep meaning. A native is lying under a banana tree on the ocean shore and doing nothing. An American comes up:
   'Why aren't you doing anything?'
   'And why should I?'
   'What do you mean, why?! Go and study. You'll learn a good profession and find a job that pays well.'
   'And why should I?'
   'What do you mean, why? You'll make a lot of money, and once a year you'll get a vacation, go to the ocean, and eat fresh tropical fruit right from the tree.'
   'But I'm already at the ocean under a banana tree.'

3. The difficulties of including education in the standard of living are amplified by political and religious education. And regarding health, by the same logic, spending in the struggle against crime could be included in the living standard.

4. One effort to measure the 'quality of life' was the publication by the US Census Bureau of the special huge book *Social Indicators* (the last was published in 1980). Here are the titles of its 11 sections: Population and the Family; Health and Nutrition; Housing and the Environment; Transportation; Public Safety; Education and Training; Work; Social Security and Welfare; Income and Productivity; Social Participation; and Culture, Leisure and Use of Time.
   This entire problem is extremely complex, if at all solvable. For example, in the US only 83 per cent of the population lived in 1977 in the same houses and apartments that they lived in in 1975. The rest had moved (*StAb–78*, p. 39). This is very high mobility, but points of view about the relation of mobility to the quality of life may differ. (There are almost no data on migration of the Soviet population, but it is many times smaller.)

5. For example, should the amount set aside for old age or the amount of pensions be considered? Or actual expenditures from pensions?

6. According to the authors' data on page 30 (hereafter I indicate the numbers of the pages referred to in brackets), in 1977 the length of the work week in the USSR, which was about 40 hours (the 'average established length of the work week of an adult industrial worker' was 40.6 hours, *Narkhos-77*, p. 388), was shorter than in Great Britain, France and West Germany and the same as in Japan. They assert that the work week in nonagricultural sectors of the US economy was about 36 hours long. For a more accurate comparison, it is necessary to

consider the working time of people employed in their own businesses and to compare holidays and vacations.

Note also that in 1979, 15.6 million USSR urban residents 'helped in agricultural work' (*Voprosy ekonomiki*, 1981, no. 9, p. 60).

7. According to my estimates, the total amount of the population's savings in savings banks, bonds and 'under mattresses' is nearing the amount of one year's money income (see my *Secret Incomes of the Soviet State Budget*, The Hague, Martinus Nijthof, 1981, and my article 'Ugroza' in *Vremja i my*, 1980, no. 53).

8. For example, all the corresponding indicators in the *NarKhoz* yearbooks speak of 'real incomes', where 'real' is supposed to indicate that price changes were taken into account. (The term *'real'nyye dokhody'* is very different from the same Western term. In particular, Soviet 'real incomes' include so-called 'consumption at the expense of social funds'). The manipulation of prices makes it possible to deliberately and greatly exaggerate the growth of the Soviet population's incomes. Not in a statistical handbook but in a newspaper with almost 10 million circulation, the chairman of the USSR State Committee on Prices, N. T. Glushkov, was not ashamed to write that 'from 1955 to 1980 the retail price index increased on the average for the country as a whole by 5.7 percentage points, including a 16.4 per cent increase in foodstuffs, but the prices on all non food goods declined by 6.5 per cent' (*Izvestiya*, 15 November 1981, p. 3).

Deliberately understating the price index and ignoring the growing monetary savings, it is stated, for example, that 'real incomes per capita have doubled since 1965' (report of the new chairman of the All-Union Council of Labor Unions, S. A. Shalayev, at the Seventeenth Congress of Labor Unions, *Izvestiya*, 17 March 1982, p. 3).

9. Although some measurements, in particular the so-called elasticity of demand, are feasible, it is impossibly far from this to an actual determination of requirements. In speaking of the 'scissors' above, I had in mind that the movement of the 'blade' characterising demand can be described only very approximately.

10. Such comparisons are an ordinary thing for economists. Readers who had occasion to (had to) read *Das Kapital* will easily remember that Marx discusses the equivalence of 10 arshins of canvas and one frockcoat. The readers of this overview should clearly understand that, in a very definite sense, we are equating one movie ticket to a kilogram of meat (in the US), and a pair of pants to 100 kg of potatoes (in the USSR).

11. It is described in a relatively old work – Milton Gilbert and Irving B. Kravis, *An International comparison of National Products and the Purchasing power of Currencies*, Paris 1954. Our authors refer to it as their methodological foundation. The book was translated into Russian: *Mezhdunarodnoye sravneniye natsional'nogo produkta i urovnya tsen*, M., 1962. The method is not the only one, but it is the most widespread and known.

12. If we put aside some substantial scientific objections (so-called price elasticity of demand, the absence of perfect competition in which prices

are fully determined by the buyers' preferences, etc.), we may mention that some people 'know how to live'; they avoid accidental spending, they buy not when they need something, but when it is cheap (thus, the 'volume of consumption' that they get for their consumption expenditures does not correspond to that of other people). The question of 'non-useful' consumption – smoking, alcohol, narcotics – is also not fully clear.

Still, it must be decisively emphasised that without the premise of the proportionality of expenditures to some 'consumer utility' practically all economic measurements lose their meaning.

13. The phenomenon is observed not only in international but also in dynamic comparisons. Thus, the growth index of any economic indicator (especially for a long time period) depends significantly upon whether it is based upon prices at the beginning or end of the period. Soviet statistics ably use this to exaggerate growth rate indicators. Let us note, incidentally, that the *Narkhoz* yearbooks finally stopped publishing the comparisons of total output (national income) with 1913 and 1929; these figures look too absurd. But the comparisons with 1940, calculated by the step index method, are still published with no allowance for the index number problem, and they are also ridiculous.

14. According to the authors' data [40, 41], 1 kg of chicken is 28 times more expensive than 1 kg of potatoes in the USSR and 7 times in the US; the corresponding ratios for white bread are 11 and 2. By the way, these data are not too accurate.

15. What is not expensive in which country deserves a special study. In the USSR, urban transport, housing, bound books (although they went up), and certain services are cheap relative to other goods. In the US, radios, record players, alcoholic beverages and clothing are cheap in comparison with those in the USSR and relative to other goods. It is also worth noting that in America, a greater gap between cheap and expensive varieties of goods exists, which is explained primarily by the possibility of buying many expensive things here (a Rolls Royce, yacht, airplane, etc.), which are not even sold in the USSR.

16. Such is the theory. In practice, under specific conditions of the Soviet economy (in general, Soviet-type economies, economies of shortages), where far from all cheap goods can be obtained, this phenomenon does not 'work' to the full extent (see Chapter 12).

17. The same is true of national product comparisons (Chapter 14). Therefore, Soviet statistics measure various economic indicators for the USSR and the US in dollars, ignoring the index number problem, and imposing on American consumption the Soviet structure of production and consumption.

18. Given the assumption of the 'market' character of prices (see Chapter 12).

19. The geometric mean is calculated in such cases as the square root of the product of the two quantities. In the example in Table 2.1 where the ratio of Soviet to American consumption is 0.51 when measured in rubles and 0.65 when measured in dollars, the geometric mean is 0.58 (coincides with the arithmetic average due to rounding).

20. Two reservations: First, this refers to the indicator of 'volume of consumption' in value terms. Indicators of the physical quantity of consumption – meat in kilograms, boots in number of pairs, etc. – are not corrected for quality. In other words, the value indicators of the amount of meat consumption (in dollars, rubles, and the geometric mean) reflect different quality, and this is equivalent to a change in quantities, although the quantity indicators themselves do not change.

    Second, the method of comparison makes the rather strong assumption of the proportionality of a large quantity of a poorer quality good to a smaller quantity of the same good of better quality. Although the correctness of this may be disputed, no alternative approach to the problem of comparison is apparent.

21. Indeed, perhaps Soviet statisticians do know but are not telling the world, for example, how much yogurt and how many pens were sold. I also do not think that in America you can find out how many of all the various kinds of automobile parts are sold.

22. Irving B. Kravis, Zoltan Kenessey *et al.*, *A System of International Comparisons of Gross Product and Purchasing Power*, 1975, p. 19.

3 Methodology Employed in the CIA Study

1. This is significantly more than the set of 165 sample goods used by the Soviet Central Statistical Administration for the comparison of retail trade in the USSR and the US (*Vestnik statistiki*, 1980, no. 12, p. 41).

2. It was done in different cities in order to take into account differences in 'price zones'. Unfortunately, differences in the quality of goods sold in various cities were ignored (see Chapter 12).

3. The study describes the example of televisions [53]. It was determined that the American black-and-white television was better than the Soviet in eight characteristics, and its price was discounted accordingly: $2 for inferior cabinet finish, $3 for manual vs. automatic switches, $10 for picture brightness and focus, etc., for a total of $47. On the other hand, the American price was increased due to the slightly larger screen size of the Soviet set ($5), an 18-month warranty instead of 1 year ($15), etc. The overall discount considering all pluses and minuses was $19, and the price of the American set was reduced by this amount before the price ratio was calculated (see Chapter 12, p. 139).

4. The authors write that differences in standard products often 'mystified' the American experts. As an example, they note that Soviet sheets and pillow cases are usually made of coarse linen fabric. They were also amazed at the way Soviet-made top sheets fit over blankets, envelope style [52–3]. I am much more mystified by the fact that the authors noted so few differences, and of such little significance.

5. The text itself does not indicate why calculations were done for 1976. Since the work was published in 1981, one may assume that it took at least five years. Just the evaluations of the quality of Soviet goods by American specialists took more than a year [52].

    It must also be noted that various types of information appear in the literature only gradually. This applies especially to Soviet data, but even for America I could not locate more recent data than those for 1972.

6. There is a suspicion that a new handbook was also published for more recent years, but if this is so, it is secret. In any event, it has already been nearly 20 years since a statistical handbook on such a 'sensitive' topic as domestic retail trade has been openly published.

7. There are no data in the literature on prices in collective farm markets after 1963. According to eyewitness accounts, in 1982 the price of beef in Moscow markets reached R8 per kg, mutton R7 per kg, and chicken R10 apiece. Prices were lower in 1976 but they were substantially higher than those given by the authors and used in their calculations.

8. Existing differences in Soviet prices, in particular those in a few price 'belts' (zones), were, of course, considered by the authors in their calculations.

9. *Narkhoz-76*, p. 471.

10. Here I cannot cite a source from the literature, and I base this assertion on personal recollection checked with other emigres.

11. The chairman of the Belorussian Price Committee maintains that the average retail price per kg of beef is R1.68 and of pork R1.85 per kg. *Promyshlennost'Belorussii*, 1977, no. 7, p. 31. See also F. S. Cheremisov, *Resursy prodovolstvennikh tovarov i ikh ispolzovaniye*, M., 1975, p. 17.

12. E. S. Karnaykhova, *Differentsial'naya renta i ekonomicheskaya otsenka zemli*, M., 1977, p. 113.

13. *Planovoye khozyaystvo*, 1976, no. 12, p. 14. Although I try to avoid criticising the American data the authors used, I must say that the prices of clothing they used seem high. This is seen in the distribution of sales of several types of clothing by price intervals; see US Bureau of the Census, *CIR, Apparel, 1977*, MA-23A(77)-1, p. 3.

14. One mistaken price is of rather special significance. The authors say [76] that the USSR price of a driver's licence is R11.40, which is absurdly high. The authors should have paid particular attention to it, because it is just this price that determines almost the largest ruble/dollar ratio – 5.182 rubles per dollar [16]. By the way, the highest ratio (5.250) pertains to a man's digital watch, and as I said, the latter should not have been used as a sample good. In other words, the dispersion of price ratios is less than that determined by the authors [16].

15. I already mentioned cigarettes and chickens. The price of eggs relates to 'dietetic' ones; the price of a man's haircut is taken as 60 kopecks, and a room in a hotel as R5 (the 'normal' price is half as much, and the special price for foreigners is twice as high. The average here makes no sense).

16. In this case, it is clear from the text [81] that 20 kopecks is not a maximum but an average (whether this is right is another matter).

17. However, there is no great certainty that the authors actually highly discounted the American prices; compare, in particular, their prices of butter and chicken with those in *StAb-78*, p. 706.

18. Apparently, the authors took the largest part of this (and other) information from R. A. Lokshin, *Spros, proizvodstvo, torgovlya*, M., 1975, which is filled with all sorts of figures. I make abundant use of this book, the authors refer to it only once.

In many instances the CIA work did not provide enough information. Nowhere indicated are the population figures used for the two countries; it takes considerable effort to work out why differing figures are given in different tables, etc.

19. *Narkhoz-77*, pp. 458, 460.

20. Generally speaking, this is not the case, which is evident, in particular, from elementary calculations comparing retail trade turnover per capita for the urban and rural population (*Narkhoz-77*, p. 456) with a direct division of state and cooperative trade separately by the number of urban and rural inhabitants. We find that a significant part of cooperative trade falls to the city. However, it is state and not cooperative trade that primarily accounts for the retail sale of consumer goods to various organisations (*melkiy opt*). In the city the share of public dining in the total volume of trade is immeasurably larger. Finally, the rural population makes many purchases in city stores. Therefore, the volume of cooperative trade can be taken as only a crude estimate of purchases of the corresponding goods by the rural population.

21. For those who do not know, I highly recommend Lev Timofeyev's essay 'Tekhnologiya chernago rynka ili krest'yanskoye iskusstvo golodat', *Grani*, 1981, no. 120.

22. There are two tables in *Narkhoz-76*, p. 512,: 'Consumption of food products by families of textile workers in Leningrad, Noginsk, and Furmanov', and 'by families of peasants in Vologda, Voronezh, Kirov, and Khar'kov oblasts'. By these data, meat consumption per capita in 1976 was 80.6 kg in urban and 50.5 kg in rural families (including fat, poultry, and subproducts). These tables are compiled 'from data of family budget studies' and we should not put great trust in the absolute volumes. But in my opinion they reflect the relationship of meat consumption in the countryside and the city quite correctly. It is also worth noting that, according to these tables, the consumption of potatoes increased sharply compared with that in pre-revolutionary times. There are also similar data in *Kommunist*, 1977, no. 13, pp. 74, 76.

23. A recent long article in *Izvestiya*, 28 April 1982, p. 2, describes the procedure by which meat processing plants receive livestock. '... the plans for collective farms, state farms, and interfarm enterprises count the live weight of livestock. Meat processing plants count slaughter weight (recorded).' All statistics (I will deal with this in Chapter 6) are based on slaughter weight. However, the authors of the article state that 'in indicators of fulfillment of the state plan, the actual weight of livestock is counted in one case and the estimated weight in another, which ... is not the same thing ... all this leads to different estimates of fulfillment of the purchase plan and to the overstatement of certain indicators of the production and sale of livestock.'

This entire question is rather complicated and, for us, too technical. However, there is no doubt that the accounting procedure permits certain manipulations, especially with 'own' consumption of meat. I am quite sure that the overstatement of these figures greatly embellishes the true picture. Apparently the situation is similar with milk.

I will add that the way the authors distributed the consumption of several agricultural products looks strange: own consumption accounts for (the rural share of population in 1976 was 39 per cent): 36 per cent of meat and poultry, 41 per cent of milk and milk products, 0 per cent of butter, 36 per cent of eggs, and 8 per cent of both fruits and vegetables [46].

24. In this particular instance, there are data in the literature – in TsNIITE-pishcheprom, *Nauchno-tekhnicheskiye referativnyye sborniki.*

25. Several years ago a special commission reported that in America we pay twice as much as is necessary for auto repair because of incompetent mechanics and deceptive practices.

26. For example, this sort of redistribution occurs when store clerks measure out less than you pay for. Regarding pilfering from food industry enterprises and collective and state farms, given the method the authors employed (as we saw, they included in total consumption various discrepancies), this should not affect the final figures for the consumption of these products. See my work (in Russian) *Second and First Economies and Economic Reforms*, Occasional Paper No. 108 of the Kennan Institute for Advanced Russian Studies, Washington, D.C., 1980.

27. *Narkhoz-76*, p. 528. Considering the varying shares of the indigenous population in the republics, it is more accurate to speak not of ethnic but geographic inequality.

A sharp difference in the average per capita consumption of goods is apparent in M. L. Dementeva and Z. S. Khodorova, *Spros i ego izucheniye v obshchestvennom pitanii*, M., 1976, p. 13. There a quite a lot of different types of data on regional differences in the literature.

28. This entire question, although extremely important, is far from our main topic. I will note only a few facts. On the one hand, this difference, based on official money income, is declining. Immediately after the war the wages of scholars were raised sharply, and scholars were the highest paid major social group (I repeat, we are speaking about *official* incomes or, more accurately, wages). A professor, doctor of science, earned (including income from additional part-time positions) up to R600–700 a month, which exceeded the minimum wage by a factor of 20–25. Since then the salaries of scientists have not increased (finding second positions became more difficult) and the minimum wage was raised rather impressively. For example, the share of the population with per capita income above R100 per month increased from 4 per cent to 40 per cent between 1965 and 1977 (*Vestnik statistiki*, 1978, no. 7, p. 56). On the other hand, social stratification increased; college degrees and high positions more and more go to the children of scientists and bureaucrats. In the mid-1970s, the ratio of incomes per worker reached at least 10 to 1, and per family member the difference might have been substantially larger (here I am not including the very few highly paid members of the USSR Academy of Sciences, marshals, and authors of mass songs).

The difference in the actual standard of living is, of course, greater. It is precisely the higher paid that receive long vacations, better apartments, admission to 'closed' health clinics, business trips abroad, etc.

29. *Narkhoz-76*, p. 522, annd *Narkhoz-77*, pp. 385, 408. In these data, 30

million pensioners are singled out as 'pensioners by old age'. One should assume that the rest, 16 million, are invalids and those who lost their providers, but this seems to be too big a number. Let us note that for the countryside the difference between the total number of pensioners and pensioners by age is insignificantly less. In 1960 that difference for the country as a whole was the same – 16 million (*Narkhoz-80*, p. 412).

30. I spoke recently to a left-leaning Italian sociologist who had nothing good to say about America. When I pointed out to him that the standard of living is incomparably higher in the citadel of capitalism than in his homeland, he sharply responded that, first, a huge part of income in Italy is hidden from taxes and thus does not enter official statistics and, second, Italian families are bigger, which reduces per capita expenditures.

31. *Narkoz-79*, p. 35; *StAb-81*, p. 45.

4 General Results

1. *XXii s'ezd Kommunisticheskoy partii Sovetskogo Soyuza. Stenograficheskii otchet*, M., 1962, vol. III, p. 295.

2. In particular, he said, 'Not only our descendants but we ourselves, comrades, our generation of Soviet people, will live under Communism!' (ibid., vol. 1, p. 257).

3. In other words, for a family of four it would have been R1392 *a month*, not counting taxes, savings, etc. This, of course, is inaccurate because total consumption includes expenditures on education and medicine, which are free in the USSR. Such spending per month for four Soviet persons was R37 (Table 4.1). If, for comparability, we subtract these expenses ($1111 per capita a year) from American consumption, we find that the American family would have had to spend 'only' R1150 in the USSR a month, which is impossibly high.

4. We are examining summary parities, which themselves result from the calculations and comparisons of consumption levels. In other words, it is not that they were somehow calculated, and then using them, levels of consumption were compared. On the contrary, these overall parities are one of the *results* of the entire study. Regarding the parities for individual groups and subgroups, they are both a necessary element and an outcome of the entire calculating procedure.

   The overall parities may be useful for various calculations. For example, since the structure of consumption changes slowly, using them we may compare the level of consumption in 'neighbouring' years with a minimum of other figures and calculations.

5. Incidentally, this exchange rate changes slower than the dollar drops under the influence of inflation. Is this not an indirect admission of fast inflation in the Soviet Union? Or, as D. Epstein noted to me, it can be caused by overevaluation.

6. In 1976, the level of consumption in these countries, relative to the US, measured in so-called international dollars, was: Italy 46 per cent,

United Kingdom 58 per cent, Japan 54 per cent, and France 72 per cent [19].

7. In 1976, foodstuffs accounted for more than 53 per cent of total trade turnover (*Narkhoz-77*, p. 457). In Table 4.1, the share of food in the total amount of goods is almost 8 percentage points higher. In part this is due to consumption of 'own' food, which does not figure into trade turnover. Collective farm markets also play some role here.

8. I did not include the figures for Hungary in Table 4.2 because they do not seem trustworthy.

9. *Narkhoz-80*, p. 42. The population grew by 9.3 per cent during this time and national income ('utilized for consumption and accumulation') by 55 per cent; so the share of personal consumption in the latter should have declined, but it grew (ibid., p. 380). Of course, there was no such growth, and the figures were obtained by some statistical tricks, primarily with prices. According to the same official data (ibid., p. 439), the index of retail prices for alcoholic beverages, 1977 as a percentage of 1970, was 103 per cent – obvious nonsense.

According to the calculations of a well-known economist who has worked in USSR Gosplan for years, V. V. Kossov, during 1966–78 the average annual growth in the supply of food, clothing, and footwear to the population was 1.8 per cent, and housing 1.6 per cent (his calculations were, of course, based upon official data, and the structure of trade turnover in 1965 was taken as 'weights') – *Ekonomika i matematicheskiye metody*, 1980, no. 1, p. 74.

In sum, there is no way to get 46 per cent for the 1970s.

10. In fact, considering that, first, the USSR lags behind the US by much more than one-third (all this is shown in detail below) and second, that the actual rates of growth of per capita consumption in the USSR in recent decades were lower than the official data show, the overall gap cannnot be bridged, even in decades.

11. *StAb-78*, p. 465; *Economic Report of the President*, January, 1980, p. 232, says that 9.4 per cent of all families and 25 per cent of all singles were below the poverty level.

Defining this level is in itself open to debate. Not long ago the media reported that the methodology of the calculation is not correct since food stamps, free medical care, and housing subsidies are not included in the income of the poor. So, the real level of poverty differs from the official statistics (*Washington Post*, 15 April 1982, p. A1).

12. *StAb-78*, p. 465.

13. Ibid., pp. 268, 440.

14. The incomes of most of the US poor are not far below the poverty level. In 1976, less than 30 per cent of the poor had incomes that did not exceed one-half of this level (U.S. Census Bureau, *Current Population Reports, Consumer Income*, Series P-60, no. 115, July 1978, p. 8).

5 Food

1. The rational norms do not always coincide in various Soviet sources.

See, for example, T. S. Khachaturov, *et al.*, *Voprosy ekonomicheskogo rosta SSSR*, M., 1976, p. 48, and also *Planovoye khozyaystvo*, 1981, no. 10, p. 117. The most detailed and recent publication of the norms is S. V. Donskova and N. Ya. Ibragimova (eds), *Ekonomika pishchevoy promyshlennosti*, M., 1981, pp. 40–41. The norms here are about the same as those in Table 5.2. Of interest is that the norms are given by republic, and there are sharp differences between them. In particular, the consumption norms for all products except vegetable oil, bread, fruits and vegetables are substantially lower in Central Asian republics.

2. Hopefully the authors did not exclude fats from the Soviet amount of pork. The American data they used apparently fully include pork fat (see Chapter 6).

3. In the words of V. Rakitskiy, (*Sotsial'naya programma pyatiletki i obraz zhizni sovetskikh lyudey*, M., 1976, p. 25) 'if we calculate in existing prices, the monthly food needs according to rational norms are: 55 rubles for a worker engaged in light work, 106 rubles for one involved in heavy work or an athlete, 46 rubles for a pensioner, 48 rubles for a school child, and 34 rubles for a preschool child.' We can compare these figures with the fact that, according to the CIA study, the actual per capita monthly expenditure on food was R45.5.

4. In particular, to consider the differences in packaging, the American prices of all food products were reduced by 5 per cent. Practically all food sold in America is packaged. The authors cite data from the Soviet literature that only 26 per cent of food products sold are packaged [8]: it seems that even this is an exaggeration (see below). Furthermore, the US prices of fruits and vegetables were reduced by 10–15 per cent, and of meat and meat products by 15–20 per cent [34].

5. There is a figure for the Soviet markup in the CIA study [44] but not for the American. The total sum paid by consumers for restaurant meals is given [45], but it apparently does not include alcohol. I determined the American markup using data from the 1972 input–output table for the US. At that time total population expenditures for restaurants were $48.8 billion, including expenditures of $21 billion for the food itself, its transport, etc. (The data were given to me by Jack Alterman.) So, the markup was 57 per cent of all expenditures for restaurants (14 per cent in the USSR). Below (Table 5.5) I use this figure, 57 per cent, for rough estimates of shares of the markup in American expenditures in subgroups.

    Understandably, my calculations are very rough. Note in particular that American consumption statistics do not take into account business expenditures in restaurants, but the corresponding amount is about a quarter of all expenditures for restaurants.

6. Here are the basic statistics on public dining. First, for the USSR. In 1976 there were a total of 280 700 'enterprises of public dining', including 238 factory kitchens, 169 000 cafeterias and restaurants, and 111 500 snack bars and buffets. The overwhelming majority of these 'enterprises' were in plants (53 000), schools (63 000), etc. Only 66 500 were 'not connected with serving a definite contingent' (in other terminology, 'open to the public'); another 7000 were in airports and railroad stations

and 6000 were in parks. The average number of employees per 'enterprise' was 8.7, and the average yearly amount of sales (including the value of goods) was R73 000 (*Narkhoz-76*, pp. 548–9, 557, 561). The last figures say that the largest part of these 'enterprises' are small. Note also that snack bars and buffets account for almost 40 per cent of all 'enterprises'. Regarding restaurants, the Ministry of Railroads admits (*Literaturnaya gazeta*, 23 December 1981, p. 12) that restaurants and buffets at small stations became places of drinking for the locals. But even without the Ministry and *Literaturnaya gazeta* we know that Soviet restaurants are primarily a place for drinking.

In 1976, 166 'courses' per capita were served (*Narkhoz-77*, p. 463). If we assume that one customer eats 2.5 courses, then during the year each person was served a little more than once a week.

On the average each 'enterprise' served 1091 people, and each that was 'open to the public' served 3200.

The overwhelming part of the entire network served school children, college students, and industrial enterprise workers. However, in 1975 only 50 per cent of all school children, 67 per cent of college students, and 63.7 per cent of industrial enterprise workers had public dining available (V. G. Bychkov, *Obshchestvennoye pitaniye i aktual'nyye voprosy ego razvitiya*, M., 1978, pp. 42, 65, 72).

Finally, in 1975 there were a total of 6872 restaurants and (in 1976) 355 in Moscow (ibid., p. 18, and *Moskva v tsifrakh, 1917–1977*, M., p. 109).

The reader should not be confused by the term 'restaurant'. In Russian it means (especially in recent years) a very expensive place, usually with live music where some specialties of higher quality and alcohol are served. Only they can be compared with American regular public dining facilities. In other 'places of eating' the quality of food is hardly tolerable.

With respect to the US, in 1977 there were 368 066 'eating and drinking places', including 93 729 'drinking places' (the distinction is made on the basis of the predominant share in total receipts). The ratio of population per eating and drinking place was 589, i.e. less than 20 per cent of that for the USSR. In this main (see below) portion of American restaurants, cafeterias, and bars, there were 15 million seats, which is simply incomparable with the corresponding Soviet facilities. An average of 10.2 persons worked in each American 'enterprise', which, given American technology, standardisation and self-service, fully explains why a customer waits for a waiter in the USSR for hours. Average annual total sales per 'enterprise' amounted to $172 000 (*StAb-79*, pp. 835–6, and US Bureau of the Census, *1977 Census of Retail Trade*, 1981, vol. 1, pp. 1–24, 2–23 and A-10).

In examining all these figures the reader must consider the fact that because of certain features of American statistics a significant number of eating and drinking places' are not accounted for. In particular, a 'place' subordinated to some firm that is engaged primarily in another activity is not counted. Thus, restaurants and cafes located in hotels are not counted unless they are operated separately on a lease basis. The same applies to cafeterias in large stores, etc. This pertains also to school, college or enterprise cafeterias. (See US Bureau of the Census, *1977 Industry and Product Classification Manual*, 1977.) An indirect indication of the possible underestimation is that in 1977 only a part of hotels and motels sold $5 billion worth of food and drink. This amount is not included in the figures given above (US Bureau of the Census, *1977 Census of Service Industries*, SC77-S-2, p. 2–15).

7.   Here is the calculation. According to Table·5.4 Soviet consumption can be equated to 34 units and American to 100 units. We decrease these figures by 5 and 20 per cent. Then Soviet consumption is equal to $(34 \times 0.95) \div (100 \times 0.8) = 40.4$ per cent of American. And the correlation in kilograms is (Table 5.1) $46 \div 118 = 39$ per cent. Hence, the quality of Soviet meat is $40.4 \div 39 = 103.5$ per cent of American.

8.   It would not be bad if public dining were singled out into an individual subgroup and examined as a separate service. There would be difficulties in selecting the corresponding sample goods and comparing their quality in both countries in order to establish price ratios, but they are surmountable.

9.   There is a fundamental difference in including public dining services and trade services in comparisons of consumption. Trade services are a direct component of the prices used in calculating price ratios, but the markups are not included in prices compared. We will discuss trade services in Chapter 12.

10.   In addition to what is mentioned in the notes to Table 5.5, I will say that there is no real substantiation for distributing the total amount of the markup for individual subgroups proportionally to expenditures on food itself in these subgroups. It was done this way simply because no other method is evident.

11.   On the one hand, as we saw in Table 4.1, food expenditures composed almost one half of all Soviet consumption spending, and only 20 per cent of American expenditures (in the currencies of the corresponding countries). On the other hand, given the incredible American choice, a small change in eating habits (and not necessarily for the worse) can make it much cheaper. And, of course, Americans who do not have enough money for food are given food stamps.

12.   It is difficult to say why just in the spring of 1982 a campaign was waged against pet dogs and cats. But one of the arguments given was 'dog owners buy thousands of tons of food products for them in stores. This reduces trade resources intended for the satisfaction of the population's needs for these products.' (*Trud*, 14 May 1982, p. 4.)

13.   The report of the special Plenum of the CPSU Central Committee on agriculture at the end of May 1982 has just arrived. Judging from the measures adopted, no improvement in the food situation is anticipated.

14.   Lokshin, p. 90.

15.   *Literaturnaya gazeta*, 3 February 1982, p. 12. The article does not say how many beer plants were checked, but there are many hundreds of them.

16.   Already in Gogol's *Inspector General* merchants were cheating their customers.

17.   According to Lokshin's data (pp. 111, 117, 137), in 1976 the shares of

products packaged in retail trade included 1 per cent of eggs, 30 per cent of meat, 2 per cent of fish products, 19 per cent of sour cream, 20 per cent of vegetable oil, 10 per cent of animal fats, and 10 per cent of fruits and vegetables. Even these figures, especially for meat and also for fruits and vegetables, are questionable.

6 Food (Continued)

1. *StAb-78*, p. 126.
2. V. G. Yusupov, *Osnovy ekonomiki truda i proizvodstva na predpriyatiyakh pishchevoy promyshlennosti*, M., 1977, p. 94.
3. N. V. Vinogradov and V. V. Vasil'yev (eds) *Ekonomika pishchevoy promyshlennosti SSSR*, M., 1976, p. 248. According to S. V. Donskova, N.Ya. Ibragimova, *et al.* (eds), *Ekonomika pishchevoy promyshlennosti*, 1981, p. 22, the bakery industry itself produces less than 80 per cent of the bread consumed in the country.
4. Professor Alec Nove says: 'In Europe bread is bought every day, in America once a week. Therefore, bread is baked here so that at the end of the week it will be just as bad as at the beginning.'
5. Here and just below, data are from Lokshin, pp. 85, 87, 89, 91.
6. According to Lokshin, 5–6 kg of bread a year per capita, or perhaps more, is used to feed livestock.
7. In 1976 the sown areas were smaller than in 1913 for millet (by 15 per cent) and buckwheat (by a third), *Narkhoz-77*, p. 224. Even if yield grew, the population also increased by 60 per cent, hence the per capita consumption of buckwheat and millet *fell in comparison with 1913*. According to *Vestnik statistiki*, 1977, no. 9, p. 92, state purchases of buckwheat in 1976 amounted to 421 000 tons, i.e. 1.6 kg per capita.
8. *Narkhoz-77*, p. 191.
9. *StAb-78*, p. 126.
10. *StAb-78*, p. 126. The use of corn in breakfast cereals is not separated here from total figures on corn flour. The figure seems too low.
11. According to *Narkhoz-80*, p. 405, per capita meat consumption did not change between 1975 and 1980. The Soviet population would decisively disagree with this: complaints increased sharply, and difficulties with meat are openly admitted now in the press. This also contradicts other data in the same yearbook – the volume of production of meat did not change during these years but the population grew by 5 per cent. Foreign trade covered no more than half of this difference. In 1975, 0.5 m. tons of meat and meat products were imported and in 1980 only 0.3 m. tons more (*SEV-81*, p. 390).

   The population is not threatened with a rapid growth of meat production. Even if the current Five-Year Plan is fulfilled (it is already clear that this will not happen), agriculture will have increased deliveries of meat and milk products by 7–8 per cent, and this is not per capita but overall (*Ekonomika sel'skogo khozyaystva*, 1981, no. 10, p. 35).
12. The authors do not give the average prices of beef and chicken.

However, an estimate based on their price list [40] shows that they took the ratio for the US to be about 2:1. In fact, retail prices of chicken were 43 per cent of the price of beef (*StAb-78*, p. 706).

13.   In some instances we may speak of the impact of tradition on the attitude of consumers, but obviously this is a case of the impact of prices and not tradition.

Traditions hardly pertain to the following. When Carter announced the grain embargo, reacting to the invasion of Afghanistan, the newspapers quickly and correctly explained that the embargo would affect Soviet consumption of meat first and most. A very visible and very liberal senator said that the embargo should be removed since it would not have an effect anyway: 'Having no meat, they will switch to chicken.'

14.   Times change even in the USSR. The production of all types of meat excluding poultry grew by 66 per cent between 1960 and 1980, and poultry by 163 per cent. In 1980 poultry accounted already for 14 per cent, instead of 10 per cent, of all meat and poultry combined (*Narkhoz-80*, p. 249).

15.   *Narkhoz-77*, pp. 191, 196; *SEV-81*, p. 113.

16.   S. F. Antonov, *Myasnaya i molochnaya promyshlennost' SSSR*, M., 1976, p. 17.

17.   Ibid., p. 43.

18.   V. G. Bychkov, *Obshchestvennoye pitaniye i aktual'nyye voprosy ego razvitiya*, M., 1978, p. 15. Such a high share is an exception. For all other products the share of public dining is lower, and overall public dining sales of all foodstuffs accounted for less than 17 per cent of retail trade turnover.

19.   *Narkhoz-77*, pp. 208, 265. Here and below, in determining the volume of sales in collective farm markets, for lack of data I ignore the sales by collective and state farms to their own workers.

20.   Let us approximate how many years it would take the USSR to catch up to the US in meat consumption per capita in kilograms, i.e. without considering quality. If we accept Soviet official data as they are published, then in 1980 per capita consumption was 57 kg compared with 41 kg in 1965 (*Narkhoz-80*, p. 405). In other words, per capita consumption of meat and meat products in 1980 was 61 kg less than in the US in 1976 (Table 5.1). Hence, if meat production in the USSR grows at the same rate as in 1965–80, reaching the 1976 American level of consumption would require $61 \div (57 - 41) \times 15 = 57$ years. The actual situation is much worse. If Soviet meat consumption is put in a form comparable to the US, i.e. excluding fats and 'subproducts', it would require 81 years. I repeat, this is based upon official Soviet data, ignoring quality, and also not taking into account that imports of meat grew by 2 kg per capita during 1965–80 (*SEV-78*, p. 381, and *SEV-81*, p. 390). Comparison with 1960 would give 79 instead of 57 years.

21.   Since 1977, the 'catch of fish, sea animals, whales, and sea products' in millions of tons has begun to decline, and in 1980 amounted to only 90 per cent of the 1976 level. Per capita consumption of fish and fish products fell by 8 per cent during this period (*Narkhoz-80*, pp. 192, 405).

22.   However, in 1976 per capita expenditures on herring were a little more

than R1, i.e. there was less than 1 kg of herring per capita. Note also that per capita consumption of herring in rubles in 1976 had fallen to 36 per cent of the 1965 level (*Narkhoz-77*, p. 458).

23. *StAb-78*, p. 126.
24. I did not find the corresponding 'direct' citations, but this is obvious. Indirectly this is said in *SEV-74*, p. 452: 'Fish and fish products are counted in market weight (*tovarnyy ves*). Also indirectly, it is proved by the fact that no textbook on the fishing industry mentions conversions to "edible weight".'
25. *StAb-78*, p. 742. About two-thirds of this is imports. One other point is worth noting. Examination of another handbook reveals that, in addition to everything else, Americans eat about 2 kg of fish per capita a year that is caught by sportsmen (*AgSt-80*, pp. 554, 556) – but the figure seems high.
   I do not think that the catch in the USSR is so great on a per capita basis.
26. *StAb-78*, p. 743.
27. In 1976, 6.3 m. standard cans of canned crab were exported (*VT-76*, p. 30); consumption within the country could hardly have been larger.
28. *StAb-78*, p. 743.
29. Ibid. and *SEV-81*, p. 113. According to Lokshin (p. 108), in 1972–4, mackerel and the like, and small fish such as *khamsa* and sprats accounted for up to 70 per cent of all fish. He speaks of the insufficient supply of cod and lancet, and does not even mention tuna.
   Those who wish to delve further into fish consumption should note that the Soviet statistics give three different figures. For 1970 they are: the catch of fish, sea animals, whales, and sea products – 7.8 m. tons (*Narkhoz-77*, p. 191); the catch of fish for food – 5.1 m. tons (N. P. Sysoyev, *Ekonomika rybnoy promyshlennosti SSSR*, M., 1972, p. 12); and the actual sales in state and retail trade – 3.593 m. tons (Lokshin, p. 107). Only the last figure characterises real consumption.
30. In itself this fact looks suspicious. The reader should take into account that in calculating these figures I encountered some uncertainties with the authors' data and it is possible that I overcame them incorrectly. On the other hand, if I understated the percentage of the markup here, the amount of the understatement is distributed among all goods.
31. *Narkhoz-77*, pp. 208, 259. This calculation, of course, is too rough, because a part of commodity output (*tovarnaya produktsiya*) is left in the countryside.
32. Yu. Markish brought this to my attention.
33. Calculated according to *Narkhoz-77*, p. 259, and *AgSt-80*, p. 369. The reference here is not to consumption but precisely to production. Consumption in the USSR in this year was 316 kg (*Narkhoz-77*, p. 430), i.e. 90.6 per cent of production.
34. The milk yield of one cow in the USSR in 1976 was 2179 kg and in the US 4935 kg (*Narkhoz-77*, p. 267, and *AgSt-80*, p. 363). However, these data must be corrected in favour of American cows (and people) for the fat content of milk.
35. The Soviet literature is silent about the fat content of milk in published

data. Certainly, we can still find something in Lokshiñ (p. 107) who speaks of the 'normalized content of fat in milk' as 3.2 per cent. The same is said in *Molochnaya promyshlennost'*, 1980, no. 2, p. 10, and in *Bol'shaya Sovetskaya entsiklopediya*, 3rd edition, vol. 16, p. 482. Apparently (this is especially evident in the last source) this pertains to the standard fat content of milk sold in retail trade but not to the production of milk or its procurement. The SEV yearbook limits itself to a skilful statement: 'The conversion of litres of milk to kilograms is made on the basis of coefficients meeting the conditions of each country' (*SEV-81*, p. 453). In the same yearbook (pp. 255, 267), data on milk production on state and collective farms (there are no data on milk production on private plots or for the country as a whole) are given in two lines – one is simply milk and the other is a conversion to a fat content of 3.5 per cent. The figures in the two lines are practically the same for various years. There is no such 'two-line accounting' for the other countries in the SEV yearbooks.

Possibly, the milk production on collective and state farms is counted at a fat content of 3.5 per cent, while milk from private plots is not even converted to an equivalent in fat content. The latter in 1976 provided about 30 per cent of total milk production (*Narkhoz-77*, p. 258), but their share of procurement amounted to only 5 per cent of the total procured (*Narkhoz-76*, p. 288). Various manipulations are quite easily possible here.

In sum, we do not have sufficient material for a confident statement, but it very much seems like the actual average fat content of milk is substantially lower than 3.2 per cent.

36. *AgSt-80*, p. 363. In other years the fat content was usually higher, and it was never lower during the past 15 years.

37. Lokshin, p. 111. That these data can be trusted is evident from the fact that in the same year 565 000 tons of cheese and *brynza* was produced (*Narkhoz-75*, p. 297).

38. *Narkhoz-77*, pp. 191, 608; Lokshin, p. 107.

39. *Narkhoz-77*, pp. 458, 460.

40. As we already saw above, this is not quite so, but, on the other hand, we are ignoring collective farm trade here, and greater accuracy in this calculation is not needed.

41. Lokshin, p. 107; *Narkhoz-77*, p. 191; *StAb-78*, p. 126.

42. *AgSt-80*, pp. 363, 369.

43. *Narkhoz-77*, p. 430, and *AgSt-78*, p. 367.

44. *AgSt-80*, p. 148. I did not discover data on the production of mayonnaise in the US, though it is very popular here. In 1975, Soviet production of mayonnaise was 0.3 kg per capita (V. D. Ivanov, *Nekotoryye itogi raboty pishchevoy promyshlennosti SSSR za 1965–1975 gg. i zadachi na 1976–1980 gg.*, M., TsNITEIpishcheprom, 1977, p. 21).

45. *Narkhoz-76*, pp. 257, 511. According to Lokshin (p. 115), 11 per cent of butter was used in producing other food products. According to V. D. Ivanov, *Nekotoryye . . .*, p. 18, the per capita production of margarine products in 1976 was 4 kg.

46. Lokshin helps us again by reporting (p. 115) that the retail price of one kilogram of salt-free butter was R3.60.
47. *StAb-78*, p. 126.
48. I avoid reference to Table 5.5 since the estimate of the markup for fats for the USSR that we got there is obviously incorrect. None the less, the 'quality' of American fats still turned out to be worse than Soviet in calculations based upon calories. Possibly, the high share of butter in the USSR had an effect here.
49. According to *Ekonomika sel'skogo khozyaystva*, 1981, no. 10, p. 32, about 15 per cent of the gross harvest of potatoes and 20 per cent of vegetables are lost. This is obviously incorrect for potatoes (several years ago *Literaturnaya Gazeta* reported that only half of all potatoes reach the consumer) so not much trust should be put in the data for vegetables either. In *Razvitiye proizvoditel'nykh sil sel'skogo khozyaystva*, M., 1981, p. 104, A. I. Okhrimchuk states: 'In the production process 12–20 per cent of output is lost, and en route from production to consumption 15–30 per cent is lost.' Note that losses of vegetables should be the greatest. In the words of F. S. Cheremisov (*Resursy prodovol'stvennykh tovarov i ikh ispol'zovaniye*, p. 30) 'the problem of storing fresh cabbage has still not been solved to date', and losses during long-term storage reach 25 per cent. We should also remember that in the USSR cabbage comprises more than one-third of all vegetables and that, even at the moment when it is put into long-term storage, much cabbage has already been lost. Losses of tomatoes are especially huge.

   In *Kachestvo produktsii i ego stimulirovaniye*, Kishinev, 1979, p. 139, R. Khalitov writes 'losses of the agricultural harvest from the field to the consumer, taking into account the reduction in quality, amount to no less than 50 per cent for vegetables in Moldavia'.

   Finally, none other than the chairman of the Scientific Council for Economic, Social, and Legal Problems of the Agro-Industrial Complex of the USSR Academy of Sciences, V. Tikhonov, said recently 'in harvesting, transporting, storing, and industrial processing, we lose about one-fifth of the gross harvest of grain, vegetables, and fruit-berry crops' (*Sotsialisticheskaya industriya*, 9 April 1982, p. 3).
50. An attentive examination of Table 6.3 leaves several questions. On the basis of personal impressions, the difference for tomatoes, which are eaten year-round here, seems small; on the other hand, it is not very clear why 40 per cent more onions should be eaten in America.
51. *Narkhoz-77*, pp. 458–60; Lokshin, p. 128.
52. I take into account that Soviet statistics might somewhat *understate* the production of vegetables on private plots. However, losses of vegetables are indeed huge.
53. This percentage of losses is obtained by direct calculations (see Table 6.4). Here is another calculation. In *Narkhoz-77*, p. 430, total consumption of fruit, including table grapes, is 39 kg per capita. Grapes are not shown separately here. According to Lokshin (p. 132), per capita consumption of fresh grapes in 1973 was 2.3 kg. The production of grape wine in 1976 increased in comparison with 1973 significantly more than

the gross grape harvest and procurements (*Narkhoz-75*, pp. 297, 381, 393; *Narkhoz-77*, pp. 191, 243, 244); therefore consumption of fresh grapes could not have increased. The total harvest of fruits and berries in 1976 was 9.8 m. tons and imports were 0.8 m. tons (*Narkhoz-77*, p. 243; *VT-76*, p. 43 – excluding grapes in both cases). Thus, we get a total of 44 kg per person. However, we did not take into account the production of fruit and berry wines, which in 1975 (there are no data for 1976) amounted to 1.1 billion litres. *Izvestiya* says (11 September 1982, p. 3) that 330 000 tons of apples are used for this production annually, saying nothing about other fruits. Therefore, in determining the per capita consumption of fruits, the Soviet statisticians could hardly have taken losses to be more than 10 per cent.

In the work cited above, *Kachestvo produktsii i evo stimulirovaniye*, p. 139, Khalitov states that in Moldavia fruit losses amount to 40–50 per cent, and for grapes they are 15–20 per cent.

According to official data, fruit and berry consumption increased by 2 kg after 1976 to 41 kg in 1977–8, and then fell to 38 kg in 1979 and 34 kg in 1980 (*Narkhoz-80*, p. 405). Perhaps production did not actually fall by so much but they began to account for losses better?

54.   Including grapes. *Narkhoz-76*, p. 322.
55.   It looks very strange that apparently fewer apples and pears were consumed in the US than in the USSR. Apples are eaten here year round, and all sorts of jams, jellies, and juices are made from them; apple pie is a symbol of America. The American superiority of only two times for 'fruits with pits' also looks understated, and it is impossible to believe that more grapes are eaten per capita in the USSR (even considering that a lot of raisins are eaten in Central Asia).
56.   There are many examples of this. The basic one is the undercounting in American statistics of fruit grown for non-commercial use. For example, *StAb-78*, pp. 772, gives apple production as 13.5 kg per capita and specially mentions that this includes production in only 34 states, and only orchards with at least 100 apple trees. '*Outlook . . .*' gives a smaller per capita production, without any explanatory notes. One might get the impression from *StAb-78*, pp. 460, 869, that banana consumption in the US is very low, etc.
57.   There are no data for the USSR on consumption of fresh fruits and berries. Lokshin (p. 129) says that trade sold about 2 m. tons in 1974, which is about 13.3 kg per urban resident a year, or 257 g a week. To this must be added, of course, fruit purchases in collective farm markets, but some part of total sales goes in the opposite direction, to the countryside.
58.   *Narkhoz-77*, p. 196, and *VT-76*, p. 43; USDA, *Outlook and Situation, Fruit*, July, 1981, pp. 34, 36.
59.   How many years will it take for the USSR to reach the per capita level of American fruit consumption in 1976? I already said that the official consumption of fruit in the USSR declined in 1979–80. We will ignore this. In 1965–78 per capita consumption grew by 13 kg and reached 41 kg (*Narkhoz-80*, p. 405). As we saw in Table 6.4, per capita consumption in the US in 1976 was 103 kg. Hence, if the production and consumption of fruit in the USSR continues to grow as in 1965–78, the

1976 American level will be reached in 62 years. If we take the 1980 production, 34 kg, this level will be reached only after 172 years.

60. Indeed, total retail sales of potatoes excluding cooperative trade sales amounted to R821 m. in 1976, i.e. 8.2 m. tons. In markets, 6.2 m. tons were sold (*Narkhoz-77*, pp. 208, 210, 458, 460), i.e. all in all, the urban population ate 14.4 m. tons. The rest is arithmetic.

61. *Narkhoz-77*, p. 430. Incidentally, the consumption of potatoes fell back to the level of 1913 (112 kg) only in 1980 (*Narkhoz-80*, p. 429), but it is well known that in 1980 (and not in 1913) it was difficult to buy potatoes in many places.

62. In 1976, 666 m. standard jars of jelly and jam were produced in the USSR (*Narkhoz-77*, p. 196). One standard jar equals 400 g. Imports of jam were 10 m. standard jars (*VT-76*, p. 43). The total is 1.1 kg per capita a year. I did not discover American data.

63. Total per capita production of confectionery goods (excluding the output of public dining enterprises) in 1976 was 13 kg (*Narkhoz-77*, p. 191). In 1975 enterprises of the Ministry of the Food Industry produced per capita 2.3 kg of caramels, 0.4 kg of chocolate and chocolate products, 0.6 kg of taffy, 0.4 kg of halvah, 2.3 kg of cookies (including 136 g of butter cookies), 0.5 kg of cakes and pies, 0.5 kg of wafers, and 0.8 kg of confections in boxes (Ivanov, *Nekotoryye . . .*, p. 25).

64. Lokshin, p. 121.

65. *AgSt-80*, pp. 97, 264; *Vestnik statistiki*, 1977, no. 9, p. 93.

66. Items consumed in the USSR include vinegar, mustard (only one type), cayenne, black pepper, and horseradish. According to *Literaturnaya Gazeta*, 7 July 1982, p. 12, clove, cinnamon, cardamom, nutmeg, and many other spices 'have not been in the stores for about 15 years and are sold in markets for exorbitant (*ludoyedskiye*) prices'.

In the US the list of the most varied spices, seasonings, herbs, sauces, etc., numbers in many dozens if not hundreds of items.

7 Food (Conclusion)

1. *Narkhoz-77*, p. 191.

2. It was planned to increase production during the last Five-Year Plan to 845 m. decalitres, i.e. to 32 litres per capita. It was anticipated that in the future (how far in the future they did not say) in Moscow, Leningrad, Minsk, Vilnius, Tallin, Riga, and the resorts on the coast of the Black Sea, per capita consumption would reach 150 litres a year, and in other capitals of union republics, 100 litres (V. E. Balashov, *Povysheniye effektivnosti pivovarennogo proizvodstva*, M., 1979, p. 7). Actually beer production began to drop in 1979–80 and in 1980 amounted only to as much as in 1976, i.e. 23 litres per capita (*Narkhoz-80*, p. 193).

In 1975, beer consumption per capita was (in litres per year) 56 in Leningrad, 47 in Estonia, 41 in Lithuania, 46 in Moscow, 27 in the

Ukraine, 21 in the Ural and Volga Regions, 19 in Kazakhstan, 17 in Central Asia, etc. (Balashav, *Povysheniye . . .*, pp. 11–12).

In 1975 less than half of all beer was sold in bottles (the rest in kegs; there is no beer in cans in the USSR), I. D. Ivanov, *Nekotoryye itogi raboty pishchevoy promyshlennosti SSSR za 1965–1975 gg. i zadachi na 1976–1980 gg*, M., TsNIITEIpishcheprom, 1977, p. 16.

3. *StAb-78*, pp. 8, 823. Per capita consumption of alcohol in the US is given for persons 18 and older.

4. V. G. Yusupov, *Osnovy ekonomiki truda i proizvodstva na predpriya-tiyakh pishchevoy promyshlennosti*, M., 1977, p. 143.

5. *Narkhoz-77*, p. 191. In 1970, 12 per cent of all grape wine produced was dry wine (Ivanov, *Nekotoryye . . .*, p. 11).

6. I. N. Zayats *et al.*, *Ekonomika, organizatsiya i planirovaniye vinodel'ches-kogo proizvodstva*, M., 1979, p. 23. I. D. Ivanov (p. 13) speaks of production in 1975 of only 277 m. decalitres of grape wine and 115 m. decalitres of fruit and berry wine. He apparently is taking into account only enterprises subordinated to the Ministry of the Food Industry (see his figures for 1970, p. 11).

7. *VT-76*, pp. 31, 44. In 1976, the import–export balance increased some-what.

8. *Narkhoz-76*, p. 322.

9. *StAb-78*, pp. 8, 823. Nothing is said here of fruit and berry wine, but presumably it is included. Only sparkling wine is given separately – 370 g per capita.

10. *Narkhoz-77*, pp. 191, 243. The explanation: state procurement was 27 per cent of the total harvest in 1940 and almost 81 per cent in 1976 (ibid., p. 224). But this must mean that the share of home wine production decreased.

11. *Narkhoz-62*, p. 203. Although it is not stated here, obviously vodka is taken which has an alcohol content of 40 per cent. For spirits it is stated (p. 672) that it is counted in 'decaliters of water-free 100 per cent raw spirits'.

12. This is amost as much per capita as was produced in 1913 in Russia – 55 m. decalitres of ethyl alcohol and 119 m. decalitres of vodka, i.e. 7.5 litres per capita (M. T. Kochubeyeva, *Ekonomika, organizatsiya i planir-ovaniye spirtovogo i likero-vodochnogo proizvodstva*, M., 1977, pp. 19–20).

13. *Narkhoz-69*, p. 266.

14. Kochubeyeva, *Ekonomika . . .*, pp. 58–9, 95.

15. Lokshin, p. 80.

16. In 1975 (there are no data for 1976), 7.3 m. decalitres of cognac were produced (Zayats *et al.*, *Ekonomika . . .*, p. 23), and the foreign trade balance (including rum) was another 2.5 m. decalitres (*VT-76*, pp. 31, 44).

17. *StAb-78*, pp. 8, 823.

18. *Molodoy kommunist*, 1980, no. 2, p. 65. This figure is, of course, horrible, but in Washington in 1981 per capita consumption was almost 22.5 litres of pure alcohol, i.e., more than in this Soviet town. True, this is the highest figure in the US, and a lot of alcohol is not for permanent

residents of the capital itself, but all the same . . . (*The Washington Post*, 8 Sept. 1982, p. C11).

19. *Trud*, 17 October 1981, p. 2.

20. *Ekonomika i organizatsiya promyshlennogo proizvodstva*, 1981, no. 3, p. 167.

21. Some sovietologists assert that the number of non-drinking Muslims should affect the per capita consumption of alcohol. This is not quite so. The Tatars, Bashkiry and some other Muslims are fully Russified in this respect. Among the Uzbeks, Azerbaijani, etc., it is primarily the elderly that do not drink. And the Uzbeks, Kazakhs, Azerbaijani, Tadzhiks, Turkmens and Kirghizi amounted to less then 12 per cent of the entire population according to the 1979 census (*Narkhoz-79*, p. 29).

22. This is what I get with our figures. The CIA study gives somewhat different indicators [8,12].

23. *Ekonomika . . .*, 1974, no. 4, p. 37.

24. A friend of mine just (September, 1982) returned from one of his periodic trips to Moscow. He says that previously he had never seen so many drunks, including women, on the streets at any time of the day.

25. Moreover, it very well may be that a certain amount of vodka, especially 'drinking spirits', is produced directly at plants making spirits.

26. Alec Nove attracted my attention to the following data. According to the yearbooks, the sales of 'alcoholic beverages' are growing (in comparable prices) very fast. In 1976, sales were: 630 per cent compared to 1940, 225 per cent compared to 1965, and 143 per cent compared to 1970 (*Narkhoz-76*, p. 508). It is quite likely that this indicator is growing fast because of the evidently wrong official index of prices for alcohol – in 1976, 1.035 times the 1965 price, and 1.019 times the 1970 price (ibid., p. 554).

 On the other hand, the indicator depends on the share of beer and wine in total alcoholic beverage sales.

27. US Bureau of the Census, *Social Indicators*, 1976, p. LXXX. Incidentally, the consumption of pure alcohol in the US was then substantially, by one-fourth, lower than the figure I got for 1976. The handbook confirms the growth of alcohol consumption after 1969, but not at the same rate. Apparently, in my calculation of pure alcohol, I overstated the alcohol content of beer and/or wine.

28. The price of American alcohol that the CIA used seems low [43], which should lead to an overstatement of American consumption.

29. It will not hurt to remind the reader that there are different aspects of alcohol consumption. As is well known, the sale of vodka was one of the best income producers in the Russian budget (R. Pipes wrote about this once again in *Russia Under the Old Regime*). The Soviet state budget in 1976 drew about a tenth of its revenue from general drunkenness.

30. I. D. Ivanov, *Nekotoryye . . .*, pp. 14, 32.

31. In *Ekonomika . . .*, p. 255, S. V. Donskova and N. Ya. Ibragimova say that the production of non-alcoholic beverages is insignificant in Uzbekistan, Azerbaijan, Kirghiziya, Tadzhikistan, and several regions of Kazakhstan. *Sovetskaya Rossiya*, 3 June 1981, p. 2, cites the workers of 'Rospivoprom' who say: 'Nonalcoholic beverages are seasonal business.

They are drunk in summer but not much in winter. They are produced accordingly. In fact, full capacity is needed for only three months of the year and then only in good weather.' However, the newspaper's team discovered that in various cities of Russia equipment does not work, there are no packaging materials, and the population's demand is not satisfied.

A lot of *kompot* and the like is drunk in the USSR, homemade *kvas* is consumed, but all of the products used in making these drinks are counted in other subgroups.

32. *StAb-78*, p. 823. I try to avoid judgements about the authors' data for the US, but here I am amazed at how, given this figure, they got total per capita consumption in retail prices of only $53.63 [20]. Note here that the markup on public dining for non-alcoholic beverages is also very high – 51 per cent (Table 5.5).

33. *StAb-78*, p. 884; *VT-76*, p. 42. I could be a little mistaken. American consumption is given on a 'green coffee' basis, and there is no indication of how Soviet imports are given.

34. *StAb-78*, p. 126; I. D. Ivanov, *Nekotoryye* ..., p. 14. The harvest of tea leaves increased a little in 1976 (*Narkhoz-77*, p. 224), and the import–export balance fell somewhat.

35. *SEV-81*, p. 115, *VT-76*, p. 44; *StAb-78*, pp. 8, 824. Of total Soviet imports in 1976, 111 m. cigarettes were bought from the US (*VT-76*, p. 304). It is necessary to recalculate per capita consumption of tobacco in the US, since it (like alcohol) is given in terms of the population 18 and older.

36. V. G. Yusupov, *Osnovy* ..., p. 197.

37. My calculating procedure allows one to compare corrected Soviet consumption in rubles (487) with American (1092-Table 4.1), and Soviet consumption in dollars (651-Table 4.1) with corrected American (1506). The result is: 487: 1092 = 44.6 per cent; 651: 1506 = 43.2 per cent; the geometric mean is 43.9 per cent, that is, 82 per cent of the CIA estimate. Roughly this is a reduction of 20 per cent. Because of computing procedures having changed Soviet consumption of food by 20 per cent in Tables 13.3 and 13.4, I obtained the final result (Table 13.2) of 43.8 divided by 53.7, which equals 81.6 per cent. If we take the price parity for food as a whole that the authors calculated [20], it turns out that Soviet consumption of food is about 44 per cent. According to Jack Alterman's calculations, the geometric mean of Soviet food consumption will be, with my corrections, 43.4 per cent. This is 81.3 per cent of the CIA estimate. He also points out that my total re-evaluation depends greatly upon the correction of the figure for meat due to its large share in total food consumption.

8 Soft Goods

1. The authors say [51] that attempts to match the classification would lead to estimation from 'inadequate data' and would not increase the

accuracy of the comparison for the group as a whole. None the less, the American data could have been regrouped separately from the basic calculation, which would have provided the opportunity for direct comparison for the majority of subgroups.

2.   The data are apparently (there are no footnotes) taken from *Narkhoz-77*, p. 431, which speaks of consumption of 'leather footwear'. According to *Narkhoz-77*, p. 244, in 1976, 744 m. pairs of leather shoes were produced, i.e., less than 3 pairs per capita, and in addition, 29 m. pairs of felt and 203 m. pairs of rubber footwear. Besdies, 70 m. pairs of leather shoes, 9 m. pairs of rubber footwear, 11 m. pairs each of sports and house shoes, and 19 m. pairs of footwear from leather substitutes were imported (*VT-76*, p. 45).

3.   But the authors did not dream up this figure. In 1976 in the US 1.65 pairs of leather footwear (excluding house slippers) were produced (StAb-78, p. 827).

4.   Using Soviet sources (*Narkhoz-77*, p. 483) the authors give per capita expenditures on shoe repair (including individual sewing) of R2 in 1976. This figure seems understated. Also, they do not say how it was established that the quantity of shoe repair in the USSR is almost five times greater than in the US [9]. American statistics do not give data on the quantity of shoe repair, and the amount of the population's expenditures on this do not include repair done by non-specialised shops (US Bureau of the Census, *1977 Census of Service Industries*, part 1, p. A–4).

5.   This norm is 3.6 pairs of leather footwear per year (V. F. Mayer, *Uroven' zhizni naseleniya SSSR*, M., 1977, p. 105). According to A. I. Levin, *Nauchno-tekhnicheskiy progress i lichnoye potrebleniye*, M., 1979, p. 108, the norms for various regions range from 4.98 to 5.98 pairs. Apparently the latter norms pertain not only to leather shoes. See also Table 18.2.

6.   American footwear distinguishes 15 widths (from A to EEE) and Soviet, three (A. M. Kochurov and K. A. Karanyan, *Spravochnik prodavtsa promyshlennykh tovarov*, M., 1974, p. 51), but I personally could not usually find shoes of large width in Soviet stores.

7.   For example, *StAb-78*, p. 827.

8.   *Narkhoz-77*, pp. 180, 185, 431, 459.

9.   *SEV-81*, pp. 112, 461.

10.   Lokshin, pp. 167–8; *Narkhoz-74*, p. 269.

11.   *SEV-81*, p. 112.

12.   US Bureau of the Census, *C.I.R, Shoes and Slippers* ..., 1976, MA-31A(76)-1, p. 8. This 786.5 m. pairs is formed as follows: production of 422.5, exports of 6 m., and imports of 370 m. The cited source includes a lot of varied information on footwear produced in the country, and very much is said about imports.

13.   Incidentally, an explanation is need for why, according to the authors' calculations, the comparative volumes of consumption of footwear and clothing in the two countries differ by a factor of more than two and half. In other words, what reason might cause Soviet consumption of footwear to be practically equal to American (in their estimation) while clothing lags behind by two and a half times?

216   *Notes and References*

14.   And not into a walk-in closet, for which there is not even a Russian
       word. Quite significant is the fact that a wardrobe chest is fully sufficient
       for a Soviet family's clothing.
15.   This is supported indirectly by the following calculation. If for clothing,
       underwear, headgear, fur goods, knitwear and hosiery we relate state
       trend to the city and cooperative trade to the countryside, it turns out
       that in 1976 the expenditures of the urban resident were 160 per cent of
       the rural resident's (*Narkhoz-77*, pp. 458–60).
          One other literary source. In *Literaturnaya Gazeta*, 24 March 1982,
       p. 11, a photograph by a reader from Krasnoyarsk was published – a
       little flock of village boys is hurrying somewhere with birdhouses. You
       must see how the boys are dressed; their appearance vivdly reminds me
       of the war (!) years.
16.   *Narkhoz-77*, pp. 271, 380–1; *StAb-78*, p. 418.
17.   *Sotsialisticheskaya industriya*, 13 May 1982, p. 4.
18.   Although entirely hypothetical, the following question relates fully to
       our topic. Assume that the chance to dress like an American fell on
       Soviet ladies from heaven. How would they look – better or worse than
       American females? Certainly, many will not agree with my argument, all
       the more so since this is literally a matter of taste, but Soviet women
       would look better. American society is less sexual and more Victorian
       than appears at first glance. Therefore, the American woman pays less
       attention to her appearance – she wants to look appealing for one but
       not for everyone. More significant is one of the results of democracy –
       the absence of a standard developed by some elite and accepted by
       society. Often the American tells herself (himself): I will dress as I wish;
       to hell with the Joneses. The point is not only the democratisation as
       such, but the fundamentally different correlations of social prestige. The
       Soviet store director, in spite of his big real income, looks up to many of
       those who are poorer, while here the newly rich establish their own
       standards.
          Both of these factors smooth out the actual difference in clothing
       between the two countries for the outside observer.
19.   *Narkhoz-76*, pp. 244; *Narkhoz-77*, p. 458.
20.   Lokshin, pp. 153–5.
21.   Ibid., p. 160.
22.   Two instances complicate the comparison. On the one hand, a lot more
       medicines can be bought without a prescription in the USSR than in the
       US. On the other, doctors usually do not write prescriptions for scarce
       medicines (see, for example, *Literaturnaya gazeta* 23 December 1981,
       p. 12).
23.   *StAb-78*, p. 100. Incidentally, Soviet-produced hearing aids are absolu-
       tely not comparable with Western.
24.   *Pravda*, 19 May 1977, p. 3. The article is titled 'Why There is a Queue for
       Eyeglasses'.
25.   *Trud*, 27 October 1981, p. 3. The article is titled 'Frames That We Have
       Long Been Awaiting". See also the material in *Literaturnaya gazeta*, 30
       April 1982, p. 13. Here we are informed of 'measures taken' – the deputy
       director of a main administration (*glavk*) was fired and some plans were

re-examined. But it is clear from the figures given that in 1982 not one order for lenses and frames will be fully satisfied. The comparison is hampered by sunglasses.

26. *Pechat' v SSSR v 1976 g.*, M., 1977, p. 18; *StAb-78*, p. 600.
27. The USSR is also ahead in the number of book stores: 19 000 at the end of 1976 compared with 13 000 in the US in 1977 (*Nakhoz-76*, p. 560 and *StAb-81*, p. 818), but in the USSR books are usually not sold in other stores, while in the US a lot of them are sold in drug stores, grocery stores, etc.
28. There is no doubt that in the USSR people know and love old and contemporary American literature incomparably more than people love Russian literature in the US. In the USSR, Poe, Cooper, O'Henry, London, Twain, Hemingway, Steinbeck, Faulkner, Updike and Vonnegut are no less revered and read than in their homeland. Americans in mass know Tolstoi, Dostoevskii, (Chekov, a little less) and Solyhenitsyn, but I have serious doubts whether they have actually read much of the works of the latter.

    In mentioning all this, it is worth noting that in the autocratic Soviet society the system by which the public informally recognises what is prestigious is different from the West. It is difficult to distinguish yourself by wealth in the USSR, and a political career is unattainable for many. Therefore, distinction and, in a sense, self-affirmation are found in how well-read and educated a person is.
29. In 1976 the average American daily paper had 55 pages and the Sunday edition 177 pages (*StAb-81*, p. 568). Of course, no one reads an American paper from cover to cover and it has a monstrous amount of advertising, but if the reader reads even 5 per cent of the printed area this is about nine pages for the Sunday edition, that is, one and a half times more than all of *Pravda* or *Izvestiya*.

    The data on per capita expenditures on printed matter in the USSR are of interest. In 1976 they amounted to a total of R9, of which more than R13 went for newspapers, more than R2 for magazines, 70 kopecks for books on art and only one third for books and periodicals have gotten more expensive. In 1977, American per capita expenditures on books amounted to more than $23 (*StAb-81*, p. 57).
30. US Bureau of the Census, *Social Indicators III*, 1980, pp. 556, 561–2.
31. *StAb-78*, p. 245.
32. In a recent satirical article in *Izvestiya*, 6 April 1982, p. 6, the author writes that in the *Santekhnika* store on Kutuzovskiy Prospekt (it, incidentally, is the only one; no other cities have such stores) he was told: 'During the entire quarter we managed to receive . . . only 4000 nipples. Can you imagine? Only one of these items (that costs one kopeck) for every two thousand Moscow residents. Not counting out-of-town buyers, of which, incidentally, we have many.'

    A comparison of the number of stores gives an indirect but very distinct impression about the comparative scale of consumption for this group. At the end of 1976 in the USSR there were 7000 state stores for housewares and hardware, 1100 kerosene kiosks and 1400 stores selling building materials (*Narkhoz-76*, p. 560). There are no similar data for cooperative trade, but the numbers should be relatively small. In the US in 1977 there were 90 000 such stores (*StAb-81*, p. 818). Moreover, first, the sizes of the stores themselves are not comparable, and second, many of these goods are sold in other places, in particular in 'drug' stores.

9 Durable Goods

1. It would make sense to divide all durables into such large subgroups as: household equipment including furniture, cars and motorcycles, and recreational and sporting goods.

2. This was the opinion of American experts. In the words of *Izvestiya*, 3 April 1979, p. 3, Soviet vacuum cleaners 'are 20 years behind modern standards'. Home air conditioners recently began to appear, but their quality is bad. The people have not been quick to buy them (*Kommercheskiy vestnik*, 1982, no. 6, p. 6), although there are no central systems in apartment buildings. Toasters have also begun to appear, but they are not selling well either.

3. *Narkhoz-77*, p. 459.

4. *Komsomol'skaya pravda*, 26 October 1980, p. 4.

5. In 1976, 0.2 square metres of rugs per capita were produced in the USSR (*Narkhoz-77*, p. 180), while in the US in 1978 consumption was more than 4.4 square metres (US Bureau of the Census, *C.I.R., Carpets and Rugs*, MA-22Q(78)-5, p. 8).

6. Here, without commentary, are data on the production of furniture in 1974, all from the same inexhaustible Lokshin (p. 194): 15 m. tables, 48.6 m. chairs and armchairs, 2.9 m. buffets and servers, 8.3 m. cabinet-closets, 648 000 divans, couches and ottomans, 3.8 m. wooden beds, 865 000 armchairs that convert to beds, 4.7 m. sleep sofas, and 583 000 furniture suites. With respect to 1976, we know only that 625 000 furniture suites were produced (*Narkhoz-77*, p. 189).

   A significant part of furniture (and rugs) go to institutions and enterprises.

7. Incidentally, this is a good reason why the Soviet comparisons of apartments built in the USSR and in the US, which is mentioned in Chapter 1, do not give the right picture. The point is not that chiefly apartments are built in the USSR and houses in the US. And it is not that quality is not comparable (see the next chapter). The main thing is that to characterise the standard of living one should speak about living space *in use* and not about the rate of housing construction.

8. E. N. Voronova (ed.), *Razmeshcheniye proizvodstva neprodovol'stvennykh tovarov narodnogo potrebleniya v SSSR*, p. 149.

9. This follows even from a Soviet estimate cited in the study [30] that 15 per cent of housework is mechanised in the USSR and 80 per cent in the US.

10. *Narkhoz-77*, p. 431. These data are calculated on the basis of figures on sales to the population for a series of years and service life norms (see N. N. Vinogradskiy, *Izucheniye sprosa na tovary narodnogo potrebleniya*,

Kiev, 1976, p. 128). According to Lokshin, p. 186, service lives are taken to be: 30 years for sewing machines, 15–20 years for refrigerators, 10–12 years for watches and televisions, 10 years for radios.

In the West, special statistical surveys are undertaken, which are of course more accurate.

11. This should be some mistake. Electric sewing machines are produced in the USSR but they cost more than R67. And sewing machines imported from the GDR are quite good, but American are much better.

12. Apparently the following point which the authors failed to take into account had an effect here. The quality ratios, as I already said, were determined by American experts who tried to calculate how much it would cost to produce a good of Soviet quality under modern American conditions. But technical progress proceeds such that consumer quality grows much faster than expenditures on production (otherwise, there would be no progress!). It is not much cheaper to produce lagging Soviet equipment in America than modern goods (see Chapter 12).

13. This is also apparent from figures that the authors give [9]. In 1976, per capita purchases in the USSR (in number of units) as a percentage of the corresponding figure for the US were: 35 per cent for televisions, 12 per cent for radios, 82 per cent for refrigerators, 62 per cent for washing machines, and 20 per cent for vacuum cleaners. In other words, the lag for purchases is sharply less than for property owned. I note here as well that for Zhiguli cars, in 12 years of use, only a 'scanty number of them were scrapped' (*Sotsialisticheskaya industriya*, 10 March 1983, p. 4).

14. *Izvestiya*, 8 January 1982, p. 2. According to *Narkhoz-82*, p. 355, in 1981, 13 per cent of the population couldn't receive TV programmes at all, and 32 per cent could not receive more than one channel.

15. *Narkhoz-77*, p. 189; *VT-76*, p. 32; *StAb-81*, p. 566.

16. *Narkhoz-77*, p. 189. Sales in retail trade were 12 000 lower (*Narkhoz-77*, p. 429). Part of these sales went to collective farms, clubs, and other organisations.

17. *VT-76*, pp. 37, 138. In 1975 both total imports and imports from the GDR were about half as large.

18. *StAb-78*, p. 652. Possibly my estimate for the USSR is overstated a little. According to Lokshin (p. 211), there were a little more than 2.6 m. cars in individual use at the end of 1974. According to another source (*Ekonomika i ekspluatatsiya avtomobil'nogo transporta*, M., 1976, p. 185), in 1975 there were already 3.5 m. cars.

19. *Narkhoz-77*, p. 429. There is a slight inaccuracy in the comparison due to the fact that in the US a certain quantity of passenger cars are in other than personal use (the Post Office, taxis, etc.), but we can safely disregard them. In the USSR this share is very high.

20. From the fact that the number of Soviet cars sold amounted to 10 per cent of the American, and the volume of consumption determined by the authors 5 per cent, it follows that the authors took the quality of Soviet cars to be half as good as American. This evaluation also is not too accurate.

21. *Narkhoz-80*, p. 404; *StAb-78*, p. 651.

22. It is not easy to calculate how many years it would take for the USSR to

'catch up to' the US in cars, if only because of the lack of data on the number in use in the USSR and the fact that in the official data on sales, as I already noted, 20 per cent are used cars. If we ignore all this, it turns out that sales of cars increased by 1.1 m. between 1965 and 1980. Then, if sales grow at the same rate, the Soviet population will buy as many cars as were bought in America in 1976 after 138 years. Considering the difference in population, the fact that the growth of production and sales has practically ceased, and that sales are overstated by the number of used cars, this should happen much, much later. In other words, the Soviet population will never see the American level of automobilisation.

23. *StAb-79*, p. 910.
24. *StAb-78*, p. 795.

10 Household Services

1. The underdevelopment of utilities in the USSR is discussed in detail below. For now I will say that in 1975 average electricity use per Soviet urban resident was 280 kwh. Of this, 34 per cent went for lighting, only 46 per cent for electrical appliances, 13 per cent for cooking, and 7 per cent for heating, hot water, and air conditioning (GOSINTI, *Obzory po problemam bol'shikh gorodov*, 1978, no. 9, p. 2). Per capita use of electricity for the same purposes in the US are 10 times greater.

2. Soviet propaganda uses every opportunity to emphasise the cheapness of housing in the USSR and the fact that its price has not changed for more than half a century. The indisputable social advantage of cheap housing is the absence of an automatic relationship between low income and poor housing. However, regardless of how you look at it, the subsidisation of Soviet housing is one of the reasons for its slow growth. Also extremely important is the fact that it is precisely the highly paid families that receive good (by Soviet standards) housing, and its cheapness thus primarily benefits these strata. Certainly, the cheapness of housing in itself (like free medicine and education) does not mean much; the determining factor is just how much of such services the population really receives per capita.

3. One might play with the idea of a comparative calculation on the basis of prices of cooperative (not state!) apartments, countryside cottage (*dachas*), and rents of apartments from private individuals in the USSR.

4. The distinction arose because of communal apartments – rent is paid there per metre of 'living' and not 'useful' space.

5. In 1976, 106.2 m. square metres of useful area was completed, i.e. 0.41 sq. metres per capita, of which 82.7 m. by state organisations and housing cooperatives, 11.4 m. by state employees with the aid of bank credit, and 12.1 m. on collective farms (by the farms and rural residents themselves) – *Narkhoz-77*, p. 411.

6. *Narkhoz-76*, p. 497. In Moscow in the same year this figure was 15. square metres (10.3 of living space), i.e. 27 per cent better than the average for all cities in the country (ibid., p. 501).

7. None the less, of interest are two recent reports by *Izvestiya*. The paper informs us (19 Jan. 1982, p. 2) that in Rybinsk 20 000 families are in need of improvements in housing conditions. The city's population is 243 000 (*Narkhoz-80*, p. 22), i.e. not less than a quarter of all residents have below-norm housing. The norm that is used in such calculations is 5 square metres of living space per person.

In the issue of 4 February 1982, p. 3, it states that the last barracks were torn down in Usol'e-Sibirsk only last year and that now there are 9 square metres per person. This presumably refers to useful area, and it is presented as a great achievement.

8. *Narkhoz-76*, p. 496. The absolute number of square metres of private housing is growing slowly, but its share of the total urban housing stock is declining sharply – from 35 per cent in 1965 to 23 per cent in 1980 (*Narkhoz-80*, p. 392).

9. A dormitory, Soviet-style, means that several (rarely two) people live in one room. Even the idle Western leftist, let us hope, would not dare to say that this is a manifestation of Soviet collectivism.

In the English language, there is not even a term 'communal apartment'; it is said like this: 'a family that shares a kitchen and bathroom with other families'. Oh, the refinement of language! I lived in a communal apartment and know what it is.

10. The *Izvestiya* editorial of 10 December 1981 says that 'eighty percent of the city-dwellers have said good-bye to communal apartments forever'. Hence, a fifth of the urban population of this socialist country, i.e. 33 million, still lives in communal apartments. But the figures presented show that even this number is understated: in speaking of communal apartments, the editors of *Izvestiya* momentarily forgot about dormitories. And, moreover, apartments where three generations live – where grandparents bump heads with their married children and grandchildren – are not considered communal.

11. *Ekonomika i organizatsiya promyshlennogo proizvodstva*, 1979, no. 5, p. 13. From the text it is not exactly clear whether the reference is to the number of persons or families.

12. *StAb-78*, pp. 43, 789–90, and also US Bureau of the Census, *Annual Housing Survey: 1976*, part A, Series H-150–76.

13. Ibid., p. 13. According to *StAb-78*, p. 43, there were 16.8 m. singles: 6.5 m. men and 10.3 m. women.

14. For comparison, in 1976 only 1 per cent of the living area in Moscow was in one-storey buildings (0.8 per cent in 1977), while 91 per cent was in buildings with five or more storeys. More than 47 per cent of living area was in buildings nine storeys and higher (*Moskva v tsifrakh, 1917–77 gg.*, M., 1977, p. 121).

15. Dick Anderson brought this to my attention; see *The Washington Post*, 24 June 1982, p. A9. Not everything here is simple. *Time* magazine asserts (13 September 1982, p. 39) that the prison standard is 6.1 square metres (60 square feet) per prisoner; however, only a fifth of all the approximately 400 000 American prisoners are confined in such conditions.

16. A. A. Bobrovnikov (ed.), *Gosudarstvennyy byudzhet Rosiyskoy Federat-*

sii, M., 1977, p. 118. One should not think that the situation is any better with respect to urban amenities in other republics; with the exception of the Baltic states, it is probably worse.

17. *Izvestiya*, 14 October 1981, p. 2.
18. *Narkhoz-76*, p.   502.
19. G. L. Bagiyev, *Osnovy ekonomiki i upravleniya kachestvom energii*, Leningrad, 1979, p. 17.
20. At the end of 1976, 59 per cent of the housing stock in rural areas was supplied with gas (*Narkhoz-76*, p. 502). But the process of extending the gas supply is moving quickly – at the end of 1980 about three-fourths of the rural housing stock was supplied (*Narkhoz-80*, p. 396).

I did not find exact figures on amenities in the countryside for the country as a whole. For the RSFSR in 1980, 62 per cent of rural housing did not have running water, 78 per cent had no sewer system, and 74 per cent had no central heating plant (*Planovoye khozyaystvo*, 1981, no. 10, p. 95).

21. When rents were established 50-plus years ago, they differed depending upon the number of storeys, location, height of ceilings, etc., but since housing prices were frozen this lost all significance.

Lacking information, the authors took expenditures on payments for dormitories to be at the level of rent for ordinary housing. Here they also transferred American experience (where dormitories are often no worse than living at home) to the USSR; but even if they had found prices for Soviet dormitories, the prices would hardly have reflected the real correlation of 'quality' compared with ordinary housing.

22. The authors correctly took into account that the Soviet state housing stock is subsidised and that the subsidy is larger than the rent. But it is not very clear how they considered these amounts in their calculations. It seems that they took them into account (as with turnover tax and agricultural subsidies) only in determining the total amount of consumption in 'adjusted' rubles [14]. Perhaps I missed something here, but it is unlikely that the study will find a more attentive reader.

23. *Narkhoz-80*, p. 49; *StAb-81*, p. 455. It is rather obvious that the general Soviet lag in capital stock in housing compared with American should be much larger than in production.

24. Here is an elementary calculation based on official data. Between 1950 and 1980 total (useful) area per urban resident increased by 1 square metre per five-year period and amounted to 13 square metres at the end of 1980 (*Narkhoz-70*, p. 546; *Narkhoz-80*, p. 392). In America it is 44 square metres for the country as a whole [10]. Thus, given existing rates of housing construction and the same growth of the urban population the living area per Soviet urban resident will be as large as in the US in 1976 after $(44-13) \times 5 = 155$ years.

Instead of commenting on this calculation, I will say that the requirements for housing are the most pressing. In a (rare in the USSR) sociological survey conducted in 1969–70, the workers of Kostroma inustrial enterprises were asked: if you had the necessary amount of money, what would you buy first? 'A cooperative apartment', answered 56 per cent of the blue-collar workers and 44 per cent of the other employees (V. M. Levin, *Sotsial'no-ekonomicheskiye potrebnosti: zakonomernosti formirovaniya i razvitiya*, M., 1974, p. 61). To evaluate this answer correctly, one should not forget that they were talking about expensive cooperative apartments; the desire to have an 'ordinary' apartment is undoubtedly much greater.

25. In 1976, fixed capital in housing amounted to R280 billion, and the average annual increment during 1975–80 was R14 billion (*Narkhoz-80*, p. 49, all in 1973 prices). Thus, calculating in money terms, fixed capital in housing would increase by a factor of four not in 155 years but in 'only' 60. However, clearly something is wrong with these figures. In particular, during 1975–80 the increase in living space per urban resident was a little more than 8 per cent, and the amount of capital in housing increased by almost 27 per cent.
26. Here it is entirely appropriate to praise the authors. For no apparent reason the Soviet yearbooks do not publish expenditures on passenger transportation either in total or by type. Therefore, the authors had to resort to various indirect calculations, and they handled this difficult problem very well. True, it seems to me that they somewhat overstated the share of business use of urban transportation and an average price for taxi rides of 51 kopecks seems too low, but overall the calculation is done well.
27. This, of course, was affected by the fact that business trips now are largely by plane, but note that, in terms of passenger–kilometres, buses (inter-city and suburban) amount to more than half of railroad trips. Railroad passenger travel is growing much slower than bus or air (*Narkhoz-80*, p. 293), so the decline of railroads in America evidently must be explained not only by the local specifics.
28. Indirect evidence of this is the fact that with the sharp increase in the price of airplane tickets in 1977, the total number of flights fell by only 7 per cent and was almost fully restored in the following year, and the number of passenger–kilometres changed even less, while taxi trips fell more and recovered only beginning in 1979 (*Narkhoz-80*, pp. 314, 320).
29. *Vestnik AN SSSR, Seriya transport*, 1981, no. 8, p. 73. When I tell this to my students and translate the figures into units of measurements familiar to them – less than 1 square foot per person – they do not believe me.
30. This does not relate to our topic, but in the West public transportation is very expensive, while in the USSR it is very cheap. The reasons for this are not entirely clear, but understandably, scale plays a large role. This is affirmed, for example, by the fact that while the Moscow and Leningrad subways are profitable, those in Baku, Tbilisi, and Kharkov receive a subsidy (*Zheleznodorozhnyy transport*, 1978, no. 1, pp. 65–9). Also a large factor is the underassessment of the value of fixed capital in transportation in the USSR.
31. *Literaturnaya gazeta* has repeatedly complained about this.
32. One reader of the manuscript remarked to me that such a car is better than a sitting car when you are travelling at night. True, but normally if an American is travelling a long distance by train at night he takes a sleeping berth.
33. *Komsomol'skaya pravda* of 31 May 1980, p. 2, describes graphically a

reporter's arrival at Sverdlovsk railroad station. The train in which the reporter arrived was two-and-a-half hours late. Other trains were also late. There are more than 1000 seats in the waiting room and at night they were all taken. Hundreds of people could not even sit down all night. The station chief told the reporter that it was a 'quiet time'; summer is much worse. The reporter concludes by saying that Sverdlovsk is far from the worst station. I should say that American trains are late quite often.

34. In the USSR a passenger gets a ticket that is good for only a particular trip. In 1970 the 'coefficient of utilization of passenger seats' in planes was 75 per cent (*Transport i svyaz' SSSR: Statisticheskiy sbornik*, M., 1972, p. 210).

35. *Novyy mir*, 1981, no. 7, pp. 142–3. *Izvestiya* of 14 February 1982, p. 2, also writes that 'in the Non-Blackearth zones . . . from 30 to 50 percent of central farmsteads still do not have stable links with regional centers'.

36. US Bureau of the Census, *Annual Housing Survey: 1976*, part A, Series H-150-76, pp. 6–7. Incidentally, in 1975, the 80.1 m. working Americans got to work as follows: 65 per cent in their own cars, alone: 19 per cent in cars together with others; 6 per cent on public transportation (two-thirds of them by bus); about 5 per cent walked, and 3 per cent worked at home. The rest got there by 'other means', evidently on bicycles (*StAb-78*, p. 657).

37. *StAb-78*, p. 647; *Za rulem*, 1968, no. 5, p. 12.

38. *Narkhoz-77*, p. 319; *SEV-81*, p. 275. There is a still greater difference between the two handbooks in the length of 'all automobile roads'. According to *Narkhoz-76*, p. 405, it was 1 406 000 km, and *SEV-81*, p. 275, gives a figure almost 30 per cent lower. It is also curious that according to the SEV handbook it fell (!) in comparison with 1960 by 26 per cent. If we accept the data in the yearbook, in 1976 a little more than half of all roads considered automobile roads were not surfaced, i.e. they were dirt roads.

39. Figures here and below are from *StAb-78*, pp. 641–3.

40. Here is what the Deputy Minister of Internal Affairs of the USSR says: 'Each year thousands of accidents connected with unsatisfactory road conditions are registered in the country. In an inspection of the Moscow/ Vorozezh/Rostov-na-Donu road by the State Automobile Inspectorate, numerous shortcomings affecting traffic safety were discovered: a significant part of the road has defects in its surface, half of all road shoulders are not reinforced, 26 per cent of dangerous spots on the road do not have guard rails . . . 20 per cent of road signs are lacking . . . plans . . . for the current five-year period do not even cover a third of the necessary work' (*Izvestiya*, 21 April 1982, p. 2).

41. Perhaps the huge territories of the Soviet North-East and Alaska should be excluded from the comparison; still, the difference is enormous.

42. During 1960–80, road construction in the USSR would seem to have been intensive. The total length of 'automobile roads with hard surfaces' (CEMA definition) almost tripled – from 271 000 to 732 000 km (*SEV-81*, p. 275). In the US during 1960–77 the total length of roads increased only 4 per cent (*StAb-79*, p. 638) but intensive improvement work was

undertaken. Thus, the length of 'surfaced rural roads' increased by 16 per cent (ibid.), and many superhighways, tunnels and bridges were constructed. Be that as it may, from 1960 to 1980 the length of roads with hard surfaces per 1000 population in the USSR increased from 1.2 to 2.8 km. In the US this indicator, as we saw, was 23.6 in 1976. In other words, if road construction in the US continues at the same rate as in the past 20 years, after 260 years the length of roads per capita will be the same in the USSR as in the US in 1976. I repeat that the quality of roads in the US and the USSR is not comparable, and this comparison is per capita – on the basis of road length per square kilometre the USSR lag would be even greater.

43. *SEV-81*, p. 295; *StAb-79*, p. 580. The figure 9.028 billion in the SEV handbook is called 'postal mailings', while *Narkhoz-77*, p. 335, says that 9 billion 'letters' were sent.
44. *Narkhoz-77*, p. 335.
45. Ibid., p. 521. But this assumption is clearly refuted by data in O. S. Srapionov, *Ekonomika in planirovaniye svyazi*, M., 1976, p. 18, where mailings of newspapers and magazines are shown separately from letters.
46. It is very difficult to compare the quality of mail services in the two countries. In the USSR, as a special experiment showed, almost all mail is delivered later than it should be, and a letter gets from Moscow to Leningrad in a longer time than in 1890 (*Literaturnaya gazeta*, 31 March 1983, p. 15). In almost all Moscow organisations, there are special messengers for 'parallel mail'. On the other hand, mail is delivered there a few times a day, including Sundays. By way of comparison: just today I received a letter from France, 21 days after it was sent; in a few cases, my mail was delivered to nearby Maryland from Washington, DC after two to three weeks.
47. *Narkhoz-77*, p. 335; *StAb – 78*, p. 588 (including also international telegrams).
48. The authors do not explain how they got these data. At the end of 1976 there were 20.9 m. telephones in the USSR and 155 m. in the US (*Narkhoz-76*, p. 417; *StAb-78*, p. 589). Considering population, the difference is about 10 times.
49. *StAb-78*, p. 589; *Transport i svyaz' SSSR*, p. 283; *Narkhoz-76*, p. 417.
50. O. S. Sharipov, *Ekonomika svyasi*, M., 1974, p. 24.
51. At the end of both 1976 and 1980, 15 per cent of the number of telephones in the 'general telephone network' were in rural areas (*Narkhoz-80*, p. 322). It is clear that practically all were in local administration, collective farm offices, etc.
52. The basic source – *StAb-78*, p. 589 – in giving a figure of 114 m., does not say what it is. The Census Bureau could not satisfy my, I hope, completely legitimate curiosity, and I readdressed the question to the American Telephone and Telegraph Company; after many calls I was finally told that this is apparently (!) the number of telephones. Only the Federal Communications Commission finally assured me that 114 m. is the number of telephones; they also gave me the above figure on the quantity of telephone numbers (lines), but could not name a publication

to cite. But *The Washington Post* (2 Dec., 1982, p. D11) says that there are 2.7 telephones per home. The reader should have sympathy with those of us who have to deal with such statistics.

53. The yearbook says that 17.4 m. telephones were automatic (*Narkhoz-76*, p. 418), but it is not clear whether this figure should be related to the quantity of phones in the 'general network' (18.4 m.) or with the total number of phones (20.9 m.). Thus, at least 1 m. telephones, but very likely 3.5 m. or about 17 per cent, were not automatic.

54. Accurate figures are lacking here also. In the USSR in 1970 there were 132 000 telephone booths (*Transport i svyaz' v SSSR*, M., 1972, p. 283), while in the US, as I was told by the Federal Communications Commission, there were 1 572 000 in 1976.

55. *SEV-81*, p. 297; *StAb-78*, p. 589.

56. Once we phoned the USSR from the beach and got through immediately. But in the USSR even six years after 1976, only 'the residents of 130 cities [out of a total of 2089 cities] have the services of automatic telephone communications between republic and oblast centres'. About 30 per cent of regional centres do not have automatic communications with the oblast center (*Izvestiya*, 7 May 1982, p. 1).

57. *StAb-78*, p. 589.

56. Since we do not have accurate data on the number of telephones in personal use, the appropriate comparison is difficult, but we can make it for the total number of telephones in the two countries. During 1965–80, the number of 'telephones in the general telephone network' increased by 17.3 m., i.e. by 1.3 m. per year, and amounted to 23.7 m. at the end of 1980 (*Narkhoz-80*, p. 322), which is 131 m. fewer than at the end of 1976 in the US. In other words, if the number of telephones grows as it has in the past 15 years, the USSR will have the same number as the US had in 1976 after 109 years, and on a per capita basis – in 130 years. Remember that the lag in the number of private telephones, as we saw, is greater.

59. Here are some data from *Narkhoz-76*, p. 569. Although they are not exactly what we need (they are in 'comparable', not 'existing' prices), they show the total volume of the corresponding services provided to the population. Expenditures per capita in 1976 were R2.02 for shoe repair, R5.28 for repairing and sewing clothing (excluding the cost of materials), R0.61 for dry cleaning and dyeing, R1.15 for laundry, R0.65 for showers, public baths, and R1.09 for film developing.

60. Recall here that the authors took the price of a haircut to be 60 kopecks. Thus, it turns out that (forgetting that a woman's haircut is more expensive and that some men in the USSR still get shaves in a barber shop) the average person gets a haircut in a barber shop three times a year.

61. *StAb-78*, p. 853. An elementary calculation with the prices that existed in 1976 shows that this figure is low. I discussed this with the head of the corresponding section of the Bureau of the Census, Sidney Marcus, and he readily agreed with me. One explanation is that services of this sort rendered by 'non-independent' barbers should not be included in this figure. Another is that a large part of the income of American barbers also is not reported.

62. *Pravda*, 8 May, p. 3.
63. There are various estimates in the literature. 'In the country as a whole about 100–120 billion hours are spent on household chores, which is equivalent to the work of 50 mil. man-years.' (*Sotsialisticheskiy trud*, 1977, no. 9, p. 20). Actually, it is, of course, woman-years.
64. In 1077 expenditures on funerals (payments for the service of 20 000 funeral parlours and crematoria) amounted to \$2.8 billion, i.e. almost \$13 per live person or \$1500 per funeral (*StAb-81*, pp. 5, 71, 824). This figure does not include cemeteries or crematoria that belong to cemeteries (US Bureau of the Census, *1977 Census of Service Industries*, part 1, p. A–3).
      K. M. Simis told me that in 1976 in Moscow he paid R250 for a coffin and two buses and another R100 for the services of a crematorium (including musicians). An additional payment on the side of R50 was also necessary. Funerals in cemeteries are more expensive than in crematoria in the USSR. Such expenditures are not necessarily typical. In particular, in the countryside funeral expenditures (not counting a funeral repast) may be only the cost of ordering a coffin from a local carpenter. Headstones are terribly expensive in the USSR – R1500 and more.
65. In 1975, 2.5 m. Soviet tourists travelled abroad (*Vneshnyaya torgovlya SSSR*, 1976, no. 9, pp. 2–4), but it is not clear how to calculate the amount of expenditures. In order to translate data on American expenditures for foreign trips into rubles, the authors used the official ruble exchange rate. Clever but not correct.
66. The statement in [11] that the geometric mean for the entire subgroup excluding hotels is 44 per cent does not square with the other figures.
67. In 1976 in the USSR, 248 full-length films were produced (including for television). Without a doubt many more television films are produced in the US, but there are no data for comparing the number of pictures shot.
      In the same year Soviet movie attendence was 16 admissions per capita (*Narkhoz-76*, pp. 610–2), which is a lot. Average expenditures on movie admissions for the year in the RSFSR were R6–6.5 per capita in the city and more than R3 in the countryside (*Voprosy tsenoobrazovaniya*, 1976, no. 5, p. 80). Judging from these figures, the authors understated expenditures on movies.
      Americans spent \$14 per capita on movies, and the average ticket cost \$2.13 (Table 10.5 and *StAb-78*, p. 245), i.e. per capita less than seven admissions per year.
      There is a widespread opinion that movies are dying and being supplanted by television. Here is what the statistics say. Per capita movie attendance in the USSR was: 6 times a year in 1950, 17 in 1960, 19 in 1970, 18 in 1975, and 16 in 1980 (*Narkhoz-70*, p. 677, and *Narkhoz-80*, p. 482). In the US the population's expenditures on movies were three times greater in 1976 than in 1960 (*StAb-78*, p. 245). In 1977 there were about 12 000 theatres with 5.4 m. seats in the US plus places for 17 m. cars in drive-ins (US Bureau of the Census, *1977 Census of Service Industries, Motion Picture Industry*, SC77-S-4, pp. 8, 21).
68. Including \$4 per capita spent in bowling alleys plus \$2.50 for food and

drink in them (US Bureau of the Census, *1977 Census of Retail Trade, Miscellaneous Subjects*, SC77-S-4, p. 33).

69.   In 1976 there were 573 theatres in the USSR including 42 for opera and ballet and 158 for children and young people. The number of admissions was 117 m., i.e. a little less than 0.5 per capita (*Narkhoz-76*, p. 608). At the end of 1979, 596 professional theatres (31 in Moscow, 16 in Leningrad, 13 in Tbilisi, 9 each in Kiev and Tashkent, etc.) had 344 000 seats. There were 227 philharmonic orchestras and independent musical groups under the USSR Ministry of Culture (*Vestnik statistiki*, 1980, no. 12, p. 74). From these data we find (assuming 365 performances a year – allowing no days off, but also no matinees) that the theatres were 95 per cent filled.

    Per capita expenditures in the US for theatre attendence and other performances, as we saw in Table 10.5 were $4.20. Thus, apparently (I do not have exact data) total attendance was about the same as in the USSR.

70.   *Narkhoz-77*, p. 189.

71.   *Narkhoz-76*, p. 606; *StAb-81*, p. 237; *StAb-79*, p. 246.

72.   Ibid., p. 121.

73.   *Narkhoz-76*, p. 526.

74.   *Moskva v tsifrakh, 1917–1977*, p. 131. *Literaturnaya gazeta* of 1 September 1982, p. 13, asserts that there are now 'a little more than 2000 courts' and '41 000 tennis players' in the country.

75.   *Finansy SSSR*, 1979, no. 5, p. 46; *Kommercheskiy vestnik*, 1982, no. 6, p. 26; *StAb-78*, p. 246.

76.   *StAb-78*, p. 656.

77.   *Narkhoz-77*, pp. 441–3. In 1976 there were: 2345 resorts and 'health resorts' (with 510 000 beds), including 1211 children's resorts with 163 000 beds; 1170 vacation houses and hotels (354 000 beds); and 954 tourist camps (312 000 beds). Most numerous were recreation camps - 5446 – belonging, presumably, to enterprises and institutions (but not labour unions), though they were small – a total of 548 000 beds. Together all 'recreation institutions', excluding those for one- or two-days, had 1.9 m. beds.

78.   *Ekonomika i organizatsiya promyshlennogo proizvodstva*, 1971, no. 1 p. 168.

79.   *Narkhoz-76*, pp. 524–5. In 1976 there were a total of 21.9 m. children in schools in urban areas, while the 'number of children served by Pioneer camps (outside the city, urban collective farm, and school)' amounted to 10.4 m. (ibid., pp. 578, 583).

80.   This is not quite accurate. According to *Moskva v tsifrakh, 1917–77* p. 123, there were 34 700 places. Also, this is only in hotels of the Ministry of Municipal Services; there are also hotels subordinated to other agencies. *Izvestiya* 26 April 1981, p. 3 says that there are 7 places per 1000 persons in the RSFSR, but this does not look true.

81.   *StAb-79*, p. 844; *StAb*, pp. 823–4. The difference between a hotel and motel is determined by the owner's answer to the corresponding census question (US Bureau of the Census, *1977 Industry and Product Classification Manual*, p. 429).

82. *StAb-78*, p. 236. I believe that this is the only case in which the handbook gives data not only in miles but also in kilometres. Of this total length, 32 km of public coast line and 48 km of private relates to the lower course of the Mississippi, and 595 and 1963 km respectively to the Great Lakes. The rest is ocean coastline, including 16 km in Alaska and 144 km in Hawaii.

83. The authors used two obviously incorrect prices in their calculations for this – R80 for a motor tune-up and chassis lubrication and R11.4 for a driver's licence [76]. On the other hand, using official statistics, they greatly understated expenditures of private owners on gasoline. Here is what *Literaturnaya gazeta* of 3 February 1982, p. 12, writes: 'In several regions of the country, the amount of coupons for gasoline sold during a month to private automobile owners were good for an average of 18–20 kilometers, while at the same time the average monthly distance driven per car was, according to the State Automobile Inspectorate, 1500–2000 kilometers. Practically all gasoline in their tanks was poured in from trucks.'

Expenditures on automobile repair and service in the US are, of course, colossal. In 1977 in auto repair shops alone Americans spent $12.8 billion on repair, $6.4 billion on renting cars, and $1 billion on parking (*StAb-81*, p. 824).

11 Education and Health Care

1. Expenditures at paid clinics, 'gifts' for doctors, paid courses (sewing, foreign languages, driving a car, etc.) and for private tutors are disparagingly low.

2. Of course the government's paying of such expenditures, instead of direct payments by consumers, is only another form of redistribution of the national product and, ultimately, education and medicine in the USSR are no more free than in the US. The actual difference might lie in the fact that in the USSR, being 'free', these services are available to everyone, while in the US they are available only to those who are able to pay for them. 'Might' because in reality things are not like this.

Regarding the USSR, there is no real equality in either education or medicine. Already in the 1960s V. Shubkin's studies demonstrated that it is primarily children of educated parents that are admitted to higher educational institutions; education is 'inherited'. At the turn of the decade a system of so-called 'preparatory schools' was introduced to help children of workers and collective farmers to get higher educational institutions, but it turned out to be not too effective. And the inequality of distribution of medical services is apparent from the special widespread network of privileged clinics and hospitals.

Regarding the US, one of the favourite themes of Soviet propaganda – that medical expenses are beyond the means of American workers – in fact looks like this. In 1976 the average American paid directly from his own pocket only 53 per cent of all expenditures on health care; 43 per cent was state expenditures and 4 per cent came from philanthropic organizations. The basic part of direct expenditures of consumers themselves was made through the insurance system. Insurance companies paid 85 per cent of the hospital bills and 47 per cent of the bills for physicians' services (*StAb-78*, pp. 100, 102). And of total expenditures on education in the same year, 74 per cent was paid by state and local organs (*Statistical Indicators III*, 1980, p. 290).

I am not asserting with all this that the US has achieved 'complete equality' in education and health, but the reality looks much better than Soviet propagandists and Western critics of capitalism try to make it appear.

3.   In order to consider illegal earnings 'on the side', the authors increased the wages of Soviet medical personnel by 5 per cent. Good intentions. None the less, first, it is hardly likely that the percentage was actually so high. Second, applying such an equal percentage for all personnel leads only to changing the correlation between wages and all material expenditures 'in favour of America' (see below). But, third, this is, of course, a trifle.

4.   There is an inaccuracy in the source in Table D–3 [95]. Therefore, the ratios I determined are approximate.

5.   These ratios are determined in the study [95]. The average wage for Soviet higher educational institutions here looks a little understated. It is, to be sure, higher than the average for science and science services (R162) but less than the wages of engineering-technical personnel both in industry and in construction (R206) – *Narkhoz-76*, pp. 472–3.

6.   This is most apparent from the figures presented in the previous footnote. The actual wages of workers in higher educational institutions turn out to be lower than those of engineering-technical personnel in industry and construction, though it is clear that qualifications are higher in the former.

7.   The auditoriums of schools in the Washington area are as much better than those of Moscow schools as an equipped theatre is better than a big room hastily prepared for an amateur performance.

Every teacher in an American college has a work place, often a separate office, while in the USSR at best (and rarely) only a department head has an office.

8.   Skipping ahead, in the same vein I will say that it is very bad that Soviet patients lie in huge halls and in corridors, while the standard room in an American hospital is intended for one or two persons and is usually equipped with a remote controlled colour television. But all this relates more to general differences in the standard of living than to differences in health care.

9.   Data in *StAb-79*, p. 109, differ somewhat from the authors' [99]. According to the authors, the average income of a doctor was $52 900 and of a dentist, $39 200, and that source gives $52 400 and $40 000 respectively. After only three years, in 1979, the average income of a doctor increased to $78 400. At the same time the average wages of a worker in a private enterprise was $12 700 (*StAb-81*, pp. 108, 407).

10. In *The Washington Post* of 16 May 1982, p. C7, an article was published

which was an extract from a speech at the National Academy of Sciences, titled 'The Lag in Mathematics and Physical Sciences'. The title adequately reflects the content of the article, which talks about schools (pre-university education), and it is clear that in the future this will also affect other levels of education. The 'Book World' section of *The Washington Post*, 8 August 1982, p. 19, gives a list of facts attested to by the National Academy of Sciences which lead to the American lag in school education in comparison with the USSR, East Germany, the People's Republic of China and Japan: the smaller number of school days (by about a quarter) and fewer hours, special subject courses are started later in American schools, including courses in mathematics, biology, chemistry, etc.; these courses are obligatory and not optional in the foreign countries, and three times as much time is spent on such courses in these countries, etc.

A couple of years ago a special commission reported on the severe lag in the study of foreign languages in the US.

11. I describe this in such detail in particular because the authors define the 'average educational attainment' in years spent in educational institutions – 8.5 on the average in the USSR and 12 in the US [11]. Such a comparison is easy but not proper. It should in no way be thought that the American school provides one and a half times more 'education' than the Soviet. A little more justified is their comparison of the share of young people of ages 18–24 who have attended universities and college-institutes: 15 per cent in the USSR and 34 per cent in the US. However, it is necessary to take into account that an American college is more like a Soviet *tekhnikum* than an institute (see below), as well as the obligatory military service at age 18 in the USSR.

12. This has its plus and minuses. I am not happy that my children did not learn poetry by heart in American schools.

13. Those who object to equating these two degrees stress the significant number of class hours in preparing for an American Ph.D., but this is sooner an argument against their position. What is important is not the number of hours listening to lectures but the amount of knowledge required. The independent (outside) work of a Soviet graduate student in a laboratory and with the literature is unquestionably an advance and not a shortcoming of Soviet training of specialists with advanced qualifications.

Such an authoritative organ as *Science* magazine, published by the American Association for the Advancement of Science, asserts (15 December 1978, p. 1, 169): 'the Soviet doctor's degree is much higher than a Ph.D., which is the equivalent of a candidate of science degree.'

The second edition of *Bol'shaya Sovetskaya Entsiklopediya* (1952, vol. 15, p. 3) mistakenly equated a doctor of science to a doctor of philosophy, but correctly asserted that both candidates of science and persons with the title professor were allowed to defend a dissertation for the doctor's degree. The third edition (vol. 11, p. 961) corrected this error and clearly states that the degree of candidate of sciences 'corresponds to the degree of doctor of philosophy existing in the US, Great Britain, and other countries'.

14. Some, for example A. Shtromas, suggest that a BA should be equated to Soviet 'incomplete higher eduction'. One might agree with this, but it remains to be determined how incomplete.

15. In addition to all else, for the first couple of years, the American college student in essence finishes his high school education – in particular, a course in English. Therefore, American two-year (junior) colleges are clearly lower than Soviet *tekhnikums*. Young people can enter a *tekhnikum* after the 8th grade and study for 4 years, or after finishing secondary schools and study for 4 years, of after finishing secondary school and study for 2 years.

16. Some understanding they do have. On the basis of the fact that students often go to *tekhnikums* beyond the tenth grade, they arbitrarily allocated half of *tekhnikums* to secondary and half to higher education.

17. According to Soviet sources, in spite of a smaller population there are more students in the US (for example, *Narkhoz-76*, p. 130). In comparing their number, excluded from the data for the US were 'those working for master's and doctor's degrees, foreign students, and students at theological and military higher educational institutions' (*Narkhoz-77*, p. 630). It would seem that the Soviet figures do not exclude foreign students or students of party and Komsomol schools or the military schools which are much more numerous in the USSR than in the US (and which, incidentally, now give diplomas for higher education). And the graduates of Soviet higher education should have been compared with the American master's holders.

18. Having a higher education in the specialty applied for is a formal requirement for becoming a graduate student (*aspirant*).

19. *Narkhoz-77*, pp. 23, 437; *StAb-77*, p. 131.

20. *Narkhoz-77*, pp. 488–9.

21. Data on the number born exist, but it is unknown how many lived to a given age. *Narkhoz-70*, p. 13, gives a distribution of the population based on the 1970 census for the age groups 0–4, 5–9, 10–15, 16–19, etc. and in general all this could be calculated.

22. Presumably the 0.8 m. still studying evenings in incomplete secondary schools are primarily adults who either could not or did not want to do it earlier.

23. See, for example, *Direktivy po pyatiletnemu planu razvitiya SSSR na 1951–1955 gg., Resheniya partii i pravitel'stva po khozyaystvennym voprosam*, vol. 3, M., 1968, p. 734.

24. *Narkhoz-76*, pp. 579–80.

25. *Narkhoz-80*, p. 459. At the beginning of the 1980/81 year there were 2.2 m. students in them – 41 per cent of those who continued their education in general education schools.

26. *StAb-78*, pp. 132, 135. According to ibid., p. 8, the combined size of the 5–13 and 14–17 age cohorts was almost 50 m. in 1976. Children usually begin school at age six (in the USSR this is still experimental) and finish at 18.

For some reason, *StAb-78*, pp. 148–9, gives enrolment as a percentage of children of ages 5–17 (and not 6–18), and this figure for 1976 is 89 per cent. Counting from age six, the percentage approaches 100 per cent.

In spite of all this, it must be considered that in 1976 35.9 per cent of the entire American population 25 years and older did not have a complete school education (3.9 per cent went to school for less than 5 years), and 15.3 per cent of the 25–9 age cohort did not finish high school. At the same time, the average number of years of study was 12.4 for all persons 25 and over and 12.9 for the 25–9 age cohort (ibid., p. 143).

27. *Narkhoz-77*, pp. 495, 501.
28. *Narkhoz-65*, p. 43.
29. *Narkhoz-77*, p. 502. Also of interest are the data for the beginning of 1976 that there were a total of 11.9 m. people in the USSR with a higher education, i.e. 4.66 per cent of the population. The number with incomplete higher education was 2.9 m. and with a secondary specialised education 18.7 m. These three categories together comprised 13.1 per cent of the population. In addition, 34.4 m. or 13.5 per cent, had a 'general secondary' education. Per 1000 persons employed in the nation's economy, the number with higher education was 113 in cities and 37 in rural areas. Among specialists and office workers (*sluzhashchiye*) in the economy, 30 per cent had a higher education (*Narkhoz-75*, pp. 36, 38).
30. *StAb-78*, pp. 160–1; *StAb-79*, pp. 168, 170.
31. *Narkhoz-77*, p. 96. In that year the number of candidates of science increased (the number defending dissertations and being certified by the USSR Higher Certification Commission [*VAK*] less the number that died) by 16 800, and doctors of science increased by 23 000 (ibid., p. 93).
    Although the number of new graduate students remained about the same during 1976–80, the increase in the number of candidates and doctors of science declined substantially after 1976. This must be due in part to the changes of statute of *VAK* and possibly also to the growing 'natural decrease' – a consequence of the sharp increase in the number of 'degreed' persons in the 1960s and 1970s. At the end of 1976 in the USSR there were 34 600 doctors of science and 345 000 candidates of science (*Narkhoz-80*, p. 95).
32. *StAb-79*, p. 168.
33. *Narkhoz-76*, pp. 133, 628; *StAb-79*, p. 113. The number of physicians here includes dentists.
34. Doctor's visits to patients at home have become such a rare occurrence in American life that *The Washington Post* wrote with amazement in a special article (21 April 1982, p. A9) that in several states in the far West where there are too many doctors, the practice of occasional home visits has again begun.
35. *Sovetskaya Rossiya*, 18 October 1981, p. 2.
36. In my years in America I have met two dozen native doctors and quite frankly none of them impressed me greatly; they are not better than the Soviet Aesculapians. Even more, the Soviet doctors, lacking wonderful American equipment and medicines, are forced to be more skilful and more attentive to patients. Certainly my opinion is subjective but who can measure these skills objectively?
37. *SEV-81*, p. 446; *StAb-77*, p. 99. Possibly, definitions of pharmacist differ in the two countries.
38. *Narkhoz-80*, p. 92.

39. The estimate of the Foreign Demographic Analysis Division of the US
     Census Bureau. This trend continued in later years. According to the
     same estimates, in 1980 life expectancy was 62.3 years for men and 73.9
     for women. However, in 1981 these figures increased slightly to 62.3 and
     73.9.

40. *StAb-81*, p. 69. Life expectancy was 68.8 years in the US in 1953 (*Social
     Indicators III*, p. 69).
          An obvious reason for the reduction in average life expectancy is the
     increase in mortality. Between 1940 and 1950, it fell dramatically in the
     USSR – from 18.0 per 1000 population to 9.7. In 1964 it reached 6.9.
     However, already in the next year it went up to 7.3, and it reached 9.6 in
     1976 and 10.3 in 1980 (*Narkhoz-65*, p. 42; *Narkhoz-80*, p. 31). In
     reporting the increased mortality in 1965, *Narkhoz-65* gives the note: 'A
     certain increase in the mortality of the population is due to the flu
     epidemic of February–March 1965.' There are no such explanations in
     subsequent yearbooks. One possible explanation is the 'aging' of the
     population. Another is that mortality falls after major demographic
     catastrophes, during which the weak die, and then rises to its original
     level (this idea is examined in detail by Maksudov – *Russia*, 1982, no. 4).
     A well-known Western specialist on Soviet demography says that the
     reasons for the increasing mortality in the USSR are not entirely clear
     but indicates that in spite of the growing number of hospital beds the
     Soviet health system is still not coping with its tasks (Murray Feshbach,
     The Soviet Union: Population Trends and Dilemmas, Population Refer-
     ence Bureau Inc., vol. 37, no. 3, August 1982).

41. *Narkhoz-74*, p. 189. Disappearance of this indicator from more recent
     editions clearly says that it is growing.

42. *Narkhoz-74*, pp. 119, 394.

43. The data relate to 1973. Boys lost 4.6 school days to illness, and girls, 5.5
     days (*Social Indicators 1976*, p. 197). For a reason I do not understand,
     according to this source (p. 198) losses of working time in 1973 were not
     4.4 days as we got, but 5.4.

44. In particular, the Soviet paid maternity leave is substantially longer.

45. *Izvestiya*, 17 March 1982, p. 3. The rise in average wages should also
     have had an impact on the increase in payments for medically excused
     absences.

46. G. A. Popov, *Ekonomika i planirovaniye zdravookraneniya*, M., 1976
     p. 159. It is not clear whether this includes visits to dentists. According to
     data for 1972 (p. 158), of the total number of visits by urban residents, 7.
     per cent were by adults and 25 per cent by children. Preventive physica
     examinations accounted for 33 per cent of all visits, and 67 per cent were
     due to illness. More than half of all visits to the home were for childre
     up to 14 years of age.

47. *Narkhoz-77*, p. 436. There are data on the total number of visits in 197
     in *Planovoye khozyaystvo*, 1972, no. 3, p. 18.

48. *StAb-79*, p. 110.

49. There are 85 m. emergency calls in the USSR annually. In Lenigrad, 40
     50 per cent of the calls are false alarms, or are not made for cases of re
     emergency (*Izvestiya*, 29 April 1983, p. 3).

50. Popov, *Ekonomika* ... , pp. 162, 166, 192. In 1978 the number hospitalised per 1000 population was 224 (*Sovetskoye zdravokhraneniye*, 1980, no. 8, p. 3).

 These data differ somewhat from those that have been given in the *Narkhoz* yearbooks since 1977: 'In 1977, 60 m. patients were hospitalised, of which 37 m. urban and 23 m. rural residents' (*Narkhoz-77*, p. 436). From this we get 233 persons hospitalised per 1000 population, including 235 in the countryside and 230 in cities.

51. *StAb-79*, pp. 112–13. Of interest are certain data on expenditures per bed-day in hospitals. There are no official Soviet data, but some data put the range of these expenditures at R3.94 to R9.02. There is also a calculation that expenditures in an oncological hospital are about R11.5 (*Izvestiya AN SSSR. Seriya ekonomicheskaya*, 1980, no. 5, pp. 92, 95). In 1976 American expenditures were $141 (*StAb-81*, p. 111), which, as I understand it, does not include payments to doctors.

52. In 1976 there were 263.8 thou. prisoners in federal and state prisons in the US. This figure is growing rather rapidly – at the beginning of 1982 it was already 384.3 thou. (*StAb-79*, p. 195, and *New York Times*, 15 December 1982, p. A8). There are no Soviet data, but it is thought that the number of prisoners is no less than 1 m. There are different opinions and estimates on this. In the mid-1970's, A. Shifrin claimed that political prisoners alone in the USSR numbered about 1 m., but most authors usually put this number close to 10 thou. Regarding the total number of prisoners, several years ago F. Neznanskii published his recollection of some secret report which indicated that this figure was on the order of 2.5 m. (*Posev*, 1979, no. 5). Recently the media said that according to CIA estimates the figure is 4 m. It seems to me that this is an overstatement.

53. In comparing expenditures of the two countries on education and medicine using price ratios on consumption as a whole, we receive absurd results – Soviet medicine and education lag even more than it is claimed by the CIA.

12 Additional Methodological Discussion

1. Several years ago I sent a leading sovietologist remarks about estimates of the size of the Soviet national product (see Chapter 14). Not discussing their essence, he advised me to make my own calculations. Foreseeing a similar reaction now, I will immediately say that alternative calculations are beyond the capabilities of a lone researcher. But why not speculatively discuss *methodological* problems?

2. It should be clear that there is no method for measuring 'aggregate consumer qualities' other than through prices. It should also be clear that the 'objective' qualities of goods here make no difference – what is important is how the consumer evaluates them.

3. To repeat, I am simplifying here. Marxist labour theory of value recognises so-called rent on naturally limited resources. Regarding

resource limitations of all types, the works of L. V. Kantorovich and his numerous followers proposes considering them in price formation using special calculations.

4. I mean primarily the so-called 'free remainder of profits' taken by the budget. Little attention is paid to all these things in sovietological literature, and incidentally there is an interesting point here: capital investment in the food and light industries is made primarily from enterprises' 'own' funds and in heavy industry from the budget. This alone is enough to make prices incomparable.

5. The most significant work on this problem was and remains the book: V. D. Belkin, *Tseny yedinogo urovnya i ekonomicheskiye izmereniya na ikh osnove*, M., 1963.

6. As Alec Nove rightly told me, one more shortcoming of this is that with such an approach, particular prices of goods are not corrected. It is clear that if Soviet prices were not distorted by the turnover tax and subsidies, the structure of consumption would be radically different. But, on the other hand, a way to make such estimates is not seen.

7. Various sorts of tax benefits and subsidies exist also 'on the American side'. Considering them for the USSR would require making corrections for the US.

8. CIA, *USSR: Gross National Product Accounts, 1970*, 197, p. 85. The differing profitability by branch is a well-known and documented fact: see, for example, *Narkhoz-77*, p. 544.

9. Strangely, this most significant fact is not mentioned in the literature and various phenomena are not studied from this point of view, though Janos Kornai devoted a special book to this. I wrote about some of its financial consequences in *Soviet Studies*, 1980, vol. XXXII, no. 4.

   In a very interesting recent article (*Problem Vostochnoy Evropy*, 1981, no. 3–4) Otă Shik indicates that as far back as L. N. Kritsman (*Vestnik kommunisticheskoy akademii*, 1924, no. 9) the theoretical unavoidability of demand exceeding supply in a socialist economy was being discussed.

10. I discussed the huge savings of the population in *Soviet Studies*, 1980, no. 1 and no. 4 and in *Secret Incomes of the Soviet State Budget* (The Hague, 1981). The political consequences of the savings are discussed in *Vremya i my*, 1981, no. 53. (in German – *Kontinent, Forum für Ost-West-Fragen*, January 1982).

11. In discussing this, the authors refer in vain to the 'marginal propensity to consume'. As I show in *Soviet Studies*, 1980, vol. XXXII, no. 4, neither the marginal propensity to consume nor the marginal propensity to save bears any relation to the realities of the Soviet economy.

12. One reason is the sharp reduction in the forced savings of the population. Another is that the population would spend money more (within the limitations of the Soviet economy) rationally – in greater correspondence to individual scales of value.

13. For the only time in the entire work, I will refer to personal experience. In the USSR our family of five had a very high gross income – more than R900 a month, i.e. much higher than the average for the country However, our standard of living was much worse than average American's, and it is unlikely that a further increase in money income would have improved our consumption.

14. It is worth noting an obvious contradiction in the position of both the authors of the work under review, and the authors whose methodology they use. Being economists of the Western school, they stand on the fact that prices are determined by buyers' preferences. This premise – that prices are proportional to consumer qualities – is fundamental to their entire study. But taking into account the index number problem presupposes an admission that costs are the basis of prices. Indeed, why is there a different correlation of prices in various countries, why is an identical good cheap in one and expensive in the other? Because, together with other reasons, their costs of production are different.

15. Several contrary examples do not contradict this in general. Although the repeated increases in the prices of gold, furs and carpets lead to a rise in demand for them, it is clear that they are bought primarily as a means of investing. The same is true of books. At the same time, we should not forget that price increases raise the 'prestige value' of goods.

  I noted in Chapter 10 that price increases for air transportation and taxis led to an immediate decline in trips. Or, the consumption of coffee declined sharply after a four-fold increase in its price. It is hard to find examples in the opposite direction; when simultaneously with price increases the prices of some poor-selling goods are reduced, their consumption does not grow since they are unmarketable.

16. Irving B. Kravis *et al.*, *A System of International Comparisons of Gross Product and Purchasing Power*, 1975, p. 23.

17. A phenomenon noted in Chapter 2 – the gap between prices of very expensive and very cheap goods is much greater in America than in the USSR – must also somehow be taken into account.

18. *Vestnik statistiki*, 1980, no. 12, pp. 41–3. In fairness I must say that the author proposes in the article a special calculating procedure that allows taking into account the 'difference in weights' in the compared countries.

19. I am not alone in my doubts. For example, A. Bergson in reporting his calculations in 1970, presented the results in rubles and in dollars but did not give the geometric mean – D. J. Daly (ed.), *International Comparisons of Prices and Output* (Columbia Press, 1972). And regarding the different significance of calculations in market dollars and non-market rubles, Rush Greenslade discussed this (ibid., pp. 188–93).

20. Considering the index number problem in Soviet–American comparisons goes far beyond the comparison of levels of consumption. In recent years F. Holzman has sharply criticised the CIA calculations of Soviet military expenditures primarily because, in his opinion, they give insufficient consideration to the effects of this problem (see, for example, his article in *International Security*, Spring, 1982, vol. 6, no. 4). In no way do I want to say that the CIA calculations of Soviet military expenditures are above improvement (there is a bit on this in Chapter 14). However, Holtzman's criticism is not valid. The point is not only that he concentrates merely on this phenomenon, does not examine a host of other varied factors, and draws the far-reaching conclusion that the CIA overstates Soviet military expenditures (in my opinion it is just the opposite). More importantly, his arguments are not very convincing. There is no proof that the USSR tries to economise in the military area, that in expenditures on arms the shares are higher for those goods that

238 *Notes and References*

are cheaper to produce. In practice his criticism boils down to a call for more careful calculation of indicators of Soviet military expenditures in rubles. But for this we must know prices and be certain that they reflect real costs. The former is unbelievably difficult and the latter does not correspond to reality – Soviet prices, especially for arms, surely distort real expenditures greatly.

21. Ya. L. Orlov, *Torgovlya v sisteme khozaystvennykh svyazey*, M., 1981, p. 15.

   Earlier he wrote (*Torgovlya i proizvodstvo*, M., 1977, p. 50) that 'many wholesale trade organisations cannot even manage with targets for checking quality that are not set very high; they sometimes just go through the motions of checking shipments . . . a survey . . . in Zhitomir wholesale-retail trade led to the rejection of 20–60 per cent of clothing. Such checks at the Kherson base showed that $\frac{1}{3}$ of the goods accepted by wholesale organisations were rejects; at the Donets base – $\frac{1}{4}$ . . . As we know almost $\frac{3}{4}$ of all goods are shipped to a retail trade directly from industrial enterprises. Under these conditions a significant part of goods entirely avoid quality checks.' In his words (p. 162), in the first half of 1975, 8 per cent of home refrigerators, 1.9 per cent of cameras, 2.3 per cent of watches, 2.5 per cent of washing machines, 4.3 per cent of vacuum cleaners, and 17.3 per cent of phonographs were returned to producers. In addition, a huge quantity of goods underwent guaranteed repair. In the words of the same author (*Trud*, 30 June 1981, p. 2), 'In 1980 about 1.7–1.8 m. families that bought televisions could not use them without preliminary repairs.'

   Even specialists do not always recognise how bad Soviet goods (not for export!) really are. In 1975 I spoke at the Russian Center of Harvard University and was stressing the abominable quality. 'What do you mean', one listener asked hostilely, 'right here in front of me is an article from *Planovoe khozyaystvo* that says that many poor goods are rejected.' It seemed to him, and according to normal logic it should be, that if goods get rejected then the consumer receives only good products. Alas, normal logic is of no help here. The 99 000 checks mentioned did not keep a huge quantity of below-standard goods from being sold to consumers.

22. Strict regionalisation of deliveries of cigarettes to the trade network prevents you from buying Moscow or Leningrad cigarettes in Rostov-na-Donu. Note also that, according to Ya. L. Orlov, (*Torgovlya . . .* pp. 72–3) Leningrad and Moscow trade organisations systematically dispose of goods that do not sell 'to other regions of the country'. The prices, of course, do not change.

23. *Pravda*, 12 August 1982, p. 3.
24. *Kommercheskiy vestnik*, 1982, no. 6, p. 30.
25. *Izvestiya*, 4 September 1982, p. 3.
26. Ya. L. Orlov, *Torgovlya . . .* , p. 144.
27. *Literaturnaya gazeta*, 14 April 1982, p. 11.
28. Ibid., 15 September 1982, p. 12.
29. *Trud*, 10 September 1977, p. 2.
30. David Epstein suggested that there are two cases in the availability-of-

goods problem. The first is when goods relatively unavailable in the USSR are included in the CIA's sample. The Soviet consumer cannot buy them, and when the goods happen to be cheaper than others, the measurement based on the sample distorts the real pattern.

The second case pertains to 'fancy' goods which are not included in the CIA's sample. The distortion results from the fact that for these goods, the CIA used price parities derived from other goods.

31.   None the less, sometimes estimates have been more precise. Somewhere above I already gave the example that instead of arbitrarily dividing canned vegetables and fruits, data from the TsNITEIpishcheprom reference handbooks could have been used.

32.   The authors' estimate of the amounts of expenditures on business trips are clearly understated, which automatically overstates the population's expenditures on transportation.

33.   *StAb-81*, p. 126.

34.   I counted in the nearest supermarket about 30 types of vinegar. True, there were only four actual 'types'; the rest was packaging, labelling and different brands, but still. At the same time don't think that in the USSR everything is absolutely identical – the number of different confectionary items has reached 2500; the canned and concentrated food industry produces 300 items, and the bakery industry, over 200 (N. V. Vinogradov and V. V. Vasil'yev, *Ekonomika pishchevoy promyshlennosti SSSR*, M., 1976, p. 33).

35.   Although not for exactly the same reason, *Literaturnaya gazeta* of 24 March 1982, p. 11 also says that the patient should have the right (I would have said possibility) to choose a doctor.

36.   Some think that the necessity of constantly making decisions is a shortcoming of diversity. It's true that choices are sometimes difficult, but, hell, I take on such a burden enthusiastically.

37.   Certainly, I am not the first to write of this. Ten years ago, Rush Greenslade pointed out that production of various goods is more expensive because of 'economies of scale' – D. J. Daly (ed.), *International Comparisons of Prices and Output* (Columbia Press, 1972), p. 187 – but there are other important points as well. For example, having refrigerators of various colours requires additional expenses. Variety also increases trade expenses sharply

Much earlier, 1944, variety was discussed by F. A. Hayek in his, *The Road to Serfdom*. He indicated that uniformity is cheaper, but equated it to the loss of freedom. Indeed, freedom is freedom of choice.

I will note as well that Western estimates of their own economic growth ignore the increase of variety. In other words, if the widening of variety were included in these estimates, they would demonstrate much faster growth of both production and consumption.

38.   In Kravis *et al.*, *World Product and Income*, p. 30, the problem is briefly mentioned, and we read: 'The ICP method of international comparisons ... simply compares the extent to which each economy delivered meat and potatoes, shoes and stockings, and other commodities to its residents without regard to the extent or nature of accompanying services. The direction and extent of the bias that result from the

omission of these general quality factors are difficult to judge.' This explains why our authors omitted the special treatment of trade. However, as I try to show below with concrete figures, in our case, 'the direction and extent' can be pointed out.

39. I remind the reader that in Chapter 4 we discussed the markup in public dining and I suggested nothing similar. The reason is clear – price ratios are established without public dining markup and are not distorted by it, but the trade markup is included in prices.

40. *Narkhoz-77*, pp. 454, 464, 472, 475, 477–8.

41. Here and below figures are from *StAb-79*, pp. 836–7. I subtract the number of 'eating and drinking places' from the total number of 'retail trade organisations'.

42. *StAb-78*, p. 416.

43. There is no need to describe in detail the endless queues, abominable packaging and other misfortunes the Soviet consumer faces. Instead I will give two citations with certain quantitative estimates. In V. T. Zhigalov, *Sotsial'noye planirovaniye razvitiya trudovykh kollektivov torgovli*, M., 1979, pp. 12–3, we read: 'In a family's time budget, buying goods takes an average of about 550 hours a year . . . the largest part of this time is spent irrationally. For example, in the overall structure of time spent on buying food products, waiting in queues amounts to 35–40 per cent, measuring, weighing, wrapping, and receiving purchases – 20–25 per cent, and paying (including waiting in line at the cashier) – 22–23 per cent'. Here is another citation from an Uzbek journal: 'It is estimated that people spend about 4 billion hours a year in the republic on buying various goods. Of this huge amount of time, 40 per cent is spent in getting to and from stores; 35 per cent on acquiring goods (weighing, packaging, trying on, discussing, getting bills for purchases); and 25 per cent in queues to sales counters and cashiers. A billion hours are lost standing in queues.' (*Ekonomika i zhizn'*, Tashkent, 1979, no. 11, p. 49.) The population of Uzbekistan in 1976 was 8.8 m. Thus, per capita (including infants) 113 hours or 14 full working days were spent standing in lines during the year. About the same amount went for weighing, wrapping, and paying for purchases.

44. *Narkhoz-77*, p. 465. Costs in wholesale and retail trade without public dining.

45. Here are the calculations in which I was greatly helped by Jack Alterman. The GNP accounts include a figure of the volume of wholesale and retail trade (below I call it just 'trade'): $297 billion in 1976 (*StAb-79*, p. 439). However, this is not quite what we need. Firstly, the figure includes public dining. Secondly, it is not only value added. Thirdly, only a part of what is sold by trade goes to personal consumption.

We will work it out with the available data from the last published input–output table of 1972. In that year trade component of GNP was $201 billion (*StAb-78*, p. 443) and value added of trade without public dining was $166 billion (*Survey of Current Business*, 1979, no. 4, p. 66). By using the 1972 ratio we establish that for 1976, without public dining the GNP trade component was $245, but not $297 billion. The next step is to transform this number from value added to gross value. In 1972 the gross value of trade was $215 billion (ibid.) and value added, as we just saw, $166 billion. Again using a 1972 ratio we establish that the gross value of trade in 1976 was $319 billion. The last step is to exclude from this what does not pertain to personal consumption. In 1976 only 64.3 per cent of all trade services pertained to goods which were used in personal consumption (ibid., 1979, no. 2, p. 51). Thus, in 1976 the marketing cost (markup) was $205 billion.

All expenditures on all goods (food, soft goods, and durables) in 1976 were $545 billion [45, 62]. Thus, trade markup was about 38 per cent. This estimate is, of course, too low, because the markup for goods which are not part of personal consumption must be much less than for other goods. So an overall estimate might be something like 40 per cent of retail price.

Such an estimate is consistent with many well-known facts. For example, in 1976 the farm prices of agricultural products ranged from two-thirds of the retail price (butter) to only one-forth (California apples), and overall the 'farm value' was only 36.6 per cent of the consumers' expenditures – *StAb-78*, pp. 705–6.

46.   David Epstein notes that in Table 12.1, line 2, the figures R2.863 and $1096 should be corrected because they are what *would* be the total *if* the asymmetry in trade services were ignored (as the CIA did). He computed that with correction, the Soviet lag in trade would be even larger.

47.   This is discussed in detail in my work, 'Ugroza', *Vremya i my*, 1981, no. 53. See as well my article, 'Will Andropov Purge the Passbooks?', *The Wall Street Journal*, March 21, 1983.

48.   The Foreign Demographic Analysis of the Census Bureau collects clippings from Soviet newspapers on various economic questions. There are dozens of clippings from *Pravda, Izvestiya, Trud, Sotsialisticheskaya industriya, Literaturnaya gazeta*, and other newspapers which tell of the shortage of tooth brushes and toothpastes, shovels, eyeglasses, skis, hosiery and socks, aspirin, photographic goods, batteries, lipstick, gloves, felt boots, soap powder, irons, alarm clocks, you cannot list them all. It is hard to name a good that at least sometime, somewhere was not in short supply.

49.   See also the article 'Nas mnogo – ona odna', in *Liternaya gazeta* of 30 June 1982, p. 13.

50.   Soviet statistical yearbooks do not compare the volume of fixed capital in the USSR and the US. Several years ago V. Kudrov, a specialist on comparisons with the US, wrote that the value of fixed productive capital in the USSR amounts to about 70 per cent of that in the US (*Mirovaya akonomika i mezhdunarodnyye otnosheniya*, 1976, no. 12, p. 33). Three years later a well-known economist, A. Kheinman, wrote that the USSR's fixed productive capital has 'caught up to or passed the US' (*Ekonomika i organizatsiya promyshelnnogo proizvodstva*, 1980, no. 5, p. 34). In both cases no explanation is given of how the estimate was obtained. In my opinion, if we count not construction cost but the real value of capital, the American advantage is very great. The difficulties of comparison result from the fact that price ratios must be

established 'by correspondence,'and also from the more rapid depreciation (in an accounting sense) in America.

51. But the approach is methodologically correct only in principle. Depreciation must be included correctly in rent payments, which is not true in the Soviet case. I also have a feeling that Soviet statistics do not take full account of the value of fixed capital in municipal services. But this should also be true with respect to fixed capital of American municipalities.

52. *Narkhoz-77*, p. 405.

53. There are, to be sure, some explanations here, but seeing in the totals a turnover tax on education and health of R2.4 billion, I still would like to see more detailed explanations.

54. *Soviet Economy in a Time of Change*, Compendium of Papers Submitted to the U.S. Congress, Joint Economic Committee, Washington, D.C., 1979, vol. 1, p. 378.

55. In my own detailed calculations (*Secret Incomes . . .*), I also ran into this riddle and could not satisfactorily solve it. Apparently, there are a set of various factors at work here, in particular, an underestimation of the share of retail trade sales not to the population.

13 Conclusion

1. First published in *The Washington Post*, 27 October 1980. The most detailed variant of this estimate was published in the text of a statement to one of the committees of Congress, *CIA Estimates of Soviet Defense Spending*. Hearings before the Subcommittee on Oversight of the Permanent Select Committee on Intelligence, House of Representatives, 3 September 1980.

2. Alec Nove reminded me of a very wise observation by Peter Wiles on such a scientific technique. The latter wrote somewhere that by stating that some factor plays some role and ignoring it in calculations, the computer does not avoid quantifying. In fact, by such a procedure the scholar gives to this factor a zero coefficient.

I would also add that in the economics profession, the skill of making estimates is fundamental. We must not avoid quantifications in cases where we are not sure; an expert must be able to give an estimate – otherwise, what kind of expert is he? Certainly, all reservations and stipulations should be made, but avoiding estimates belongs to political rather than economic skills.

3. David Epstein noted to me that in applying the corrections for 'unquantifiable factors', I may involve 'double counting'. Indeed, as he rightly indicates, variety and quality figured in my discussion on meat, fruit, transportation, etc. However, I hope that I am not guilty here. First of all, far from all the factors are mentioned in our concrete discussion – for example, non-observance of standards. Much more important is that my estimates of their impact are very low – 10–20 per cent (Table 13.1). I will again remind the reader that I suggested in Chapter 12 a correction of 20

per cent only to take variety into account. So once again I suggested very small, probably minimal corrections, and it answers the question about 'double counting'.
4. My calculations in Tables 13.1, 13.2, 13.3 and 13.4 are for illustration. That is why I apply the same percentage in each group to both Soviet and American consumption (for example, 40 per cent for medicine as in variant I). Of course, this is not 'exact', but simplifies the calculations.
5. The corrections below for medicine and education are very arbitrary, but, once again, they are better than a 'zero coefficient'. Also, to repeat, I consciously make these corrections larger than coefficients for other factors in the opposite direction. The reader can note that my corrections for medicine and education upwards are larger in dollars than corrections for goods and household services downwards (Table 13.4).
6. Kravis *et al.*, *World Product and Income*, 1982, pp. 234–5.
7. Indirectly some Soviet calculations also support this conclusion. A book edited by T. T. Timofeyev, *Sotsial'no-ekonomicheskiye problemy truda i byta rabochego klassa*, M., 1979, part 1, p. 59, says that 'rational consumption' can be attained with a family money income of R200 a month, and that since 50 per cent of the population works average earnings should be R400. The average monthly wages for workers and employees in 1976 was R151 (*Narkhoz-77*, p. 385), i.e. 2.6 times less. Consider that the number of workers and employees was not 50 per cent but 40 per cent and that the earnings of collective farmers were even less. Pensions were much less. A significant part of money earnings went into increased savings. And 'rational consumption' itself corresponds to 'rational norms', of which we already spoke many times and which we will run into again in a couple of pages; they are *much lower* than the level of consumption reached in the US in 1976.
8. *The Washington Post*, 1 July 1982, p. C6, published an editorial on our standard of living which said that its actual growth in the 1970s was much better than we imagine. The main thing is the increase in life expectancy from 70.8 years at the begininning of the decade to 73.6 years in 1980. They note further that during the decade housing conditions and the availability of education improved. Characteristically, on the one hand, as we see, growth was primarily 'qualitative', but on the other, people were not satisfied, the 'scissors' did not come closer.
9. I already discussed this probelm in *Slavic Review*, vol. 39, no. 4, 1980.
10. I avoid using official data on the 'growth of the population's real income', although they also demonstrate a sharp reduction in growth rates – 33 per cent in 1965–70, 24 per cent in 1970–5, and less than 12 per cent in 1975–80 (*Narkhoz-80*, p. 380). There are at least two reasons not to trust them. One – they include the increase in money savings of the population which under today's specific conditions greatly distorts the picture. Another is that they are based on incorrect price indexes. Even in the Soviet literature we can read: 'Analysis of data of the USSR TsSU shows that in recent years there has been a tendency for the average price of some goods, including food products, to increase due to the rise in the share of sales of first-class and higher category goods.' (F. S. Cheremisov, *Resursy prodovol'stvennykh tovarov i ikh ispol'zovaniye*, p. 52.)

To characterise the price indexes it is sufficient to say that the 1980 index for 'alcoholic products' relative to 1970 is 1.03 (*Narkhoz-80*, p. 437).

11. Here is another calculation based upon official data. In the 15-year period, 1965–80, gross agricultural output increased by 37.3 per cent and the population by 14.8 per cent (*Narkhoz-80*, pp. 7, 201–2). Hence per capita production increased by 20 per cent. If we now accept the CIA conclusion that the USSR lags in food by a factor of two, then Soviet agriculture and food industry will need no less than 60–70 years in order to achieve the American level. And this is on the assumption that the rate of development of agriculture will be the same, but it is dropping sharply.

12. *SEV-81*, p. 183.

13. Norms are not the only issue; there are several other factors. First, the norms themselves are significantly lower than the level of consumption already actually achieved in America. Second, a basic proportion of Soviet durables is relatively 'young'. Soon the process of replacing old units will sharply intensify. Third, and probably most important, Soviet consumers already want to replace black and white televisions with colour, refrigerators with bigger ones, washing machines with those that actually wash, etc.

14. *Narkhoz-70*, p. 664; *Narkhoz-80*, p. 468.

15. See my article in *Russia*, 1981, No. 2.

Not very long ago a very interesting study by G. Khanin appeared (*Izvestiya AN SSSR Seriya ekonomicheskaya*, 1981, no. 6). The author (in very Aesopian language) proves that the official indicators of industrial growth are greatly overstated. He proposes his system in indicators, and if the reader is not too lazy to do some calculations he will see that in the 1970s Soviet industry hardly grew.

Appendix 1

1. *Allocation of Resources in the Soviet Union and China, 1975*, Hearings before the Joint Economic Committee of the US Congress, 1975, p. 14.

2. Soviet indicators of so-called gross social product (*valovaya produktsiya*) are in principle not comparable with GNP indicators. They are also losing their significance in the USSR.

3. *Secret Incomes of the Soviet State Budget*, pp. 228–32.

4. CIA, *USSR: Gross National Product Accounts, 1970*, Wash., 1975, p. 1. This percentage is somewhat overstated (!) since some other expenditures were also included here. In essence, with this estimate the CIA agreed with Soviet official data on military expenditures!

5. Apparently one cannot speak of the 'incorrectness' of the GNP indicator in rubles. Ultimately it is determined in those prices that actually exist in the Soviet economy. At the same time, at least the structure of GNP thus turns out to be distorted. In particular, the share of military expenditures is especially reduced.

6. *Soviet Economy in A Time of Change*, 1979, V. I, p. 378.

7. *Narkhoz-76*, p. 95.
8. Ibid., p. 98.
9. When my overview was already finished, I noticed that this strange fact was observed in 1970 when a Hungarian, Zoltan Kenessey, spoke on this with clear irony (D. J. Daly, *International Comparisons . . .* p. 169).
10. Curiously, the CIA avoids comparison of the Soviet and American economies on the basis of the SNI indicator, although a comparison of Soviet indicators are calculated by both the TsSU and the CIA – see the very interesting work by J.Pitzer: CIA, *USSR: Toward a Reconciliation of Marxist and Western Measures of National Income*, October 1978.
11. Regarding depreciation, the estimate by A. Kheinman of the equality of fixed productive capital in the two countries (see Chapter 12, n. 50) should in no way be believed. But even if this were so, it would be necessary to consider the large value of American capital in the service sphere as well as the significantly faster rate of depreciation in the US.
    And regarding services, this, as a Russian saying goes, even a kitten could understand.
12. Of course, not only the methodology must be known. Here is some evidence from *Literaturnaya gazeta*, 3 February 1982, p. 12, that requires no commentary: 'Competent people believe that on the average . . . the amount of work actually undone (overreported) is no less than 20 per cent of all work for the RSFSR Ministry of Automobile Transportation. They also say here that this is a very 'careful' figure. And they added that for other departments with their own freight transportation this figure is even higher.'
13. From articles by the late head of the TsSU, V. Starovskiy, *Voprosy ekonomiki*, 1960, no. 4, and also the late head of the Summary Department of TsSU, V. A. Sobol', *Vestnik statistiki*, 1963, no. 7 (there is also an article by V. Kudrov in the latter with 'criticisms' of American calculations); it is apparent that the more or less generally accepted method of international comparisons was well known to Soviet statisticians and that they made significant 'corrections' to it. But these and other publications do not contain a concrete description of the Soviet method actually used.
    The most detailed is a recent article by an old TsSU hand, L. Tsyrlin (*Vestnik statistiki*, 1981, no. 4). We learn here that the main concern is reclassifying American indicators into a form comparable with Soviet. 'Sample goods' are mentioned vaguely, the index number problem is not mentioned at all, nor is the fact that the comparison is made in dollars. The general direction of comparative calculations can be judged from the fact that in comparing labour productivity in agriculture, the number of American agricultural workers is increased by 44 per cent relative to official American data (p. 39). In the author's words, the 'double counting of services' in the US is taken to be 25–30 per cent of the amount of national income. (p. 40), which fully supports my assertion that the comparison of GNP should give results that are better for America than comparison on the basis of SNI.
14. A. Korsunsky asserts that the absurdity of the TsSU comparative estimates is clear from the following. The Soviet statistics simultaneously say two contradictory things:

a) from 1959 to 1981, Soviet National Income, compared with American, increased from 60 per cent to 67 per cent, that is, the comparative sizes of the two economies are very much the same (*Narkhoz-59*, p. 117, *Narkhoz-81*, p. 91); and

b) since 1960, Soviet National Income increased, by 1981, by 335 per cent, and American National Income increased by 204 per cent (*Narkhoz-81*, p. 93).

Soviet statisticians are very slowly increasing the indicators of Soviet National Income as compared with American (63 per cent in 1967, 65 per cent 1969, 67 per cent in 1975 – *Narkhoz-67*, p. 139; *Narkhoz-69*, p. 94; *Narkhoz-75*, p. 120), and ignore the decreases in production in the US during depressions. So they hope that gradually their estimate will approximate the truth. It will only if the Soviet economy develops faster than the American. As a Russian proverb says, it will happen only when a lobster whistles.

15.   I am simplifying a little here. But, incidentally, in the study on national product in *Soviet Economy* ..., for some reason science is not distinguished.

16.   The USSR sells many arms, much was captured in the Arab–Israeli wars, and thanks to V. Belenko we got acquainted with the MiG-25.

17.   CIA, *Ruble–Dollar Ratios for Construction*, Feb. 1976, and also CIA, *USSR and the United States: Price Ratios for Machinery, 1967 Rubles-1972 Dollars*, vols I and II, Sept. 1980.

18.   The CIA economists contend that they determine Soviet military expenditures by a methodology other than that described in my overview. Namely, the expenditures are determined directly in dollars, and the amount is then translated into rubles using some coefficients. Although formally this methodology differs a little, in essence its basic idea is the same.

19.   New wholesale prices for machinery were introduced beginning in 1973 and coefficients for construction-assembly work were lowered in 1976. The authors might have at hand only official indexes, which, as specialists well know, are suitable only for determining the volume of financial and not physical volumes.

20.   But here also far from everything is in order. It is more or less obvious that such a low percentage was obtained because expenditures for this element of GNP are composed primarily of wages, and the standard of living in the USSR in the opinion of the authors is three times lower than in the US. But then the parity is too low! And I would not have said that the 'quality' of administration in the USSR is much worse than in America; the bureaucratic apparatus here is also no present.

21.   At the end of the 1950s the difference was huge – see V. D. Belkin, *Tseny* ... But even now the difference is still very great. This is evident at least from the fact that in 1976 the profitability of all industry (calculated excluding turnover tax) was 14.4 per cent, in light industry 26.6 per cent, and in the food industry 21.2 per cent (*Narkhoz-77*, p. 544).

22.   *Soviet Economy* ..., p. 378; *Narkhoz-76*, p. 96.

23.   It is obvious that the actual volume of investment must be significantly less than in America. The American volume of production is larger,

American factories are much better technically equipped, and equipment is modernised sooner, which requires incomparably higher expenditures on the replacement of equipment. The question of *new* equipment is debatable since there are no reliable measures of the relative rates of growth of output, but even if Soviet growth rates were somewhat higher, the effect of this would be largely offset by the factors just mentioned. Regarding non-productive investment, the volume of services tremendously exceeds that in the USSR and the service industry itself is still farther outdistancing the Soviet in its equipment. As we saw in Chapter 10, although the number of housing units completed in the US may be lower, this is much more than offset by the significantly larger size of each unit. Possibly Soviet investment is larger in terms of the amount of expenditures but in no way by their results.

Alec Nove pointed out to me that though their results are not the best, Soviet investments in agriculture are huge, and apparently larger than American. Very true, but this is very far from exceeding the Soviet lag in other categories.

24. A few comments are needed here. First of all, when I say that very large amounts of military expenditures cannot be 'hidden' in the Soviet budget, the emphasis is on 'very' – rather large amounts actually are hidden. The point is, that as my own research of the expenditure side of the budget showed, the room there for total Soviet military expenditures is not enough. Precisely because of this, I suggested a few years ago that military expenditures are partially funded from outside the budget (see my book, *Secret Incomes . . .*).

Second, we think that the CIA's estimate takes into consideration the 'opportunity cost' effect, but the very fact that the price parity for military expenditures is practically equal to the parity for the economy as a whole proved beyond a doubt that it does not.

In February 1983, I discussed the matter with a special working group of the CIA (Abram Becker, Bob Campbell, Vlad Treml), and was very surprised to hear from Becker that the CIA does take into account the opportunity cost effect.

Thirdly, it would be difficult to think that the CIA changed the estimate because they raised the price parity for military expenditures – I see no reason for the parity to be lower, and hope that the CIA economists did not see such reasons.

Fourthly, in considering the real size of Soviet military expenditures in rubles, the basic obstacle is quantifying the opportunity cost effect – or, in other words, the correction of the price parity. I dare to estimate it as close to a ratio of 2. That is, Soviet military expenditures are close to 20–25 per cent of GNP.

25. See, in particular, Andrew W. Marshall, 'Comparison of US and SU Defense Expenditures', in *Allocation of Resources in the Soviet Union and China – 1975*, Hearings before the Subcommittee on Priorities and Economy in Government, JEC, Congress of the United States, Ninety-fourth Congress, First Session, part I, 1975.

26. See my article in *Russia*, 1984, No. 10.

27. The overview was already completed when I became acquainted with an

unpublished work by G. Pugh (Decision-Science Applications). In it he did the following calculation. He compared the estimates of Soviet imports and exports for 1972 in domestic prices with corresponding estimates in so-called foreign trade prices, and calculated conversion coefficients from domestic prices to dollars. Multiplying estimates of the components of Soviet GNP by these coefficients, he determined that it is much less than existing CIA estimates in dollars. This calculation, though conditional on many assumptions, is still quite revealing.

28.   Statement of Henry Rowen before the Joint Economic Committee, 1 December 1982, p. 11.

29.   In particular, it seems that in comparing the Soviet and American economies, the following fact is not taken into account. The share of production of intermediate products is much larger in the Soviet economy, and its, so to speak, total volume is much closer to the American than 'final' production (this is discussed in my work 'Protivorechivyye protivorechiya' in *USSR: Vnutrenniye protivorechiya*, no. 1, New York, 1981).

30.   On this, see also 'A Reply to Professor Pickersgill', *Soviet Studies*, vol. XXXII, 1980, no. 4.

31.   As far as I know, no one has subjected these calculations to detailed criticism; at least nothing of this sort appeared in the press. However, in recent years two critics – William Lee and Stephen Rosenfielde – have contended that the comparative CIA estimate of Soviet GNP is too low.

32.   C. J. Daly (ed.), *International Comparisons of Prices and Output*, Columbia Press, 1972.

33.   The growth of per capita consumption expenditures in constant prices relative to 1940 was 112 per cent in 1945, 131 per cent in 1950, and 141 per cent in 1955 (*StAb-60*, p. 305).

34.   From this, generally speaking, one may conclude that, since 1955, the gap in the levels of consumption in the USSR and the US has declined. Apparently, this is more or less so, especially due to the relatively rather slow growth of the standard of living in the US from a very high level. None the less, the gap was narrowed primarily in physical volumes. After the 1950s, consumption in the US did not, so to speak, increase as much as it improved – the quality of life became better. But precisely the quality of life is most difficult to measure.

35.   The 'hawks' said that we must 'outspend the Soviets' and force them to spend more than they are able to on military purposes. Not a bad idea, but it was not implemented – the US for years has not outspent the USSR in military expenditures.

36.   This is aside from our theme, but I will use the opportunity to emphasise most decisively that detente helped the Soviet chiefs to avoid (to long delay) structural reforms of the Soviet economic system. At the beginning of the 1970s we in Moscow came to the opinion that without such reforms the economy would start rolling downhill. True, we saw various roads to reform – quite a few proposed that it was necessary to 'strengthen planning and the centralisation of management' – but the need for reform of some type was fully recognised. However, detente and the broad growth of foreign trade that took shape then, and the foreign

technology obtained provided the possibility of avoiding serious reform – things were limited to another organisational shake-up (the creation of associations). I remember well how conversations began to fly – we will expand trade, get advanced technology, re-equip industry, and solve our temporary difficulties.

I say all this also because many in the West persist in speaking of the fatal danger of 'putting the Kremlin in a desperate position', 'destabilisation' – in such a position they would 'push the button'. This, of course, is not so – maybe they are gangsters in the Kremlin, but not lunatics. And by putting them into a 'desparate position', more likely we would stimulate various reforms within the country.

37. In *The Washington Post*, 27 October 1980, I proposed the following explanation. Previously Moscow did not have the possibility of overtaking America militarily; a more powerful economy gave the US an advantage in arms. Under conditions of detente, and after Vietnam, when America sharply reduced miltary spending, the Soviet rulers saw a rare opportunity – to exert themselves, stretch out the technological renovation of industry still further, delay the real increase in the standard of living still more, and instead, to further increase the efforts and resources flowing into military industry, to overtake and surpass America in military might. Which they did. I have seen no objections to this explanation.

38. Today, 1 April 1982, as I write these lines, *The Washington Post* reports that Massachusetts senator Paul Tsongas, questioning a Pentagon official in the Senate, asked: if the Soviet rulers today in peacetime cannot feed their population, how will they do this in a military cataclysm?

39. There is another thing that disturbs me. As the reader now knows, Soviet consumption was compared only for 1955 and 1976. One gets the impression that investment also was compared no more than twice. Though the CIA works on military expenditures continuously, its estimate was changed only once, in 1976. From this is follows that estimates of Soviet GNP for the entire period were made on the basis of a simplified method, i.e. by multiplying 'base-year' figures by growth rates. But why such confidence in these growth rates? And why, all the same, after a sharp revision of military expenditures, after special detailed calculations for consumption and for investment, did the total estimate of GNP not change? Does this mean that they continue to trust both the 'base' and these growth rates?

Appendix 2

1. My disagreements with those views were first published in *The Washington Post*, 27 Oct. 1980 (the full text was included in the text of Hearings before the Subcommittee on Oversight of the permanent Select Committee on Intelligence, US House of Representatives, 3 Sept. 1980). No reaction has followed.

2. Not less than 20 per cent of the reported grain harvest is garbage, weeds, and excessive moisture – *Novy Mir*, 1985, no. 8, p. 35.

3. The project was performed by the Foundation for Soviet Studies for the Director of Net Assessment, US Department of Defense.

4. See my exchange with Professor J. Pickersgill in *Soviet Studies*, vol. XXXII, no. 4, Oct. 1980. See also *Soviet Studies*, vol. XXXVII, no. 4, Oct. 1985.

5. *Vestnik Kommunisticheskov Akademii*, 1924, no. 9 (it was noticed recently by Ota Sic).

6. Recently a sovietologist said to me, 'What are you talking about? Kornai's book was published, so you cannot say that we ignore this phenomenon.' Alas, I can. Although nobody denies that there are shortages, no one, as far as I know, tries to use the point in theoretical considerations, and nobody has so far agreed with me that among other reasons, the phenomenon of shortage forces us to have a *special* theory of a Soviet-type economy.

    On the other hand, Professor Alec Nove pointed out to me recently that because the monetary incomes of the Czechoslovakian population are not 'excessive', there are no queues to the stores, so in the macroeconomic sense, the economy is not one of shortage. The problem deserves special discussion.

7. Said Pasternak: 'A solitary few seek the truth, and they break with those who love it insufficiently.'

8. During the discussion at Harvard, Professor Abram Bergson spoke against the 'non-quantified approach'. Professor Richard Pipes argued that great scientific discoveries have been made on the basis of intuition, and only then supported by formulas and experiments.

9. For example, the CIA study of Soviet and US consumption published in 1981 reached numerically the same result as previous studies.

10. *USSR: Measures of Economic Growth and Development, 1950–80*, Washington, DC, 1982.

11. Professor Bergson pointed out that in Western GNP accounts, profits from governmental activities are not counted, either. First, this practice is questionable – why, for example, should the same health service be counted differently, depending on whether it was performed by a private doctor or by one who is employed by a government agency? That is why, second, in many calculations of productivity, the government sector is excluded. Third, the real shares of the government (state) sector in the US and the USSR are very different.

12. *USSR: Gross National Product Accounts, 1970*. Washington, DC: Nov. 1975.

13. Strikingly, I saw no discussion of the latest version of the model, or of the calculations of GNP for 1950-80.

14. Professor Bergson argued that my alternative approach – taking the price ratio for trade service as equal to the average ratio for all goods – is wrong. I agree that it is arbitrary, and that attempts to compute a special ratio for trade services should be undertaken. But what I did is much better than Professor Bergson's taking the ratio as equal to zero.

15. For example, *Soviet Economy in a Time of Change*, 1979, vol. 1, p. 378.

16. 'If all personnel costs are removed from both sides . . . the Soviet level is

about 30 per cent greater than the United States in 1978' (*Allocation of Resources in the Soviet Union and China – 1979*, p. 46).

17. During the discusion, Professor Bergson argued that he had written six pages discussing the problem, and had even given a table with pluses and minuses for each factor. True, but in his *calculations and resulting figures*, neither his considerations nor pluses and minuses was included.

18. In D. J. Daly (ed.), *International Comparisons of Prices and Output*, Columbia University Press, 1972.

19. In the words of Academician Tigran Khatchaturov, ' . . . the USSR produces less agricultural production than the US' (*Voprosy Ekonomiki*, 1985, no. 4, p. 75).

20. See, for example, *Statistical Abstract of the US*, 1981, p. 422, where it is shown that in 1976, agriculture, forestry, and fisheries together constituted less than 3 per cent of GNP.

21. *USSR: Measures of Economic Growth and Development, 1950–80*, p. 61 (for 1980, the figure is even lower – 13.9 per cent). In itself, this claim is ridiculous – the Soviet estimate is much higher.

22. In 1984, 85.5 m. tons of potatoes were produced (*valovaya produktsiya*), and only 24.3 m. tons left the producers (*tovarnaya produktsiya*) – *Narkhoz-84*, 224, 233.

23. I insist here on intuition, especially because it is not only mine, but that of practically all other former and present Soviets who have spoken on the subject.

24. *The Soviet Economy in a Time of Change*, vol. 1, p. 379. The ratios are a little different with Soviet and US weights, but in geometric mean measurement, they are very close to each other.

25. The question is not simple. I claim that Soviet GNP is overestimated *as compared with American*, but here we are talking about the share. However, as I said, the CIA's calculating procedure dertermines the size of military expenditures *through* a dollar estimate.

26. See my *Secret Incomes of the Soviet State Budget*, Martinus Nijhoff, 1981, 'Financial Crisis in the USSR', *Soviet Studies*, vol. XXXII, no. 1, Jan. 1980, and 'Will Andropov Purge the Passbooks?', *The Wall Street Journal*, 21 March 1983.

27. During the last few years it was not, but the USSR still owes a lot to the West.

28. Those figures can be calculated rather precisely on the basis of data in the statistical yearbook of the COMECON (for example, the yearbook of 1978, p. 42), and estimates for forestry and 'other branches' from input–output tables. I wrote on this in *The Wall Street Journal*, 31 March 1985. See also my piece in *Soviet Studies*, vol. XXXVIII, no. 4.

29. See *USSR: Measures of Economic Growth and Development, 1950–80*, p. 135.

30. Laurie Kurtzweg and David Epstein pointed out that my logic is not convincing, because in spite of the negative productivity, the economy was developing with additional labour and capital. Very true; still, in considering prospects of an economy, its productivity is the most important indicator. The moment when productivity growth became negative is the mark of a crisis.

31. *Soviet Economy*, 1985, no. 1.

Name Index